ice
Institution of Civil Engineers
Publishing

NEC4: Defined Cost and Compensation Events

Patrick Waterhouse
CEng FICE FCIArb FCInstCES
Bowdon Consulting

Published by ICE Publishing, One Great George Street, Westminster, London SW1P 3AA.

Full details of ICE Publishing representatives and distributors can be found at: www.icebookshop.com/bookshop_contact.asp

Other titles by ICE Publishing:

Managing Reality, Third edition: Complete Set
Bronwyn Mitchell and Barry Trebes. ISBN 978-0-7277-6195-8
NEC4 Practical Solutions
Robert Alan Gerrard and Stuart Kings. ISBN 978-0-7277-6199-6
NEC4 Resolving and Avoiding Disputes
Robert Alan Gerrard and Patrick Waterhouse. ISBN 978-0-7277-6404-1

www.icebookshop.com

A catalogue record for this book is available from the British Library

ISBN 978-0-7277-6560-4

ICE Publishing is a division of Thomas Telford Ltd, a wholly-owned subsidiary of the Institution of Civil Engineers (ICE).

Cover photo: Pearl River, Guangzhou, China. Sean Pavone/Alamy Stock Photo

Commissioning Editor: Michael Fenton
Production Editor: Madhubanti Bhattacharyya
Marketing Specialist: April Nagy

Typeset by The Manila Typesetting Company
Index created by Madelon Nanninga-Franssen
Printed and bound in Great Britain by Page Bros, Norwich

NEC4: Defined Cost and Compensation Events

Contents

Preface

The NEC contracts are 30 years old this year. Since the publication of the first consultative edition, considerable experience has been gained in their use by organisations around the world. The subsequent publication of NEC2, NEC3 and NEC4 has always aimed to benefit from the experiences of the contracts' users. Writing a book of this nature similarly relies upon other peoples' experiences. I have drawn upon the contributions of a number of experienced and capable construction contracts practitioners, and my thanks go to Hayley Drever, Bill Edwards, Charles Edwards, Robert Gerrard, Sean Gibbs, Ross Hayes, Kelvin Hughes, David Hunter, Nasir Khan MBE, Stuart Kings, Lisa Molloy, Richard Patterson, Andy Thompson, Peter Tosland, Barry Trebes and David Woodhouse.

My own experience of NEC contracts dates back to their first publication when many people thought they were an excellent idea, but fewer fancied using them until they were proven. The subsequent 30 years have seen the contracts firmly establish themselves.

My current practice is in training, advisory services and adjudication. Each type of work brings its own valuable experience of NEC contracts, but the contributions of my panel have broadened the knowledge needed for this book from people working on major, multi-billion pound contracts, to those advising second- and third-tier subcontractors with lower-value contracts but with equally difficult issues to deal with. The contributions of my panel members have hopefully ensured that the advice given in this book is representative of life at the 'coal face' and reflects the flexibility that is one of the NEC's objectives.

I have planned this book to provide stand-alone advice for each of the six main options of the Engineering and Construction Contract. There is some overlap in the contract between each of the main Options, particularly C, D, E and F. Therefore, there is some repetition in this book in the later chapters dealing with those main options. The repetition is deliberate so that the reader can gain a complete understanding of each main Option without having to repeatedly refer to multiple parts of the book at once.

I thank the supportive team at ICE Publishing for the help provided and also their counterparts at the NEC for advanced sight of the new facilities management contracts referred to in chapter 16.

I look forward to revising this book, on the publication of NEC5, whenever that is. The pace of change in the industry's working practices will surely see the fifth edition arrive quicker than the 12 years interregnum between NEC3 and NEC4.

Patrick Waterhouse
June 2021

About the author

Patrick Waterhouse CEng FICE FCIArb FCInstCES is a construction adjudicator, accredited mediator and contract consultant. He is a recognised expert in the NEC forms of contract and has adjudicated numerous disputes under NEC contracts. Patrick delivers training in all forms of contract and is an examiner for ICE's law and contract management examinations and for its adjudicator qualification examination.

List of abbreviations

ALC	NEC4 Alliance Contract
DBO	NEC4 Design Build and Operate Contract
ECC	NEC4 Engineering and Construction Contract June 2017 with amendments January 2019 and October 2020
ECS	NEC4 Engineering and Construction Subcontract June 2017 with amendments January 2019 and October 2020
ECSC	NEC4 Engineering and Construction Short Contract
ECSS	NEC4 Engineering and Construction Short Subcontract
FMC	NEC4 Facilities Management Contract
FMS	NEC4 Facilities Management Subcontract
HGCRA	Housing Grants Construction and Regeneration Act 1996 as amended
PSC	NEC4 Professional Service Contract
PSS	NEC4 Professional Service Subcontract
PSSC	NEC4 Professional Service Short Contract
SC	NEC4 Supply Contract
SSC	NEC4 Supply Short Contract
TSC	NEC4 Term Service Contract
TSSC	NEC4 Term Service Short Contract

ICE Publishing

Patrick Waterhouse
ISBN 978-0-7277-6560-4
https://doi.org/10.1680/necdcce.65604.001

Chapter 1
Introduction

The NEC4 suite of contracts is the fourth generation of a series of contracts conceived in the mid-1980s and first published in 1991. Initially there was the New Engineering Contract, from which the NEC name was derived. The principles of that initial contract were then rolled out to a series of related contracts for the industry when NEC2 was born in 1995. Much has been written on the provenance of the contracts, and I don't provide a detailed history lesson here. But the New Engineering Contract (as it then was) introduced a number of new concepts into standard form contracts for the first time. Defined Cost was one of those concepts, and the principles of compensation events were another departure from traditional practice. (Note: terms defined in the NEC have capital initial letters, with terms identified in the Contract Data in italics.)

Defined Cost plays a central role in the operation of NEC contracts. It forms the backbone of financial assessments for change in all six of the main Options of the Engineering and Construction Contract (ECC). In addition, for four of these main Options (C, D, E and F), Defined Cost is used to assess routine payments due to the *Contractor*. Similar arrangements exist in many other of the NEC4 suite of contracts.

A thorough understanding of Defined Cost is needed for users in all areas of the contract. *Contractors* need to understand when pricing a tender or negotiating an agreement how they will be paid for routine work and for compensation events. They need (certainly for main Options C, D, E and F) to set up suitable cost tracking and reporting systems that will produce the accounts and records demanded by the contract. *Clients* and *Project Managers* also need to understand the pricing and reporting systems to be used. The regular forecasting, reporting, assessing and certifying of payments require the *Contractor* and *Project Manager* to collaborate; these four activities are contractual requirements that cannot usually be undertaken unilaterally in an administrative vacuum.

The management of change creates tension and the potential for dispute in all forms of construction and engineering contracts. The system of compensation events in NEC contracts provides more prescriptive mechanisms than can be seen in other standard forms. The operation of the four-stages process is eased with collaboration, but may still be concluded without the active involvement of one of the protagonists if necessary. The compensation events processes, unlike say Joint Contracts Tribunal (JCT) contracts, provide for the assessment of both the time and financial aspects of change in a single process. Where the *Contractor* is entitled to additional time to complete the *works*, it will almost always be allowed payment for its time-related overhead costs too. There is no separation of time and money as is seen in JCT or Infrastructure Conditions of Contract (ICC) contracts. The financial impact of compensation events is based around Defined Cost. This is the case in all main Options of the ECC and the other 'full' contracts. The contract requires the *Project Manager* and the *Contractor* to forecast the effect of the event on future Defined Cost, something that many contract administrators are reluctant or uncomfortable to do. The ability to forecast is a key skill required of people in both organisations.

In theory, a particular event can be a compensation event even without an impact on Defined Cost or the Completion Date, albeit the response of the *Project Manager* to such a notification is likely to be a notification to the *Contractor* that the Prices, Completion Date and Key Dates will not be changed (clause 61.4). *Contractors* need to be able to identify (*a*) when a specified compensation event has occurred, (*b*) what effect it will have on Defined Cost and (*c*) what effect it will have on time. The third point is just as important as the second; there is close correlation between time and money on all construction projects.

The assessment of Defined Cost uses many of the other skills that *Contractors* and *Project Managers* need. Of additional importance where compensation events are concerned is speed. The processes are all time limited, for example the default time period for the *Contractor* to provide a quotation is 3 weeks if a different period has not been agreed. The *Project Manager* can be required to make the assessment of a compensation event in a number of scenarios, each of which is where the *Contractor* has been remiss in some way. Again, close collaboration is needed to optimise the process. Both the *Project Manager* and the *Contractor* will have something to learn from the other about most activities.

The ECC allows the *Project Manager* to obtain quotations from the *Contractor* about proposed compensation events. In other words, the *Contractor* is being asked what the effect on the contract's time and payment provisions would be if a proposed event occurred. Such a quotation must be prepared with the same level of accuracy as those quotations for definite compensation events. New to NEC4 contracts is the creation of a further compensation event to compensate the *Contractor* for its quotation efforts where such a proposed event does not then proceed. I explain more of this in Chapter 8.

The implementation of compensation events is hopefully the culmination of the process. The loose drafting of the contract suggests that, once implemented, assessments of compensation events cannot be amended. The drafting isn't sufficiently strong enough to achieve this certainty, but the aim is certainly to avoid continuing negotiation or argument in the majority of cases.

This book looks at the time assessment of compensation events in sufficient detail to understand the impact upon financial assessments. It does not set out to provide a detailed commentary of planning and programming issues – they are better dealt with elsewhere by the relevant experts. But those assessing the financial aspects of compensation events must understand the role of time. If a *Contractor* is delayed or disrupted, this will ordinarily impact upon the time-related overheads: salaries, welfare facilities, offices, telecoms, security, etc. The list is lengthy. Other standard forms of contract deal with time and money claims under separate processes; NEC contracts do not. The compensation event processes consider time and money simultaneously, and sometimes *Contractors* omit the time element, intending to revisit the subject later.

Defined Cost is a defined term used in NEC contracts to attach a financial value to the net cost of work or services prior to the addition of a Fee to allow for overheads and profit away from where the work or services are taking place. The definition of Defined Cost varies according to the main Option selected, but essentially there are three different definitions across the six main Options. The aim of the term is to properly pay the *Contractor* for the resources used to Provide the Works while protecting the *Client* from overpaying for those things. A number of checks and balances are in place in the core clauses, the main Option clauses, the secondary Option clauses and the Schedules of Cost Components. In most contracts, particularly those using main Options C, D, E and F, *Clients* will typically add Z clauses to the contract to provide further protection by way of audit and records.

The only role of Defined Cost in main Option A and main Option B contracts is for the financial assessment of compensation events. This is done using the Short Schedule of Cost Components, its only role in the ECC. The Fee is added to the cost of components in the Short Schedule to establish the full amount payable to the *Contractor*.

Defined Cost in main Options C, D and E is used to assess the amount payable to the *Contractor* to all of the work it provides. Separately Defined Cost is also used to assess compensation events and the eventual impact on the total of the Prices. In these main Options, Defined Cost is the cost of components in the (full) Schedule of Cost Components. The Fee is added to the cost of components in the Schedule in both calculations.

There is no role for either Schedule of Cost Components in a main Option F contract; the definition of Defined Cost is much simpler, being the amount paid to Subcontractors plus the prices for work done by the *Contractor*. This latter amount is already included in the Contract Data, and will usually have been established by competitive tender. While the contract does not expressly say so, it is designed to be used in a relationship where the *Contractor* does little work itself other than the management and administration of the *works*, and therefore the majority of the cost will be incurred through Subcontractors.

In contracts formed using main Options C, D, E and F, there is a role for Disallowed Cost, which is one of the protections in place for the *Client*. Its name is apt.

The assessment of compensation events in main Option C and main Option D contracts (target contracts) affects the total of the Prices, and ultimately the share of any underspend or overspend between the Parties. In main Option E and main Option F contracts, the amendment of the total of the Prices merely affects the forecast of the total Defined Cost of the *works*.

Final assessments are a relatively recent feature of NEC contracts, first introduced in the NEC4 suite. As with all NEC terminology, the authors have steered clear of using familiar terminology from elsewhere in the industry, but these have already been labelled as 'final accounts' by many users. The concept of final assessments does differ from the traditional final account of JCT or Institution of Civil Engineers (ICE) vintage as there are processes to finalise assessments of Defined Costs in contracts formed of main Option C, D, E or F when part of the *works* has been finalised. The primary use of final assessments, though, has been in the assessment of the final amount due and its certification by the *Project Manager*. This ability to draw a line under a finished project and allow everyone to move on is to be welcomed.

Other NEC contracts, by design, contain similar provisions for Defined Cost and compensation events as the ECC. By necessity these do differ in places. The ECC regulates the sale of a physical product; other NEC contracts concern the sale of intangible services. Other contracts contain simpler terms or different ways of managing relationships. So, the contracts in question adhere to NEC principles while being relevant to their specific aims.

A book on the use of any standard form of contract would not be complete without a mention of the impact of additional or amended clauses. Given a proper title, Z clauses on 'planet-NEC' could possibly spawn a book of their own. Well-written Z clauses should add to the utility of a contract. More often I see poorly written ones that detract from the aims of the published contract. Many Z clauses affect Defined Cost and particularly compensation events, and I describe some of the more worrying examples later in the book.

Finally, a note about disputes. Regardless of the form of contract, commercial relationships can and do need external resolution from time to time. NEC contracts emphasise the importance of collaboration, but they still produce a steady stream of adjudications, as do other standard form contracts. Many disputes involve Defined Cost and, inevitably, compensation events. Some of these can be avoided by good drafting and good contract administration. I explain how later in the book.

Patrick Waterhouse
ISBN 978-0-7277-6560-4
https://doi.org/10.1680/necdcce.65604.005

Chapter 2
What is the role of Defined Cost in NEC4 contracts?

Defined Cost has the benefit, unlike many contract terms, of meaning what it says. The NEC4 suite of contracts relies on a common series of rules, principles and procedures to establish a relationship between the Parties. In Chapter 16 I have provided a commentary on the role of Defined Cost in each of the other NEC4 contracts.

Put simply, the Defined Cost of work undertaken by the *Contractor* is the amount of money that the contract requires the *Client* to pay to the *Contractor* for that work. The term is defined in clause 11.2, with the definition depending upon which main Option of the ECC has been selected. There are a number of regulators on the amounts that are assessed.

In most situations where Defined Cost is due to the *Contractor*, there is also an obligation to pay the Fee, another defined term. There are two clauses that help us to understand the Fee and its relationship with Defined Cost.

Clause 11.2(10)

The Fee is the amount calculated by applying the *fee percentage* to the amount of Defined Cost.

Clause 52.1

All the *Contractor's* costs which are not included in the Defined Cost are treated as included in the Fee. Defined Cost includes only amounts calculated using rates and percentages stated in the Contract Data and other amounts at open market or competitively tendered prices with deductions for all discounts, rebates and taxes which can be recovered.

Defined Cost contains many restrictions, regardless of the main Option selected. One of the restrictions is that it generally refers to expenditure in the Working Areas when dealing with people costs. There are exceptions in terms of people costs for design, and for manufacture and fabrication, and where people ordinarily based on site are working elsewhere.

The wider organisation of the *Contractor* will include overhead activities such as accounting, human resources, learning and development, sales and marketing, company secretarial, senior management, compliance, etc., and these activities are likely to be based outside the Working Areas at, say, head office. These activities need paying for whether directly or indirectly. The Fee is the opportunity for the *Contractor* to recover its overheads and costs where these are incurred outside the Working Areas. Most arguments and disputes about the interpretation of this differentiation tend to revolve around the periphery of the definitions. I often see disputes about whether people who are based in the Working Areas need to be there or whether their desks have been moved to site merely to qualify for inclusion as Defined Cost. The work done by people is as important as their location in the analysis of whether they should be paid for in Defined Cost.

The COVID-19 pandemic led to huge changes in workplaces, not least of all in the construction industry. Previous reluctance to allow working at home was swept aside by necessity. You can't install steelwork from home, pour concrete or excavate for foundations. But many administrative, design, management and procurement actions can be undertaken remotely. Prior to the pandemic we had already seen changes in the workplace with flexible working, meetings in coffee shops and the like. Changes to the Schedules of Cost Components in the NEC4 suite reflected this by allowing payment to be made for the work done by people ordinarily resident in the Working Areas for what they did elsewhere.

The role of other people, perhaps planners or compliance specialists, when they work outside the Working Areas is not recognised by the Schedules of Cost Components for inclusion as Defined Cost. This is probably for the best, as verifying what such people do or how long they spend doing it is difficult once it takes place away from the main areas of interest.

The Schedules of Cost Components have long provided for the payment in respect of people who design or manufacture or fabricate outside the Working Areas. With the rise in prefabrication and offsite manufacture, these provisions are likely to be used more than previously, and I explain later how they are probably inadequate for even the current level of offsite work.

So, what of the Fee? Let's consider something happening as part of the *works* under a contract which requires a person, either directly employed or through a Subcontractor. An employee of the *Contractor* needs to be recruited, appointed, trained, assessed, given personal protective equipment, and transported to/from the Working Areas. All of these supporting services are provided for by people or departments that aren't within the Working Areas and therefore don't qualify for payment as Defined Cost. In a similar way, a Subcontractor working on the project will need procuring, a legal department to draft the sub-contract, the compliance department to check its credentials and so on. There are activities away from the Working Areas that are necessary but are not reflected in the Schedules of Cost Components. The cost of doing these things is recovered through the Fee, as a fixed percentage of the Defined Cost assessed for core operations.

So why does this distinction matter? Simply put, because work undertaken and classified as Defined Cost is likely to lead to an increase in the amounts due to the *Contractor* and therefore make the project more expensive for the *Client*. The classification of a cost as Defined Cost or Fee is an important distinction in contract situations that, frequently in NEC contracts, reflects an agreement between the Parties as to how *works* are paid for. Agreements to reimburse the *Contractor* must contain detailed prescription as to what is paid for in the Working Areas – pound for pound – and what is paid for as a fixed percentage for the events that happen elsewhere and (most probably) cannot be easily verified. Any contractual process that requires verification must avoid the potential for uncertainty, and therefore the Fee is often deployed to pay for things where such verification would be difficult. Applying x% to a verifiable cost is much simpler than, say, verifying the part-time input of a health and safety advisor done partly at home and partly at head office – both locations being away from the Working Areas.

In later chapters I will explain the details of Defined Cost in each of the six main Options. Its importance to the NEC4 suite of contracts cannot be undervalued as it is essential to the assessment of change in all six main Options, and crucial to all payments in four of the main Options. Each main Option contains a definition of Defined Cost and several other important terms, including the Prices. The Prices are closely aligned to what the *Client* pays for the *works*. In main Options E and F, it merely provides an indication of the likely outturn cost of the *works*.

The assessment of changes to the Prices is undertaken through the compensation event provisions, and these, in clause 63.1, assess the financial impact of each event by considering the actual and forecast impacts on Defined Cost. A limited number of events in the contract allow a reduction in the Prices but, where this is provided for, it is a reduction in Defined Cost that must be calculated. The same rules apply as in the opposite scenario, but I often see *Project Managers* and *Contractors* suddenly reversing their arguments for reasons of self-interest. The equivalence of the use of Defined Cost in each scenario appeals to me and supports the fair allocation of risk in the contract.

The definitions of Defined Cost are used in different ways, depending on (*a*) which main Option is used and (*b*) whether the assessment is for a compensation event or for business as usual. For example, the use of main Option B or D requires a Bill of Quantities to provide the Prices. The various intricacies that these involve (frequently misunderstood due to their apparent simplicity) include provisions to reassess rates where a significant difference happens between the estimated quantities listed in the original bill and the actual work undertaken. In the scenario where the value of such a change exceeds 1/200th of the original total of the Prices, there will be a re-rating. But the decision to do this is based on a Defined Cost calculation. I explain this in more detail in Chapter 6.

Defined Cost is used in main Options C, D, E and F for payment of amounts due as the Price for Work Done to Date. That pays for the work the Parties knew of at the start and the effect of other events since. As the primary form of payment assessment in those main Options, it requires considerable attention to detail. The definition of Defined Cost also includes, by reference, Disallowed Cost. Its definition runs to half a page of exclusions. Any contract that is based on a form of reimbursement requires protection for each party. One of the planning tools incorporated into the ECC is the requirement for the *Contractor* to produce, in consultation with the *Project Manager*, a regular cost forecast. This assists the *Client* with planning for its own cash flow.

I explain later in the book how the assessment and reimbursement of the *Contractor's* Defined Cost are further restricted. The avoidance of an open-ended liability for the *Client* is important, as is an entitlement for the *Contractor* to be paid the right amount. The contract has a number of provisions requiring that the costs needed incurring (each schedule of cost components), that costs for compensation events were incurred competently and reasonably (clause 63.9), and that the amounts are reasonable and net of discounts and rebates (clause 52.1). Several other levers also apply, details of which are explained later.

Some of the secondary Options refer directly to Defined Cost: Options X1 (price adjustment for inflation), X2 (changes in the law) and X22 (early contractor involvement). Others, while not making a direct reference, will have an impact on Defined Cost.

Proof of compliance is important, even in a contract where the parties have agreed to work in a spirit of mutual trust and cooperation. The late US President Ronald Reagan used to say, sometimes to his opposite number Mikhail Gorbachev's annoyance, that he would 'trust, but verify' the USSR's compliance with arms treaties. Much the same principles apply here: the parties must work together, but the trust must be earned through vigilance.

The use of Defined Cost in the assessment of the Price for Work Done to Date in main Options C, D, E and F requires the *Project Manager* to forecast what will be paid in the next period. That relies on the *Project Manager's* skill and also the *Contractor's* cost forecast. Records of expenditure are key to this process. Much of what will be paid in the future will already be documented through invoices and the like. Proof of payments can be obtained from bank statements and reconciliations.

While we hope that our projects are concluded successfully, the contract has to include termination provisions. These are also, in part, reliant on Defined Cost provisions. Amounts due on termination in the ECC refer to Defined Cost in three of the four amounts listed in clause 93. Many terminations involve disagreement and dispute. Having an agreed mechanism that quantifies the liability can be helpful in avoiding such disputes, or at least narrowing down the items in dispute. Payments due to the *Contractor* on termination include the same Defined Cost definitions as those used for 'business as usual'; this again points to reciprocal obligations and supports the collaborative approach of this contract. Termination payments in main Options C and D also include a calculation of the *Contractor's* share.

We also hope to avoid formal dispute resolution where possible, but Option W1 includes a reference to Defined Cost. The Dispute Reference Table, in clause W1.1, includes disputes concerning the treatment as correct of Defined Cost: these occur where the *Project Manager* has failed to respond to compensation event correspondence within the timescales of the contract, or at all.

The remainder of this book will look at the detail of Defined Cost, how it is assessed and how it is used in assessing the Price for Work Done to Date, and the effect on the Prices of compensation events. In most situations the ECC's drafters have carefully considered the interrelationships between the various contractual terms; occasionally they have not. But I have set out the best advice that I have for users of the contract.

ICE Publishing

Patrick Waterhouse
ISBN 978-0-7277-6560-4
https://doi.org/10.1680/necdcce.65604.009

Chapter 3
What is a compensation event?

Change

The process of change is a significant topic in any commercial contract. Within the construction industry we dedicate significant resources and money to dealing with the consequences of change. How much will it cost? When will you finish? How can such a small change cost so much? Questions such as these abound from clients and contractors alike. All construction contracts contain provisions for change, and legally there would be huge problems if they didn't and then changes occurred. They need to explain what changes are allowed, who can suggest them, who can formalise them, how they will be valued and so on.

The process of change is allowed for in some detail in the ECC. Changes to the contract, as distinct to changes to the *works* and their delivery, are covered in clause 12.3. That clause requires changes to the contract to be evidenced in writing and to be signed. Those are very specific requirements that seem to avoid the less prescriptive demands of communications in clauses 13.1, 13.2 and 13.7.

Compensation events

The system of compensation events is administered by the *Contractor* and the *Project Manager*. So, the *Client* is not directly involved here, just as the *Project Manager* isn't involved in a change under clause 12.3. It is likely though that both the *Client* and the *Project Manager* will be involved in the background of both processes.

Compensation events in the ECC must be managed by the *Project Manager* and the *Contractor*. Complaints about the bureaucratic nature of these processes are common from users of the contract, but I often hear complaints of dispute, delay and costs overruns from the same people. The level of administration is deliberate, to enable control and to monitor progress. Compensation events usually lead to changes in cost and changes in timescales. *Clients* paying for projects need visibility as to the likely impact of change on time and cost. *Contractors* need to be able to forecast these things too. So, the system of control in the compensation events is important and must be followed. Doing so will lead to better outcomes for both Parties.

So, how do the processes work? Compensation events provide the *Contractor* with an entitlement to additional payment and additional time to complete the *works* when there is one or more occurrences of a specified event. This includes the assessment of changed Prices in the event that the *Project Manager* instructs a reduction in the Scope. Some, but not all, compensation events allow for the Prices to be reduced as well as increased.

What is a compensation event?

The official explanation

> Compensation events are events which, if they occur and do not arise from the *Contractor's* fault, entitle the *Contractor* to be compensated for any effect the event may have on the Prices, the Completion Date and any affected Key Dates.
>
> NEC4 ECC user guide

The principle is a sound one – a robust mechanism for handling the effect of change on time and money. In all construction contracts the subject of change probably provides the most vexed challenges for the parties and the contract administrators. As with many simple concepts, the detail is more difficult, particularly as compensation events usually involve both Parties being paid, or paying, additional money. The starting point is to establish what that payment should be, and involves assessing the impact of the event anew. The default position is that rates and prices already in the contract will not be used without the combined consent of the *Contractor* and the *Project Manager*. The exception to this principle is for the calculation of the Fee. For example, in a main Option B contract where the *Contractor* has a loss-making rate in the Bill of Quantities, then it will not be required to use that rate for compensation events, nor would it be able to profit from an excessive rate in the opposite scenario. The *Contractor* and the *Client* would be required to use such a rate for the original Scope stated in the contract, but not for further work.

Compensation events are now an established process in NEC contracts. Imitation, being the sincerest form of flattery, sees other contracts (often cited as 'bespoke' by those charging fees to write them) now using the same terminology and procedures.

Compensation events are listed in the contract (the term isn't defined). Broadly speaking, they fall into these categories

- Additional (or reduced) work being instructed by the *Project Manager*. Primarily, this results from the *Client* changing its mind, perhaps with new requirements. Occasionally, this results from errors in the contract documents.
- The failure of the *Client*, *Project Manager*, *Supervisor* or Others to do something either at all or on time.
- The occurrence of a risk-based event, such as weather or physical conditions, which has exceeded the acceptable risk that the Parties had agreed the *Contractor* should bear. In theory, at least, where the *Contractor* has accepted that initial threshold risk, it will be able to recover payment and time for the consequences of that risk being exceeded.

The events are clearly explained, and it is relatively easy to say that a specific compensation event either has or has not occurred, which is undoubtedly the drafters' intention. The first part of any dispute is often about the event itself. Has it happened? 'Of course', says the *Contractor*. 'Of course not', says the *Project Manager*. But that is the reasoning behind the notification provisions: don't waste time and effort dealing with a compensation event assessment if it hasn't happened or is unlikely to do so.

The wording of each description tries to be as objective as possible, relying on documents or actual events. Subjectivity does creep in with some of them, for example clause 60.1(12), where we are asked to compare the actual conditions encountered by the *Contractor* (that should be straightforward with good records) with the theoretical benchmark of the experienced contractor and what that organisation might have allowed for. But, overall, the objective tests vastly outnumber the subjective ones, which is what is needed in a contract that seeks to encourage collaboration.

Administering compensation events

In the ECC the compensation events provisions are linked to many other parts of the contract: payments, programmes, early warnings, communications, etc. So, understanding the detailed requirements of those other parts of the contract is just as important as knowing what to do to operate the compensation events processes properly.

The compensation events provisions provide a robust administrative approach to the management of change: dealing with the time and money aspects simultaneously. The four-step process is intended to provide a manageable route to the implementation of change under the contract, and should, in theory, be capable of being concluded by one Party without the other's participation. That scenario isn't desirable nor hopefully common but needs to be provided for. The most desirable scenario is where the Parties agree on the consequence of change. But agreement isn't necessary to implement a compensation event.

The aim of creating a final, unchangeable compensation event is stated in clause 66.3. If revision is needed after implementation, then the *Project Manager* is unlikely to have a further role, as the *Senior Representatives* (by agreement of the Parties in secondary Option W2) and then the *Adjudicator* are the next steps when using Option W1 or W2. The Dispute Avoidance Board would be the next step where Option W3 is used. Alternatively, the Parties can make an agreement subject to clause 12.3 to vary the assessment, but this is rare.

The four stages of the process are

(*a*) Notification, where the occurrence of a compensation event must be recognised and notified to the other Party. The time-barring provisions of the contract encourage the *Contractor* to notify compensation events at the first sign of one possibly occurring. *Project Managers* too have the obligation to notify certain compensation events. Although the contract doesn't expressly say so, the notification should identify which compensation event by clause number has occurred.

(*b*) Quotation, where the *Contractor* will provide its own assessment of the contractual impact of the event in accordance with the contract's assessment rules. This is a helpful way of starting the assessment process, and a quotation is subject to the same assessment rules in clause 63 as assessments produced by the *Project Manager*. Even where the *Project Manager* does not accept the *Contractor's* first, or subsequent, quotation, it is likely that useful information will have been gleaned from the quotation(s).

(*c*) Assessment, where the *Project Manager* will establish if the *Contractor* has provided a correct quotation. If the *Contractor* has not done so, the *Project Manager* will make an assessment that will then be implemented. This process is time barred, to motivate the *Project Manager* to do it quickly. The *Project Manager* is subject to the same assessment rules and the same timescales as the *Contractor* was when producing its quotation.

(*d*) Implementation, where the *Contractor's* quotation (if accepted by the *Project Manager*) or the *Project Manager's* assessment will lead to the changing of the Prices, the Completion Date and the Key Dates where appropriate. The word 'implementation' does not refer to the implementation of any physical works connected to the compensation event.

Are compensation events just in clause 60.1?

Although clause 60.1 is the primary location where you will find compensation events, they are also found in four additional places

- main Option clauses
- secondary Option clauses
- Contract Data (if used, via clause 60.1(21))
- Z clauses (with the addition in NEC4 ECC of clause 60.1(21), additional compensation events created through Z clauses are likely to be rare – Z clauses are more likely to remove or amend compensation events from the standard form in my experience).

Clause 60.1(1) in the core clauses has 20 compensation events listed together with the link to any additional ones in the Contract Data.

Additional compensation events are listed in

- clauses 60.4, 60.5 and 60.6 (main Options B and D) (these refer to issues with the Bill of Quantities: significantly changed quantities, failure to adhere to the identified *method of measurement*, and time consequences of situations with varied quantities)
- secondary Option clauses X2.1 (change in law), X12.3(6)(7) (multiparty collaboration), X14.2 (advanced payment), X15.2 (*Contractor's* design) and Y2.5 (suspension).

Where *Clients* consider it to be commercially desirable, the provision of additional compensation events is provided for twofold: (*a*) in clause 60.1(21), and (*b*) with Z clauses to allow the Parties to amend the risk profile of a contract. In most situations such a change will either be created by the *Client* acting unilaterally or by the receipt of qualified tenders from potential contractors provoking a change. Why might a *Client* do this unilaterally? I have seen this clause used where a project faces unpredictable risks with potentially high-value outcomes, for example the treatment of contaminated materials such as asbestos, or protester/security problems. These risks may lead to additional time and cost that is impossible to estimate in advance and that would have a material impact on the project. If the *Contractor* were to face such risks, it is likely that the *Client* would face amounts being added to the tender figures. The *Client* would end up paying for these risks even if they didn't materialise. So, by adding an additional compensation event(s), the *Client* will remove such risks from the *Contractor* and will only face additional costs if the risk materialises.

Clauses for the addition of further compensation events should be drafted carefully. As with all bespoke additions or amendments to the contract, the wording should be written by someone who is appropriately skilled in drafting and who is familiar with the standard version of the contract. Additional compensation events must dovetail with the rest of the contract. Legal interpretation tends to favour the amended provisions over the standard wording where a conflict between the two is found, so poor drafting of additional provisions may count against a party wanting to rely upon the default clauses. Parties contracting based on an amended term need to have certainty as to what their respective obligations and entitlements are.

I will next describe the compensation events in turn, how they are used and the challenges they pose to the Parties and the *Project Manager*. To assist with the structure of this book I have divided the compensation events into three chapters, in the order in which the events appear in the contract

- Chapter 4: compensation events 60.1(1)–60.1(10)
- Chapter 5: compensation events 60.1(11)–60.1(21)
- Chapter 6: compensation events in the main and secondary Options.

ice Publishing

Patrick Waterhouse
ISBN 978-0-7277-6560-4
https://doi.org/10.1680/necdcce.65604.015

Chapter 4
Compensation events 60.1(1)–60.1(10)

> Clause 60.1(1)
>
> The *Project Manager* gives an instruction changing the Scope except
>
> - a change made in order to accept a Defect or
> - a change to the Scope provided by the *Contractor* for its design which is made
>   - at the *Contractor's* request or
>   - in order to comply with the Scope provided by the *Client*.

This is probably the most common compensation event. Changes to the Scope of the project are commonplace in construction for all sorts of reasons, and the contract must remain flexible enough to accommodate them after the Contract Date. The *Project Manager* may instruct changes to the Scope under clause 14.3 and, where this is done, the *Contractor* must obey the instruction. The *Project Manager's* instructions should comply with clauses 13.1 and 13.2. In the real world, changes to the Scope aren't always obvious in written instructions. Revisions of drawings are a common source of disagreement: is the amendment a change to the Scope, or just design development? Hand sketches issued on site by the (main) *Contractor* to a Subcontractor in response to a technical query may lead to a compensation event. Does a handwritten sketch comply with clause 13? The issue of design development is not new, but it's important to remember that the phrase isn't mentioned in the ECC, nor is it suggested in any way. Both the *Contractor* and the *Project Manager* must remain alert to changes in the Scope, large and small, and inform each other through the notification provisions in clause 60.1. Where the *Project Manager* is aware of a change and hopes that the *Contractor* won't spot it, there is a risk of a compensation event being notified very much later when the *Contractor* notices the change and the 8 weeks time bar in clause 61.3 won't apply. *Contractors* should view instructions from *Project Managers* in the same way they view tender documents at the outset. Is there sufficient information? Is it clear what the *Contractor* has to do, and how? If the instruction is not clear enough, then further information should be sought by the *Contractor* before preparing a quotation.

For the changes that do lead to a compensation event, ideally there needs to be an instruction from the *Project Manager* that can be clearly identified. Not all such changes are accompanied by an explicit instruction. Should there be a letter? A transmittal note? An email? Is an automated notification from a communications system stating that a new document has been uploaded sufficient? These are things for the Parties to work out well before the subtleties become important. It doesn't take too much imagination to see that such situations were the reasoning behind clause 13.

There are two exceptions given in clause 60.1(1) to this compensation event. The first is where the change has been made in order to accept a Defect. There is a direct link here with clause 45.2, although that clause refers to the *Project Manager* changing the Scope, not to the giving of an instruction.

Careful documentation of the correspondence required by clauses 45.1 and 45.2 will assist with avoiding any misunderstanding.

The second exception is where the *Contractor's* Scope for its design is changed at the *Contractor's* request or to comply with the *Client's* Scope. This is relatively clear: it is this bullet in the clause that ensures that the *Client's* Scope takes precedence over that of the *Contractor's*. The wording must be read carefully though. If the *Client's* Scope is changed to match the *Contractor's*, then a compensation event will ensue. Again, careful documenting of the changes will be needed.

A change to the Scope can also see the removal of works. There could be several reasons why an instruction to remove work from the Scope is necessary

- the *Client* may have changed its mind on the quantity or specification of an item
- affordability or budget constraints
- to save time
- a change in the law
- a value engineering proposal by *Contractor* (clause 16.1)
- a proposal by the *Contractor* to reduce the cost of operating and maintaining an asset (whole life cost – secondary Option X21).

Removal of Scope, in most circumstances, will lead to a reduction in the total of the Prices. The flexibility to remove work, as well as add to it, is just as important. Case law suggests that a *Client* cannot take work off the *Contractor* merely to award it to another contractor, possibly one willing to be paid less for the task. But as a *Client's* needs change, the ability to amend the Scope in either direction is important. The same rules of assessing Defined Cost apply to omissions as they do to additions, and it is often fascinating to see Parties' approaches to assessment reverse when suddenly it suits them. While the contract provides for a reduction in the total of the Prices, the compensation event provisions only refer to a delay to the Completion Date in clause 63.5, not to a reduction in the time available to the *Contractor*. This is sometimes not realised by *Clients* and *Project Managers* when removing significant quantities of work and not understanding why the project doesn't automatically finish earlier. Of course, an earlier finish can be mutually agreed under the acceleration provisions in clause 36. But on their own, the compensation event provisions guarantee the *Contractor* the full period of time originally agreed for the project, with a potential increase in time where work is added.

All compensation events under clause 60.1(1) are simpler and quicker to process with a well-written Scope. That doesn't just include the use of good-quality text but also a user-friendly structure with easy cross-referencing between the various documents that make up the Scope. Where the Scope is poorly written, it will be difficult to identify the change. For example, where an underground pipe has to be laid at an unspecified depth, how does the *Contractor* demonstrate additional costs where the pipe has eventually been laid much deeper than originally intended?

Clause 60.1(2)

> The *Client* does not allow access to and use of each part of the Site by the later of its *access date* and the date for access shown on the Accepted Programme.

Access to the Site is clearly necessary for most construction projects even if, say, design and fabrication activities are taking place elsewhere. Note the distinction between the Site and the Working Areas; this compensation event only refers to the Site. The contract anticipates that the non-Site parts of the Working Areas will be the choice of the *Contractor*, and therefore access to them will be for the *Contractor* to arrange. In such circumstances it would be clearly inappropriate for compensation to be paid to the *Contractor* for their unavailability.

The impact of delayed access can be significant, particularly where scarce resources are needed that may be required elsewhere in the event that the *Contractor* cannot start work on the expected date(s).

Contractors can suffer all sorts of access difficulties with their projects, and not all of these will create compensation events. The impact of rare events, such as the COVID-19 pandemic or the 2001 foot and mouth outbreak in the UK, may lead to external bodies preventing access to premises. That is different to the *Client* not allowing access. The wording of clause 60.1(2) is clear: it is the *Client's* denial of access that must occur to create a compensation event here, not a general denial of access. So where, for example, a particular road or area is inaccessible due to government regulation or perhaps other unrelated construction works, this will not satisfy the test in clause 60.1(2).

This compensation event relies upon two other things being properly in place

- The Contract Data must identify the *access date(s)*, and the *Client* needs to be able to provide access by those dates.
- The Accepted Programme must be administered properly by the *Contractor* and the *Project Manager* so that the occurrence of a compensation event can be demonstrated. *Access date(s)* and the date(s) for access need to be shown on the programme, which can be seen from clause 31.2. The *Contractor* should show that information on each programme submission, and the *Project Manager* should ensure that the dates are compliant before accepting the programme. Where Sites are subdivided into different sections, each with its own *access date*, further complications can arise. If multiple dates are to be used, then the part of the Site to which they refer must be spelt out clearly. Some projects have works taking place on multiple sites, and careful management of each location's access arrangements are needed.

Example – delay in access to the Site

A *Contractor* working on a project to replace a bridge over a dual carriageway road has constructed the new bridge in land adjacent to the highway. The old bridge is due to be demolished on weekend 1, with the new bridge being transported into place on weekend 2. The jacking and movement of the new bridge by a Subcontractor requires specialist hydraulic jacks, self-propelled modular transporters and skilled people who are frequently allocated to projects months in advance.

The *Client* on this project suffers planning delays, and the project is delayed by 3 months. The Equipment and people needed for the bridge movement are allocated to other projects and are not available until 5 months after the initial installation date. So, a 3 month delay by the *Client* has led to a 5 month delay on this subcontract. It is not usually possible to equate a delay in access of x weeks to a delay in the entire project of x weeks overall.

Where access delays occur at the start of a project, they sometimes can be mitigated in subsequent activities.

> Clause 60.1(3)
>
> The *Client* does not provide something which it is to provide by the date shown on the Accepted Programme.

This compensation event reflects the reality of many projects: that the successful completion of the *works* will rely upon the actions of both Parties, and Others. *Clients* often provide free-issue Plant and Materials or perhaps access their own staff for specialist advice and input. The use of the word 'something' is deliberately wide in its application, and therefore enables this clause to be used in many different circumstances.

Of course, for this compensation event to happen, the *Client* must have had an obligation to provide something that was contractually binding. There is a link here to clause 25.2, where it states that such obligations will be stated in the Scope. If time is critical to the provision of such 'services and other things', then the dates should also be stated in the Scope, and this can be reflected by the *Contractor* in the programme.

If the *Client's* provision is late or non-existent, then this needs to be measured against the Accepted Programme: that is what the words in the clause say. There is no compensation event due if the *Contractor* points to some other record such as meeting minutes, correspondence or discussion. The *Contractor* must ensure that where it wants to rely upon the timeliness of the *Client's* provision of 'something', then that provision is shown on the next programme submission. When deciding whether to accept the programme, the *Project Manager* needs to check that the *Client* can provide what's needed on the dates stated by the *Contractor*. Late provision under this compensation event is in respect to the Accepted Programme, not to any other part of the contract.

> Clause 60.1(4)
>
> The *Project Manager* gives an instruction to stop or not start any work or to change a Key Date.

The contract gives the *Project Manager* considerable authority. This compensation event links to clause 34.1, which allows the *Project Manager* to instruct interruptions to the *works*. The *Project Manager* must comply with the contract's communications clauses and clearly state which activity(ies) is (are) subject to the instruction. Good records must be kept by both the *Contractor* and the *Project Manager*. What has happened during the stoppage? Which resources were affected? What knock-on impacts might the stoppage have? All these things must be documented at the time.

This compensation event also links to clause 14.3, the ability of the *Project Manager* to instruct a change to a Key Date. This is a significant provision, as it allows a Key Date to be brought forward, as well as put back. Typically, a Key Date is changed to suit the requirements of Others, perhaps specialist providers engaged directly by the *Client*. Where the *Contractor* is required to adapt its planning to facilitate such a change, there is a likelihood of additional costs and perhaps a delay to sectional Completion Dates and the overall Completion Date.

While this compensation event doesn't need to be notified by the *Contractor* to avoid the time bar in clause 61.3, it's advisable that the *Contractor* does notify the *Project Manager* as soon as becoming aware of a notification not having been received from the *Project Manager.*

The considerable financial burden attached to the lengthening of time-related obligations has always meant that the Parties are reluctant to stop the *works* but are keen to avoid liability when they do. The ECC gives the *Project Manager* the ability to stop the *works* or amend Key Dates for good reasons, and many of those then become a compensation event. If the *Contractor* wants to be compensated, then it must follow the rules in the contract, which will always include keeping accurate records.

Clause 91.6 allows for either Party to terminate the *Contractor's* future involvement in the project in the event that an instruction to restart work is not given within 13 weeks.

Clause 60.1(5)

The *Client* or Others

- do not work within the times shown on the Accepted Programme,
- do not work within the conditions stated in the Scope or
- carry out work on the Site that is not stated in the Scope.

This compensation event relates to clauses 31.2, 25.1 and 25.2, although, in line with the normal NEC drafting protocol, it doesn't expressly cross-refer to those clauses. The *Contractor* must be able to rely upon the information in the contract and in the Accepted Programme. The contract refers to the Accepted Programme in one bullet, and there are references to the Scope in the remaining two. This clause must be read carefully, and the reference to the Accepted Programme is another warning for the *Project Manager* when checking a programme before accepting it. Can the *Client* and/or Others comply with the times stated in the programme by the *Contractor*? Once a programme is accepted by the *Project Manager*, then the *Client* is at risk for its own failure to perform to those times and for the failure of Others too, so the *Project Manager's* diligence is vital.

The quality of Scope drafting is referred to repeatedly (and unapologetically) by me in this book. It is crucial to the success of projects for many reasons. Here, we see how a compensation event can result from two aspects of the Scope. In the event that the conditions on the Site or the work of Others changes, there will be a need to compare what actually happens with what the Scope says. A clear, well-structured description in the Scope will be a good starting point for that assessment.

The likely outcome of this compensation event is delay and/or disruption. Disruption claims, as distinct from delay claims, are difficult to demonstrate and evaluate under any form of contract, and the ECC is no different. Once again, the Parties can make things easier for themselves by keeping accurate records of the actual effects of events. Forecasting the effects of compensation events such as this one (as required by clause 63.1) is not likely to be straightforward, and so records will be doubly important.

The conditions or works referred to in the second and third bullets, by the nature of the Scope, must be included in the contract at the outset. If not, then an instruction from the *Project Manager* will be needed to include them.

> Clause 60.1(6)
>
> The *Project Manager* or *Supervisor* does not reply to a communication from the *Contractor* within the period required by the contract.

Almost all of the important clauses in the contract contain time limits for the *Project Manager* to do certain things, and the Scope is likely to contain more for the *Supervisor* too in respect of the duties in section 4 of the core Clauses. The failure of anyone in a project to reply to communications can be frustrating for the innocent party, but it isn't always easy to demonstrate any financial or time impact of the failure, thus making any claim difficult for want of causation.

Where the *conditions of contract* and the Scope contain time restrictions, then there is often a remedy for the failure to respond on time. For example, the compensation event provisions and programme submissions allow for the *Contractor* to submit a reminder to the *Project Manager* and for the relevant submission to be treated as accepted after 2 weeks. But the system of reminders, designed to nudge a recalcitrant *Project Manager* into action, is optional. The *Contractor* does not have to issue a reminder. So, there is a possibility that a silent *Project Manager* or *Supervisor* could be adding to delay and costs without being alerted to this, at least until notified of a compensation event. The compensation event in clause 60.1(6) then provides for the effect of the delay that is incurred in that situation.

There is a similarity between this compensation event and that in clause 60.1(9), the latter one relating to the *Project Manager's* withholding of an acceptance. This compensation event is broader and covers a range of communications. Clause 60.1(9) refers to the withholding of acceptance, which covers a smaller number of breaches. It could be argued that clause 60.1(9) only applies when the *Project Manager* states that it does not accept a submission, as distinct from remaining silent. But more of that later.

There is also a similarity between this compensation event and that in clause 60.1(11), the latter one referring to the *Supervisor* causing unnecessary delay in tests and inspections. Clearly, where the *Supervisor* does not reply to communications about tests and inspections, then unnecessary delay is likely to ensue. The complexity of tests in the construction process, and the increasing prevalence of off-site manufacture, requires the *Supervisor* to have effective administration systems in place to avoid the *Client* being exposed to compensation events for poor communications. The effect of off-site manufacture is to extend the travel obligations of the *Supervisor* so that visits to manufacturing sites can be undertaken. These take more time and require more planning than the work of a *Supervisor* permanently based in the Working Areas.

Cooperation between the *Contractor*, *Supervisor* and *Project Manager* should minimise the occurrence of this compensation event. But if such collaboration is rare, then there is a risk that some communications will be answered tardily and that compensation events will follow. As with many other provisions for the administration of this contract, communications systems will provide for more efficiency.

> Clause 60.1(7)
>
> The *Project Manager* gives an instruction for dealing with an object of value or of historical or other interest found within the Site.

This clause links to clause 73.1, where the *Contractor* is required to notify the *Project Manager* when such an object is found. The *Project Manager* must then instruct the *Contractor* how to deal with that object. Clause 73 is designed to ensure that all Parties on the Site avoid sanctions, possibly criminal ones, for damaging objects that may have historical significance and may not be owned by the *Client*. Any instruction given by the *Project Manager* will presumably follow consultation with the relevant authorities.

The discovery of valuable objects or historical items typically involve other legal considerations in most legal jurisdictions, and the Parties to an ECC will not have the freedom to decide what to do when, say, human remains are found. Usually, the police are the first port of call when this happens, and they will hand over to archaeologists once and if criminal conduct has been ruled out. Discovery of other historical items is also covered by this clause. Where there is delay in receiving advice from the relevant authorities, the *Project Manager* may instruct a pause in the *works*, at least in the immediate vicinity to the discovery, under clause 34.1. That would create a separate compensation event, as this clause only relates to 'dealing' with the object.

This compensation event is not triggered by the mere discovery of such things but, instead, by the *Project Manager* giving an instruction. Clause 73.1 requires the *Contractor* to notify the *Project Manager* of such a finding and for the *Project Manager* to give an instruction. There is an assumption that it will act quickly when such things are discovered. In the absence of an instruction, the *Contractor* is probably well advised to ask for one.

If the *Project Manager* did not provide the necessary instruction and the *Contractor* were to continue works that could damage the items discovered, then this would possibly be illegal, and therefore a notice under clause 17.2 might prompt the *Project Manager* into action.

As with other situations involving delay and disruption, good records should be retained by all concerned: that will make subsequent administration of claims easier.

Clause 60.1(8)

> The *Project Manager* or *Supervisor* changes a decision which either has previously communicated to the *Contractor*.

This clause has debatable impact, and it isn't immediately clear what it refers to by a 'decision': it isn't a defined term, and therefore should be considered to have its ordinary meaning. In most projects, the *Project Manager* and *Supervisor* will make many thousands of decisions; almost every acceptance, certificate, etc., involves a decision. Therefore, it might be argued that each change of mind could be a compensation event under this clause, provided it has been communicated to the *Contractor*. I suggest that such a broad interpretation is unlikely to be effective here and that the clause only operates where the contract contains an express obligation for the *Project Manager* or *Supervisor* to decide something or issue a decision. There are no such obligations for the *Supervisor* in the *conditions of contract*, but the Scope might contain such references if the drafters have used the words 'decide' or 'decision'.

The mere existence of this compensation event suggests that the *Project Manager* may be able to change decisions somewhere in the contract. The oft-claimed possibility is to reassess a compensation event, under duress from the *Contractor*. Clause 66.3 says that an implemented compensation event assessment is not changed except as stated in the *conditions of contract*. But such a statement does not appear to exist in the default contract. Does the contract need to expressly state that the *Project Manager* can change an assessment, or does the original entitlement to make an assessment lead to the entitlement to reassess? Is that assessment a decision? In the absence of clear words to say such things, I have always worked on the basis that the *Project Manager* cannot reassess an implemented compensation event. Perhaps clause 66.3 is referring to the ability of the Parties to change an assessment relying on clause 12.3?

The *conditions of contract* have seven references to the *Project Manager* 'deciding' something

- clause 25.3: the achievement of a Condition for a Key Date
- clause 30.2: the date of Completion
- clause 50.1: the first assessment date
- clause 50.9 (main Options C, D, E and F only): Defined Cost assessments
- clause 61.5: the *Contractor's* failure to give an early warning
- clause 64.1: the *Contractor's* failure to assess a compensation event correctly, leading to the *Project Manager* making the assessment
- clause 63.17 (main Option F only): changes to Prices and time.

There is also a reference to decisions in early warning meetings at clause 15.3, but they are not made unilaterally by the *Project Manager*; rather, they are made in collaboration. So, I consider that a decision made at an early warning meeting is unlikely to lead to a compensation event if it is subsequently changed.

Perhaps the most likely place for decisions to be controversial is in compensation events themselves. In clauses 61.1 and 61.3 the *Project Manager* is required to notify the *Contractor* of a compensation event that results from a changed decision.

The revision of decisions by either the *Project Manager* or *Supervisor* should be carefully documented. The wording of the new decision and any analysis of its contrast from the original one should be carefully drafted with the active consideration of how it might be interpreted later.

Clause 60.1(9)

> The *Project Manager* withholds an acceptance (other than acceptance of a quotation for acceleration or for not correcting a Defect) for a reason not stated in the contract.

I referred to this compensation event earlier when comparing its use with that of clause 60.1(6), the failure of the *Project Manager* or *Supervisor* to reply to a communication. This clause only refers to the *Project Manager's* withholding of an acceptance, so, if the Scope refers to the *Supervisor* having to accept something, then this compensation event will not apply. I think that for this compensation event to be demonstrated, the *Project Manager* must have expressly said 'no' to a request. The continued silence in the face of a request is covered by clause 60.1(6).

The *Project Manager* accepts or does not accept many things in the ECC, and I have listed them all below to alert readers to the myriad different situations that could be caught by this compensation event.

It's worth referring too to clauses 13.4, 13.8 and 14.1, to demonstrate the wide-ranging ability of the *Project Manager* to decline acceptance of something. These clauses regulate the *Project Manager's* conduct in these matters and explain that where acceptance is withheld for a reason not stated in the contract, a compensation event will ensue. The *Project Manager* can say 'no' to anything that is proposed by the *Contractor.* The circumstances of saying 'no' then dictate what commercial process follows. For example, the *Contractor* may submit a design package for acceptance that complies with both the Scope and the applicable law. But if the *Project Manager* is aware of a possible change in approach from the *Client* that will affect the design, the package should not be accepted, to avoid the abortive costs that might follow. By withholding acceptance, the *Project Manager* will create a compensation event, but that will probably have a much-reduced impact than allowing abortive work to proceed instead.

The items for the *Project Manager* to accept (or not as the case may be) are

16.2 *Contractor's* proposals
16.3 Adding to the Working Areas
21.2 Design (of permanent *works*)
23.1 Equipment design (temporary works)
24.1 Replacement of a *key person*
26.2 Subcontractor
26.2 Subcontract documents
26.4 Pricing data from proposed subcontracts (main Options C, D, E and F)
31.3 Programmes
40.2 Quality plan and quality policy statement
50.9 Defined Cost finalisation (main Options C, D, E and F)
55.3 Revised Activity Schedule (main Option A)
62.3 Compensation event quotation
65.2 Proposed instructions
84.1 Insurance certificates
X4.2 Alternative guarantor for the ultimate holding company guarantee
X10.1 Information Execution Plan
X13.1 Bank or insurer to provide a performance bond
X14.2 Bank or insurer to provide an advance payment bond
X16.3 Bank or insurer to provide a retention bond
X21.3 Whole life cost quotation
X22.2 Defined Cost forecasts
X22.3 Design proposals for Stage Two
Y1.4 Banking arrangements for the Project Bank Account
Y1.6 Adding a Supplier to the Named Suppliers.

This list provides a useful explanation of just how many issues that the *Contractor* must involve the *Project Manager* with. The blanket rule in clause 13.4 requires the *Project Manager* to 'state the reasons in sufficient detail' when not accepting something. That reason can therefore be considered by the *Contractor*, and an assessment can be made as to whether the *Project Manager* has effectively generated a compensation event in declining to accept something. Of course, such interpretations can be subjective, and a lack of description by the *Project Manager* can make things difficult. For example, the *Project Manager* may not accept a design submission, stating that it doesn't comply with the applicable law. But if the legal point is not explained in enough detail, as required in clause 13.4, then the *Contractor* will not be able to assess whether the *Project Manager* is correct or not and will most likely proceed on the basis that the *Project Manager* is not correct. This type of communication leads to a lot of festering problems that, with time, will lead to dispute.

The successful management of the acceptance process requires

- the *Contractor* to provide enough detail of what is being submitted for acceptance
- where the *Project Manager* does not accept the submission, the accompanying explanation to be clear and sufficiently detailed to explain the methodology
- the *Project Manager* and *Contractor* to meet to discuss items that have not been accepted and allow others to attend, particularly if an early warning has been given and an early warning meeting is being held.

The two exceptions in this compensation event refer to the actions in clauses 36.1 and 45.2. The acceptance of an acceleration quotation and of defective work is exempt from time restrictions, as these are optional actions that the *Project Manager* and *Contractor* are free to use or avoid as they wish. Agreements for acceleration or accepting Defects are commercial 'deals' between the Parties, freely entered into, or not. So, the various rules of compensation events do not apply.

Clause 60.1(10)

The *Supervisor* instructs the *Contractor* to search for a Defect and no Defect is found unless the search is needed only because the *Contractor* gave insufficient notice of doing work obstructing a required test or inspection.

This compensation event reflects the *Supervisor's* authority in clause 43.1 to instruct the *Contractor* to search for a Defect. A lot of construction work gets covered up by succeeding work, for example drainage pipes in trenches, brick ties in cavities, building services in ceiling voids and so on. Therefore, where the *Supervisor* has concerns about defective work, an instruction may be needed to uncover work. The compensation event does not occur in the following situations

- Where **a** Defect is found. It does not have to be **the** Defect specified by the *Supervisor* (note the emphasis).
- Where the *Contractor* had given insufficient notice of doing work, in other words the *Supervisor* was not afforded the opportunity to inspect works prior to them being covered up. For this to work effectively, the Scope must contain detailed procedures for the coordination of the *Contractor's* and *Supervisor's* duties for testing and inspection. Items such as hold points and notice periods must be carefully identified.

Instructing the *Contractor* to search for a Defect can involve dismantling or even destroying completed works, so the *Supervisor* must ensure that this is a last resort and that no other route exists to satisfy a concern. For example, quality records, photographs and CCTV images could all be used to analyse the previous installation processes.

The reality of life on site means that this clause relies heavily on interaction with other areas of the contract, most probably the Scope. What is 'insufficient notice'? Most probably it is a notice period that is less than the period stated in the Scope for a required test or inspection. If the Scope is silent on such things, then we are left with an interpretation problem.

The specifics of each site will need to be considered when setting such periods. Is there a full-time presence for the *Supervisor*, or is it an occasional, visiting role? These considerations are also relevant to the compensation event in clause 60.1(11). For inspections outside the Working Areas, look at clauses 27.2 (access to work being done) and 42.1 (testing and inspection before delivery). The costs of delaying work on a production line in a factory can be significant, so close adherence to the Accepted Programme is vital for the *Supervisor*.

ICE Publishing

Patrick Waterhouse
ISBN 978-0-7277-6560-4
https://doi.org/10.1680/necdcce.65604.027

Chapter 5
Compensation events 60.1(11)–60.1(21)

Clause 60.1(11)

A test or inspection done by the *Supervisor* causes unnecessary delay.

This compensation event is similar to the previous one in clause 60.1(10), in that we can minimise its occurrence by drafting the Scope carefully and then resourcing the *Supervisor's* role sufficiently to comply. All tests and inspections will cause delay, but presumably the tests and inspections are necessary, so the delay is too. This compensation event matches the wording in clause 41.5. By drafting the Scope properly, the Parties can ensure that the *Contractor* and the *Supervisor* know of each other's requirements for testing and inspection. They are required to communicate with one another under clause 41.3. The programme is an important tool in communications: the *Contractor* should show tests and inspections and the necessary notices on the programme, particularly in the short term. This is often a requirement of the Scope. The *Supervisor's* role covers work wherever it is happening, and this will necessitate visits elsewhere, perhaps in other countries. Planning for trips abroad can take time, so the provision of a factory acceptance test should not be sprung on the *Supervisor* – it should be shown on long-, medium- and short-term programmes. In addition to quality checks, the *Supervisor* is also responsible for marking Plant and Materials under clause 71.

To ensure that compensation events under this clause are minimised, the *Supervisor* and the *Contractor* should ensure that

- The *Supervisor* only does those tests recognised in the *conditions of contract* and the Scope and does not demand testing or performance of a higher quality merely as a matter of personal preference. This is a routine feature of disputes where the *Supervisor's* conduct is involved.
- The proper contractual notice periods are given by the person(s) undertaking the test to the others.
- Close coordination is undertaken, and those involved remain flexible to each other's needs.

Clause 60.1(12)

The *Contractor* encounters physical conditions which

- are within the Site,
- are not weather conditions and
- an experienced *Contractor* would have judged at the Contract Date to have such a small chance of occurring that it would have been unreasonable to have allowed for them.

Only the difference between the physical conditions encountered and those for which it would have been reasonable to have allowed is taken into account in assessing a compensation event.

This compensation event is a common one, and the situation in question affects many construction contracts. Those of us of a particular age will recall the ICE Conditions of Contract's (the predecessor to NEC contracts) clause 12, which dealt with the same problem. I've always assumed that the numbering of this compensation event was more than a mere coincidence. Typically, the wording refers to ground conditions being more expensive and slower to work with than some level of expectation of the Parties at the outset. Physical conditions, particularly those below ground, are difficult to predict even where there has been some site investigation prior to the Contract Date. Actual conditions may, and often do, differ from those predicted conditions, leading to additional costs and delay. Material predicted to be soil may turn out to be rock when excavated, water may be experienced at a higher level than predicted and so on. The final sentence of this clause causes some debate, and the marginal differences can be difficult to demonstrate.

This clause and its equivalents in other contract forms have often been applied in imaginative ways. In one instance when 'encountering' of several hundred environmental protesters on site, and the consequential cost of removing them and keeping them at a safe distance. In another by a Subcontractor that had to lift move and drop a new bridge deck, manufactured by the (main) *Contractor*, into place found that the bridge was heavier than it had been led to expect. It then started a claim based on the Site's physical conditions being different. The drafters of the ECC probably did not have either of these scenarios in mind, but they demonstrate why some *Client*s remove or amend this clause.

For *Clients*, these claims are difficult to explain to a lay audience. More expenditure on foundations creates no additional value in whatever sits on top of those foundations, so claims of this nature often lead to a puzzlement in those sanctioning the payments. Where this clause is removed, it doesn't transfer physical conditions risk entirely to the *Contractor* as, particularly where the design is provided by the *Client*, instructions by the *Project Manager* may be required to overcome the conditions found, and then a compensation event will occur because of those instructions.

This clause also links to clauses 60.2 and 60.3 and to the Site Information. All three clauses must be read together. It is not clear why these clauses are provided separately to clause 60.1(12).

Looking at the provisions overall, the Parties need to consider the following

- The conditions experienced must be within the Site. If they are found elsewhere in the Working Areas, then, whatever the impact, there won't be a compensation event. The Site has been selected by the *Client*, while the Working Areas were most likely selected by the *Contractor*. If conditions within the Working Areas, but away from the Site, are unfavourable, the *Contractor* can choose to use other areas instead.
- They must not be weather conditions. Rain and snow can create physical conditions, but are covered in the next clause. Occasionally there are disputes about flooding: is that a physical condition, or a consequence of weather conditions? If flooding on the Site is caused by heavy rainfall say 20 miles (30 km) upstream, the weather provisions in clause 60.1(13) will not apply.
- The subjective test as to whether an **experienced** contractor, as distinct from the *Contractor*, would have judged this to be a sufficiently large risk to have allowed for it. As with every other test in the ECC, it is immaterial what the *Contractor* allowed for. The drafters have tried to create an objective test here, but inevitably its interpretation will lead to different, possibly subjective, views. Once physical conditions are encountered that lead to a compensation event, the *Project Manager* and *Contractor* will pore over the information available at the tender stage and that in the Site Information to suggest what an experienced *Contractor* would have allowed for.

Differing opinions are common in this analysis. Industry people often refer to what a **competent** contractor would have allowed for. The ECC, and indeed all of the NEC4 forms, do not make reference to such an entity.

- Where it is demonstrated that the physical conditions were different from those that an experienced *Contractor* would have allowed for, it is only the effect over and above that level that is compensated for. For such a comparison to take place, accurate records must be kept during the *works*, not just those of the resources deployed but also of the physical conditions in question. As an industry we often leave the debates about these issues until the building, the bridge, the road or the railway has been built and the opportunity to check the conditions has gone. Accurate records, as with all claims, make the process of dealing with them very much easier.
- Clause 60.2 sets out several assumptions as to the level of knowledge that the *Contractor* is assumed to have had when making the decision on what to allow for in its prices. It is still a feature of many disputes that the *Contractor* has not visited the Site before the Contract Date. I have seen a *Contractor* surprised to discover water ingress while excavating in gravel next to a river, another *Contractor* struggling with the removal of rock just below the surface when working on a hillside punctuated with visible rocky outcrops. Physical conditions are a difficult enough subject without the *Contractor* failing to avail itself of the information available and opportunities to visit the Site.
- Clause 60.2 assumes that the *Contractor* has taken into account
  - the Site Information
  - publicly available information **referred to** in the Site Information
  - information available from a visual inspection of the Site
  - other information that an experienced contractor could reasonably be expected to have or to obtain.
- Clause 60.3 provides some direction in the event of an ambiguity or inconsistency, but this is only in relation to the contents of the Site Information and not any difference between the Site Information and other documents. This latter situation would be dealt with under the remaining provisions of the contract.

The additional works caused by these events tend to be demanding of resources, particularly Equipment and people. Detailed records are needed of the impact of physical conditions, and these must be maintained by the *Project Manager* and the *Contractor*. Ideally, the records will be agreed while they are contemporaneously prepared.

Clause 60.1(13)

A *weather measurement* is recorded

- within a calendar month,
- before the Completion Date for the whole of the *works* and
- at the place stated in the Contract Data

the value of which, by comparison with the *weather data*, is shown to occur on average less frequently than once in ten years.

Only the difference between the *weather measurement* and the weather which the *weather data* show to occur on average less frequently than once in ten years is considered in assessing a compensation event.

The issue of weather has caused difficulty to construction projects since records began, or certainly records that survive to this day. Even with modern-day construction increasingly reliant upon off-site manufacturing, there will always be work to do outside. Work inside is still subject to problems caused by extreme temperatures, as many construction processes are temperature dependent. Wherever work takes place in the world, *Contractors* must plan for routine weather conditions, but it is the extremes that cause difficulties in relationships.

Other forms of contract provide relief for ‘exceptionally adverse weather’ or other similar, subjective words. Such phraseology has created difficulties over the years and can contribute to disputes because of the inherent bias of the decision-makers. One person’s exceptionally adverse rain is another’s predictable rainfall. The ECC has a mechanism designed to avoid such subjective arguments, one that should produce a binary result. Where bad weather stops work, the *Project Manager* may say that the stoppage was merely a health and safety issue for the *Contractor* and therefore isn’t a compensation event under either clause 60.1(13) or 60.1(4).

As with all the compensation events, the wording must be read carefully. The mechanism provides compensation to the *Contractor* for weather conditions that are in excess of the stated threshold. But the comparison is month by month. In other words, the *Contractor* needs to experience weather worse than the 10-yearly average in, say, November this year. The actual weather measurements for November this year will be compared with the 10-yearly average for all Novembers on record. If the *Contractor* suffers 30 days of bad weather from, say, 15 November to 14 December, then this might not qualify as a compensation event if milder conditions were experienced in early November or late December.

The poor weather must be experienced before the Completion Date. So, if the *Contractor* is running late, it won’t receive any compensation for the effects of the weather, nor will it gain relief from delay damages.

And, of course, the weather must be experienced at the place stated in the Contract Data. Often this is the Site, if no nearby and relevant monitoring facilities exist already. This could mean, for example, that weather-related interruption away from the Site, but within the Working Areas, may not qualify for relief.

Those negotiating or setting contract conditions should consider how weather will affect the *works*. Wind will affect craneage and will bring lifting operations to a standstill once the speed exceeds the maximum allowed under health and safety regulations. But wind conditions aren’t listed in the Contract Data of the standard ECC form, so Parties will need to create their own entries. Wind speed is usually measured for the use of cranes for safety reasons, so consider if an automated measurement and recording system can be established to ensure that both Parties are working from the same source data. Wind is usually a very localised problem due to the topography of an area, so generic wind speed results are unlikely to be relevant. When I encounter wind-related compensation events I typically see Z clauses deployed to create bespoke risk-sharing provisions. As with all bespoke amendments, these must be written to dovetail with the original wording. Fog is another weather condition that can cause delay but is rarely mentioned in contracts.

The Contract Data contain entries for the effects of rainfall and temperature extremes. Extreme high or low temperatures affect the ability to undertake wet trades such as concreting, plastering and brickwork. Rain affects the ability to install materials that require compaction or high-quality surface finishes.

Of course, these risks can and should be mitigated by the provision of shade, shelter, heating and so on. And all these weather extremes affect productivity because they impact on the ability of human beings to work manually. Perhaps one of the best arguments in favour of factory-based manufacture?

Working with weather data requires

- thought and knowledge being applied when the contract is drafted
- consideration of the effects of the weather risks by tenderers and the ultimate *Contractor*
- monitoring of weather data by the *Contractor*, *Project Manager* and *Supervisor*
- careful interpretation of the data by the *Contractor* and *Project Manager*, although it is usually the former that is keener to undertake this role, particularly as this compensation event will need to be notified in most situations by the *Contractor*
- cooperation between the *Contractor* and the *Project Manager* for assessing the impact of the compensation event, for example sharing the acquisition of historic data.

The assessment of this compensation event requires the Parties to judge the marginal increase in cost and time experienced by the *Contractor* over and above the 10-yearly average that the contract requires the *Contractor* to provide for. So, if the *Contractor* has experienced 5 days of excessive rainfall during November and the historic 10-yearly average states that only 2 days of rainfall of that level would have been experienced, then compensation is due for the effect of the additional 3 days. That sounds simple, but the reality of demonstrating the cost and time effect of those additional 3 days is never as straightforward as it initially sounds.

Parties should remember that, without a Z clause amendment, clause 60.1(13) entitles the *Contractor* to additional payment as well as time. This is different from most other contracts, where time is usually the only relief available. Z clauses often do make the amendment so that only additional time is an entitlement for the *Contractor*.

Clause 60.1(14)

An event which is a *Client's* liability stated in these *conditions of contract*.

This clause relates to the *Client's* liabilities listed in clause 80.1. That list does not require explanation here, but this clause ensures that the compensation provisions and assessment rules will apply to the occurrence of any of the *Client's* liabilities. The liabilities can be extended by the final bullet in clause 80.1, which cross-refers to the Contract Data. For such a liability to be effective, the additional liability should be in the Contract Data and not, say, in the Scope or in a poorly drafted Z clause.

The *Client's* liabilities can be summarised as

- a consequence of the *Contractor* Providing the Works in accordance with the *Client's* requirements
- a fault by the *Client* or part of the *Client's* team
- broader societal problems (war, etc)
- loss or damage after take over or termination
- **additional** *Client's* liabilities in the Contract Data.

I can't provide a description of the likely circumstances of each of the *Client's* liabilities listed in clause 80.1, but my experience suggests that the most common one is a fault in the *Client's* design. This is a problematic subject, given the creative nature of design. Demonstrating that a design is faulty can be a difficult task, and forecasting its effects (as per clauses 63.1 and 63.5) even more so.

The *Client's* liabilities include 'A fault of the *Client* or any person employed by or contracted to it, except the *Contractor*.' This includes the *Project Manager*, the *Supervisor*, and any other suppliers or contractors whose work affects the *Contractor*.

Clause 60.1(14) states that the occurrence of a *Client's* liability will be a compensation event. In addition, clause 82.2 allows the *Contractor* to recover costs paid to Others from the Client. These costs might not otherwise be recoverable under clause 63.1 as Defined Cost. Clause 60.1(14) will potentially allow a change to the Completion Date and Key Dates in addition to a financial entitlement.

> Clause 60.1(15)
>
> The *Project Manager* certifies take over of a part of the *works* before both Completion and the Completion Date.

This compensation event relies on the *Project Manager* issuing a certificate, as opposed to the action of take over itself. In my experience many contractual users do not read the last part of this clause, take over has to happen *before* both Completion *and* the Completion Date. There is a link here to clause 35.3, which requires the *Project Manager* to certify the date on which the *Client* takes over any part of the *works*. The *Project Manager* must certify within 1 week of take over. So, we have the possibility that take over may occur and that the *Project Manager* may be late in the certification or perhaps not do it at all. In that situation, the *Project Manager* would be in breach of clause 10.1 by not acting as stated, and there isn't an express remedy in the contract for the *Project Manager's* failure in this regard, aside from following the dispute resolution procedures or possible as a *Client* liability.

The need for this compensation event is to reflect the disruption and additional costs that might be incurred by the *Contractor* if the *Client* 'moves in' and starts using the *works* while the *Contractor* is still trying to construct them, having not been allowed the agreed time period to reach Completion. Once the Completion Date has passed, there will not be a compensation event, as the *Contractor* will be in breach, and the *Client's* actions will be mitigating its own losses as a result of the delayed Completion.

If the contract's programming obligations have been complied with, then any early take over by the *Client* will have been expected and planned for. This would hopefully reduce the time and cost impact of such actions.

There are situations on some sites where the *Client's* early use of the *works* is programmed into the project, for example switching highways traffic onto a newly constructed carriageway to allow an existing section of carriageway to be refurbished or amended. In that scenario there would not be a compensation event if that methodology was agreed in the contract. Equally, where the early use of the asset is included in the Scope and necessary for the *works*, then there will be no compensation event. An example of this type of arrangement is in the commissioning of a treatment plant for household waste where the lengthy commissioning activities need the provision by the *Client* and the treatment by the *Contractor* of actual household waste well before Completion or take over.

Clause 60.1(16)

The *Client* does not provide materials, facilities and samples for tests and inspection as stated in the Scope.

This compensation event relates to the *Client's* (reciprocal) obligations in clause 41.2 to provide these things to the *Contractor* as stated in the Scope. This is similar to the compensation event in clause 60.1(3); that differs from this one from its reference to the Accepted Programme. Here, the reference is to the Scope. Some sites may benefit from laboratory services provided by the *Client* or the *Supervisor*, and typically we see these stated in the Scope. Where they are subsequently not provided, there will be a consequential impact on costs and possibly timing too. Where samples are not provided, then these will cost money to acquire if the *Contractor* must do so instead. Any instruction to provide such things may trigger a compensation event under clause 60.1(1).

As with most compensation events, good records will assist with the assessment of this type of incident. The express reference to the Scope will capture those things specified in the Scope, but any post-contract ad hoc agreement made by the Parties will need to have been formalised as an implemented compensation event before the *Client's* failure to honour it can qualify as a compensation event.

The example of the household waste treatment plant in the discussion on the previous compensation event is relevant here too. Typically, in those circumstances the *Client* will be required to provide specified weights of waste for treatment, and if it fails to do so, presumably with some agreed call-off provisions, it will delay testing and commissioning. Those provisions must be contained in the Scope.

Clause 60.1(17)

The *Project Manager* notifies the *Contractor* of a correction to an assumption which the *Project Manager* stated about a compensation event.

This compensation event links to the *Project Manager's* ability in clause 61.6 to state assumptions before instructing the *Contractor* to submit a quotation for a compensation event. Where there is some doubt, the *Project Manager* can state an assumption. For example, will additional works be undertaken overnight on a weekend or during normal working hours midweek? Should the *Contractor* use method X, or method Y? The answer to this question will have a bearing on the forecast Defined Cost of people, Equipment and the other constituents of the Schedules of Cost Components. The *Project Manager*, having stated assumptions, takes the risk of uncertain costs away from the *Contractor*. If, once the event has happened, the assumptions turn out to be incorrect, then a further compensation event will occur to correct the effect on the Prices and dates of the error. The clause needs to be read carefully, as the 'event' is the notification by the *Project Manager* of a correction to an assumption. The *Project Manager* is obliged to notify such a correction by the final sentence in clause 61.6.

The original assumptions and the later correction should be clearly described by the *Project Manager*, to aid the assessment of the correcting compensation event under this clause. Depending upon the cause of the original compensation event and the main Option selected, the correcting compensation event may lead to a reduction in the Prices.

> Clause 60.1(18)
>
> A breach of contract by the *Client* which is not one of the other compensation events in the contract.

This clause leads to compensation event provisions dealing with the consequences of an otherwise-unspecified breach by the *Client*. It needs to be read in conjunction with clause 63.6, which sets out to create the compensation event provisions as a sole remedy for both Parties. Whether the drafting successfully achieves this end is probably best answered by those with legal qualifications, so I will comment no further.

I think that the aim of this clause is to provide a mechanism for assessing the effect of a *Client* breach that isn't otherwise contemplated or included in the drafting. The intent is probably to avoid such a breach being entirely at large. Given my earlier concern, I think that the Parties should take advice before investing too much effort in this compensation event should a breach be alleged. The interaction of this clause with other remedies for breach of contract has yet to be tested in the courts to give us any guidance as to its predominance or otherwise.

Occasionally, disputes referred to me as an adjudicator contain arguments about implied terms. The contract in its published form cannot contemplate what implied terms may come into existence, nor what any express remedy might be for the breach of an implied term. This compensation event is typically relied upon by the innocent party to a breach of an implied term.

> Clause 60.1(19)
>
> An event which
>
> - stops the *Contractor* completing the whole of the *works* or
> - stops the *Contractor* completing the whole of the *works* by the date for planned Completion shown on the Accepted Programme,
>
> and which
>
> - neither Party could prevent,
> - an experienced *Contractor* would have judged at the Contract Date to have such a small chance of occurring that it would have been unreasonable to have allowed for it and
> - is not one of the other compensation events stated in the contract.

This compensation event is sometimes referred to as the force majeure clause. The term force majeure doesn't have a defined meaning in law, so perhaps on its own it doesn't help much in understanding this clause.

The COVID-19 pandemic has focused attention on clauses such as this that, previously, attracted little attention from all but the most diligent of lawyers. The effect of the pandemic on the industry's costs and speed of progress will now see such clauses being closely scrutinised in the future. The provision of a contractual remedy for a generic event will always leave gaps in its provisions, so this clause must be read and used very carefully. It is often quoted by *Contractors* for inappropriate events because, simply put, the event in question provides no entitlement anywhere else in the contract. Examples of inappropriate usage include Subcontractor insolvency, weather events where clause 60.1(13) has been removed, and material price rises caused by foreign exchange movements.

The first two bullets refer to the event stopping the Completion of the *works*. But on closer reading the second bullet is effectively referring to something that slows down the achievement of Completion by reference to the Accepted Programme. Again, we see the importance of having an up-to-date Accepted Programme and how it interacts with other areas of the contract. The effect of such an event on sectional Completion would not be captured by this clause. The reference to 'the whole of the works' clearly excludes such matters from the reach of sectional Completion in clause X5.1.

For this compensation event to be triggered, the final three bullets must be satisfied. Events of this nature tend to be rare (fourth bullet), an example being extreme natural conditions such as a pandemic, flooding or, as happened in the UK in 2001, an agricultural disease epidemic that caused large areas of rural land to be inaccessible. Finally, the event must not be one of the other compensation events in the contract.

The unpredictable nature of events such as these mean that, more than ever, good records must be kept. The industry in the UK struggled to deal with the commercial aftermath of the foot and mouth outbreak in 2001 due to the 'act now, record later' nature of events. That is possibly understandable given the unique circumstances, but some thought should be given to these issues at the time.

The impacts of the COVID-19 pandemic are still being experienced at the time of this book's publication, but I have already seen a large number of claims, disputes and adjudications for related delays and additional costs. Many of those claims, predictably, are poorly particularised and/or suffer from a lack of evidence. As with all such claims, good record keeping is vital for a smooth administration process.

Within all four territories of the UK, the respective government authorities provided generous relief to the effects of the pandemic. In places, that goodwill was abused by suppliers to the public sector that saw such relief as a 'blank cheque' to absolve them of the consequences of all delays. Unsurprisingly, government clients did not intend this to be the case. We also saw some representatives of government clients trying to enforce stricter rules of evidencing the claims than that set out in the various rules. These approaches made some of the claims difficult to assess, even if the majority of participants stuck to the rules. Records are important, but so too is a sensible, business-like approach from both sides.

Clause 60.1(20)

The *Project Manager* notifies the *Contractor* that a quotation for a proposed instruction is not accepted.

This compensation event refers to clause 65, which provides for the *Project Manager* to instruct the *Contractor* to submit quotations for proposed instructions but where the *Contractor* does not immediately put an instruction into effect, thereby avoiding the need to comply with clause 27.3. This provision allows the *Project Manager* (presumably on behalf of the *Client*) to explore the effect of a proposed instruction without committing to it. If the quotation is acceptable to the *Client*, then the *Project Manager* can instruct the *works* (clause 65.2). If not, the *Project Manager* must notify the *Contractor* that the quotation is not accepted, and notify a compensation event for the effect of preparing the (abortive) quotation.

The effect here is to compensate the *Contractor* for the time and cost of preparing a quotation – sometimes this may be considerable if design and planning are required. The clause will also protect the *Contractor* against being used as a free estimating service and being distracted from the 'day job'.

Demonstrating the cost may prove challenging in some situations, particularly if the people preparing the quotation are already paid for under Defined Cost applications in a main Option C, D, E or F contract. Good records, as ever, are important. I describe the operation of clause 65 later in this book.

Experience of the NEC4 contracts has shown that this clause 60.1(20) is widely ignored by the Parties until they dispute something else. *Project Managers* and *Clients* are often keen to assess the cost impact of potential changes, and *Contractors* are often keen to try and earn additional revenue. Frequently, therefore, the quotations don't lead to additional compensation events under this clause unless there is a disagreement elsewhere on the contract.

I explain the use of the clause 65 provisions in Chapter 7, and its practical implementation. Regardless of what the contract says, there is always scope for disagreement when someone charges for an activity that, as here, has not led to something of value being created. This compensation event recognises the value of the people who prepare such quotations: estimators, builders, designers, engineers, temporary works specialists, planners and, of course, a supply chain connected to the *Contractor*. The costs of an abortive quotation can be significant, so I recommend that the *Project Manager* and the *Contractor* discuss the likely abortive costs that would be assessed under this clause before an instruction is given by the *Project Manager* that would lead to those costs being incurred.

Clause 60.1(21)

Additional compensation events stated in Contract Data part one.

I explained earlier in this chapter about the need for good drafting when amending or adding new compensation events. This clause allows additional compensation events to be stated in Contract Data part one. The wording is specific to Contract Data part one, thus avoiding the potential for an erroneous entry in part two by a tenderer that could lead to an unintended change in risk profile.

Additional compensation events may be desirable, and I provided some examples earlier. These tend to be for specific risks that may deter companies from bidding for a contract or that may lead to disproportionate pricing from those who do. The inclusion of additional compensation events under this clause should be considered carefully as part of an overall package of risk management that might also include Z clauses and additional *Client* liabilities.

Patrick Waterhouse
ISBN 978-0-7277-6560-4
https://doi.org/10.1680/necdcce.65604.037

Chapter 6
Compensation events in the main and secondary Options

There are further compensation events that only apply to contracts using main Options B and D, where a Bill of Quantities has been used. These recognise that the Bill of Quantities is usually prepared by the *Client* and that the risk in its accuracy therefore rests with the *Client*.

The correct preparation and use of a Bill of Quantities requires considerable professional skill, and it is my experience that these skills are less common in the industry than they once were due to the reduced use of bills in construction contracts. Ironically this is probably something caused partly by the success of NEC contracts, where only a third of the main Options involve a Bill of Quantities and where, in my experience, main Options A and C predominate. These two main Options use an Activity Schedule for part of their pricing mechanisms.

Despite the welcome advance of technology and the part-automation of taking off quantities from designs, we still need people with an understanding of how bills should be used and the role of a *method of measurement*. The following three additional compensation events require administering by people with the relevant skills. Bills of quantities can appear to be deceptively simple, yet the consequences of getting them wrong can be considerable.

The ECC provides a choice for the selection of the *method of measurement* – it is identified in Contract Data part one. Several are published, for example the *Civil Engineering Standard Method of Measurement*, 4th edition, revised (CESMM4), which is accompanied by a handbook and a series of worked examples. Such accompanying texts to any method of measurements are a useful guide to the Parties and their advisors.

Clause 60.4

A difference between the final total quantity of work done and the quantity stated for an item in the Bill of Quantities is a compensation event if

- the difference does not result from a change to the Scope,
- the difference causes the Defined Cost per unit of quantity to change and
- the rate in the Bill of Quantities for the item multiplied by the final total quantity of work done is more than 0.5% of the total of the Prices at the Contract Date.

If the Defined Cost per unit of quantity is reduced, the affected rate is reduced.

This compensation event leads to a re-rating of individual items where there is enough change in quantity for that item, but not where the change in quantity results from a change to the Scope. Where a change to the Scope creates a compensation event, that is covered by clause 60.1(1). The principle in clause 60.4 recognises that the larger the volume of work needed under a particular rate, the more efficiently (i.e. cheaply and quickly) it can usually be executed due to economies of scale and vice versa. While it is the change in quantity that leads to the compensation event, the threshold at which this happens is specified financially; this must be more than 0.5% of the total of the Prices at the Contract Date, in other words the value of the contract on day 1. Bills of Quantities always contain estimated quantities when first prepared. Some of those quantities, for example structural steelwork, are unlikely to change without a change in the Scope. But others, for example earthworks, can experience significant changes from their original estimated quantities. This compensation event provides a re-rating and, as explained in the final sentence of Clause 60.4, the rate can be reduced too.

Changes to rates need to reflect the contract's assessment rules, such as the Schedules of Costs Components, the provisions for Defined Cost, clause 52.1 and the Fee. The assessment of amounts in this process will involve some judgement, with the potential for conflicting views. Therefore, good records are essential, and all calculations should follow the contract's rules in clause 63. Joint assessment by the *Project Manager* and the *Contractor* will help in this regard.

Clause 60.5

A difference between the final total quantity of work done and the quantity for an item stated in the Bill of Quantities which delays Completion, or the meeting of the Condition stated for a Key Date is a compensation event.

This compensation event recognises that, with significant increases in quantity over that originally stated in the Bill of Quantities, the change in rate envisaged under clause 60.4 will not compensate the *Contractor* for its prolongation costs. These are the time-related overheads that accrue while the *works* are lengthened in duration. As before, the assessment needs to stay faithful to the ECC's assessment provisions for cost and time. The delay to Completion, and any sectional Completion or any Key Date, will also lead to amendments to those dates where that is due.

Clause 60.6

The *Project Manager* gives an instruction to correct a mistake in the Bill of Quantities which is

- A departure from the rules for item descriptions or division of the work into items in the *method of measurement* or
- Due to an ambiguity or inconsistency.

Each such correction is a compensation event which may lead to reduced Prices.

The impact of this compensation event is not often well understood in the industry. After all, in this scenario there is no additional or varied work. The issue here is that the *Contractor* has taken the Bill of Quantities at the tender stage as being correct and consistent with the *method of measurement*, and will have made pricing decisions based on the data provided. If an error has crept in and subsequently needs correcting by the *Project Manager*, post-contract, then either the *Contractor* or the *Client* will be compensated for the effects of the incorrect documents. The provisions for faulty Bills of Quantities work on the assumption that the *Client* prepared those documents and is therefore responsible for any errors therein.

This compensation event also allows the reduction in the Prices.

There is a reference to an ambiguity or inconsistency that does not specify that the error has to be entirely in the Bills of Quantities. Where an inconsistency is corrected (but not an ambiguity), say between the Bills of Quantities on one hand and the Scope on the other, then clause 60.7 says that the *Contractor* is assumed to have taken the Bills of Quantities to be correct.

Clause 60.7

In assessing a compensation event which results from a correction of an inconsistency between the Bill of Quantities and another document, the *Contractor* is assumed to have taken the Bill of Quantities as correct.

This is one of just a small number of clauses[i] in the default ECC form that establishes an order of precedence between the various constituents of the contract.[ii] Such instances of inconsistencies are common but, in my experience, they rarely involve significant amounts. Any such compensation event should be administered by someone who understands the subtleties of Bills of Quantities and the *method of measurement* and how the Bills of Quantities interact with the remainder of the contract.

Clause X1.5

The Defined Cost for compensation events is assessed using

- the Defined Cost at *base date* levels for amounts calculated from rates stated in the Contract Data for people and Equipment and
- the Defined Cost current at the dividing date by one plus the PAF [Price Adjustment Factor] for the last assessment of the amount due before that dividing date, for other amounts.

I have only quoted part of secondary Option X1 (price adjustment for inflation) here to show the effect of the clause on Defined Cost. This final clause of X1 explains how amounts assessed for compensation events will be indexed to match the effect of the agreed index movement. Secondary Option X1 only works with main Options A, B, C and D. The cost-reimbursable nature of main Options E and F means that amounts actually incurred are reimbursed, so no inflationary adjustment is required.

Clause X2.1

A change in the law of the country in which the Site is located is a compensation event if it occurs after the Contract Date. If the effect of a compensation event which is a change in the law is to reduce the total Defined Cost, the Prices are reduced.

[i] See also clauses 60.1(1) (second bullet), 60.3 and 63.10).

[ii] Of course, many Clients add such a provision as a Z clause, but that falls outside this book's remit.

This compensation event occurs when a change in law happens after the Contract Date, even if the change was known about by the Parties prior to the Contract Date. The change in law must occur in the same country as the Site. So, for example, if a change in law occurs in another country where Plant and Materials are being manufactured, this will not lead to a compensation event.

The aim of this X clause, when included in the contract, is to fully transfer the risk of change in law to the *Client*. Even where changes in law are known about in advance in many countries, the date of the change becoming effective can be at large, so requiring the *Contractor* to take this risk may lead to higher tender prices unnecessarily.

If secondary Option X2 is included in the proposed Contract Data, tenderers bidding for an ECC contract should not include for a known change in law at the Site in their proposals if it is likely to occur after the Contract Date. Once the change actually affects the *works*, then the Parties should also recognise that the choice of the *law of the contract* may be irrelevant to the occurrence, or not, of a compensation event under this clause.

Clause X12.3(6)

The Core Group may give an instruction to the Partners to change the Partnering Information. Each such change to the Partnering Information is a compensation event which may lead to reduced Prices.

Clause X12.3(7)

The Core Group prepares and maintains a timetable showing the proposed timing of the contributions of the Partners. The Core Group issues a copy of the timetable to the Partners each time it is revised. The *Contractor* changes its programme if it is necessary to do so in order to comply with the revised timetable. Each such change is a compensation event which may lead to reduced Prices.

These compensation events refer to changes in the multiparty collaboration arrangements, where secondary Option X12 has been incorporated. Changes instructed by the Core Group to either the Partnering Information or to the timing of contributions in the *Contractor's* programme will create a compensation event. Each is self-explanatory, and the methods of assessment will reflect the main Option used. The *Contractor* will be compensated for the effect of the changes in the Core Group's arrangements once they are known and instructed.

The aim of the secondary Option X12 provisions is to make the provision of works more effective in terms of cost, time and quality. The use of common key performance indicators assists with achieving the aim. But in such arrangements it is common that, for the common good, an individual partner will be required to do additional work, or change the order of its work or amend how its collaboration is provided. In any of these situations, a compensation event will arise for the consequences to the *Contractor* of its changed collaboration, including a reduction in Prices as appropriate.

Clause X14.2

Delay in making the advanced payment in accordance with the contract is a compensation event.

Secondary Option X14 allows for an advanced payment from the *Client* to the *Contractor*, usually to pay for something being manufactured in advance of the *works*, perhaps requiring a long lead time before reaching the Working Areas.

Should a delay occur in the *Client* making the advance payment where secondary Option X14 is incorporated, this compensation event will occur. The payment is due under the second bullet of clause 50.3. The failure to pay that amount on time will surely lead to an obligation to pay interest under clause 51.3. But the reality of advanced payments is often that the payment is needed by the *Contractor* as a down-payment to a supplier or Subcontractor for a major piece of off-site manufacture. Without access to working capital, and where the *Contractor* will have relied upon this payment, it will suffer through late payment, perhaps leading to a delay in delivery with a consequential delay to the *works*. Demonstrating the impact of this event may be difficult, even considering the clear inconvenience that the late payment will cause. In the example suggested, the effect of a delay in delivery will lead to a need to compare the delay and its effect on planned Completion, as with other compensation events.

Clause X15.1

The *Contractor* is not liable for a Defect which arose from its design unless it failed to carry out that design using the skill and care normally used by professionals designing works similar to the *works*.

Clause X15.2

If the *Contractor* corrects a Defect for which it is not liable under the contract it is a compensation event.

Secondary Option X15 is included in design and build contracts to reduce the design obligation of the *Contractor* to the standard often referred to elsewhere as 'reasonable skill and care'. Within secondary Option X15 there is provision for a compensation event if defective work has to be corrected, where that work arose from its design and the design was provided to the standard required by clause X15.1. This clause X15.2 is potentially contradictory, albeit its intent is clear. If there is a Defect then, according to the definition in clause 11.2(6), it is a breach by the *Contractor* and there is therefore a liability for the *Contractor* to correct. If the design has been provided with the skill and care required, then there is no Defect according to this clause. I have assumed here that clause X15.2 is read in conjunction with clause X15.1 and is not a stand-alone provision.

Clause X15.2 will compensate the *Contractor* for rectifying issues that arise where the *Contractor's* design has been provided with the skill and care required, but where the design has not achieved the result specified elsewhere in the contract. If the *Project Manager* instructs the *Contractor* to remedy such an issue, there would be a compensation event.

A Defect is defined in clause 11.2(6) as a part of the *works* that is not in accordance with the Scope. Where a part of the *works* is defective, it may be that the design was provided to the required standard, and therefore we need to differentiate between works and design here.

Clause Y2.5

If the *Contractor* exercises its right under the Housing Grants, Construction and Regeneration Act 1996 as amended by the Local Democracy, Economic Development and Construction Act 2009 to suspend performance, it is a compensation event.

The ECC is succinct on this issue. The legislation named in clause Y2.5, effective in England, Wales and Scotland (and its equivalent in Northern Ireland), allows the *Contractor* to suspend performance in certain situations of non-payment and requires[iii] contracts (for them to comply with the legislation) to contain provisions for the *Contractor* to recover its costs in those situations. That is the sole purpose of this clause. The drafters of the ECC do not elaborate further, albeit the usual assessment rules of clause 63 apply to any such event. This is a process that will require good record keeping and the Parties' cooperation at the site level, even if more senior people in the respective organisations have differences.

The NEC drafters have provided for the minimum provisions required by the HGCRA 1996 to avoid intervention through one of the schemes. For example, the contract does not mention when or how suspension would occur: that is left to the act, and is outside the remit of this book. Also, nothing is included to explain what happens in the event of the *Project Manager* failing to certify a payment despite a payment application from the *Contractor*. Again, that is provided for by the HGCRA 1996.

This provision limits the *Contractor's* remedy in the event of suspension to the Defined Cost plus Fee provisions of compensation events. Where suspension occurs, the contract will set out how costs are dealt with through the rules in clause 63.

[iii] Housing Grants Construction and Regeneration Act (HGRA) 1996 as amended, section 112(3A); Construction Contracts Order (Northern Ireland) 1997 as amended, article 11(3A).

ICE Publishing

Patrick Waterhouse
ISBN 978-0-7277-6560-4
https://doi.org/10.1680/necdcce.65604.043
ICE Publishing: All rights reserved

Chapter 7
Notifying compensation events, producing quotations and proposed instructions

Compensation event processes

Compensation events feature in all NEC contracts and share common processes. The processes might appear excessive, but they are designed to assist the Parties to deal with the consequences of change and other project risks. Many of the contract's requirements are for communication so that the *Contractor* and the *Project Manager* are aware of each other's actions. The processes contain several time bars, intended to incentivise the right behaviours or at least to deter the wrong behaviours. There are four stages to the compensation events processes that are summarised here. The first two stages, notification and quotation, are explained in this chapter, and the remaining two are explained in the next chapter.

- **Notification**. Before committing resource to dealing with the commercial niceties of compensation events, the Parties need to establish if a compensation event has occurred. The obligations to notify compensation events are clearly set out and should be simple to observe. But I repeatedly see problems caused by the reluctance of *Project Managers* to notify compensation events, supposedly in the hope that the *Contractor* will not notice that something has changed or that a risk event has occurred. Clause 61.1 requires the *Project Manager* to notify compensation events that have arisen from specific sources. A *Project Manager* that omits to notify a compensation event runs the risk that the *Contractor* will do so long after the event and may still have the entitlement to do so, with ensuing difficulties for the *Client's* budget. Dealing with such issues at the time is usually easier than explaining the cause of additional payments to the *Client* much later.
- **Quotation**. Having established that a compensation event has occurred, the first step is for the *Contractor* to prepare a quotation once instructed to do so by the *Project Manager*. Collaboration at this stage will certainly aid the smooth administration of change. Rather than preparing a quotation alone, the *Contractor* can obtain the input of the *Project Manager* before starting the process. There is a greater likelihood that the quotation will be accepted if it has been prepared with the *Project Manager's* knowledge and contribution. There are formal ways for the *Project Manager* to make an input, but I also emphasise the importance of less formal collaboration being deployed.
- **Assessment**. The contract, in clause 63, sets out the assessment rules for compensation events. These rules should be used by *Contractors* preparing quotations and by *Project Managers* undertaking their own assessments. These rules cover the impact on both time and money. They detail the *Contractor's* entitlement and the *Client's* obligations, and the sole remedy clause (63.6) explains this. I look at the assessment processes in detail in later chapters in this book.
- **Implementation**. This phase of the process concerns the implementation into the contract of the revised Prices, Key Dates and Completion Date(s). (There may be more than one Completion Date if secondary Option X5 (sectional Completion) forms part of the contract.) It does not refer

to the physical implementation of any works that might be the subject of the compensation event. This is the conclusion of the process and the point, after which, the compensation event cannot be reassessed except by mutual consent (clause 12.3) or the intervention of the *Senior Representatives*, the *Adjudicator* or the *tribunal* as appropriate. I look at the implementation processes in detail in the next chapter.

Notification

The purpose of the notification clauses is to ensure that both Parties are aware of the progress of change in the *works* or the occurrence of another event that might affect time and money. Managing change is difficult, and if control is not maintained the Parties will struggle to understand the true position in the project of time and money. It cannot be overstated how important this process is in the aim of correctly administering projects. The starting point of the compensation events process is the notification: where either the *Project Manager* or the *Contractor* notifies the other as to the occurrence of a compensation event. No other administration is needed at this point, such as a quotation or a programme. The first stage is to accept that there has been, or is likely to be, a compensation event. Where the *Project Manager* makes the notification, that communication should also include an instruction to submit a quotation (clause 61.2).

The *Project Manager* has the ability, in clauses 61.2 and 61.4, to notify the *Contractor* that the Prices and dates will not be changed when the event

- arises from the *Contractor's* fault
- has not happened and probably won't
- has not been notified in accordance with the time requirements of the contract
- has no effect on dates or Prices
- is not one stated in the contract.

The ability to say 'no' at this point, prior to the preparation of any quotations or assessments, is designed to avoid unnecessary effort. Interestingly, if and when the *Project Manager* notifies a compensation event that might not suit the *Contractor*, for example a reduction in Prices from a change to the Scope, the *Contractor* has no formal route to argue against this.

Clause 61.1 requires the *Project Manager* to notify the *Contractor* of a compensation event that arises from the *Project Manager* or *Supervisor*

- giving an instruction (clauses 60.1(1), 60.1(4), 60.1(7), 60.1(10) and 60.6)
- giving a notification (clauses 60.1(17) and 60.1(20))
- issuing a certificate (clause 60.1(15))
- changing an earlier decision (clause 60.1(8)).

The relevant compensation events should all be known to a competent *Project Manager*, hence the obligation to notify them to the *Contractor*. The notification should be provided at the same time as the communication that created the compensation event. Failure to notify a compensation event at this point is not a rare event. Some *Project Managers* have the (mistaken) belief that if they don't notify a compensation event then somehow the *Contractor* will miss the relevance of the communication, and a change to the Prices may be avoided. That is unlikely, and the omission of this important contractual process is likely to cause unnecessary problems later.

Where the *Project Manager* notifies a compensation event to the *Contractor* in this manner, the notification must be accompanied by an instruction to submit a quotation. Potentially, therefore, we may have three items of communication covering the same event

- the original instruction, certificate or decision
- a notification of a compensation event
- an instruction to submit a quotation (although this can be included in the notification).

In clause 61.2 (and 61.4) the contract allows for the *Project Manager* and the *Contractor* to agree that there is a compensation event, but for the *Project Manager* to state that there is no impact on time and money. While such a provision may seem like a futile exercise in contract administration, it does leave open the door to a revision to the latter opinion through adjudication and the *tribunal*.

Clause 61.3 describes the process to be followed when the *Contractor* is obliged to notify a compensation event and when the *Project Manager* has not notified it.

The important part of this clause is the time bar of 8 weeks on the *Contractor's* notification of a compensation event, by when that event should have been notified by the *Contractor*. Failure, by the *Contractor*, to notify a compensation event within the stated period means that 'the Prices, the Completion Date or a Key Date are not changed'.

This clause is frequently amended by a Z clause reducing the time-barred period from 8 weeks to a much lower number. The lowest period that I have seen is 5 working days, which appears to be far too short, albeit it related to a design and build subcontract flowing down from a private finance project agreement, itself with short time bars. The purpose of this time bar is to encourage the *Contractor* to make the *Project Manager* aware of a compensation event when otherwise the *Project Manager* might not be aware. The obligation is not to make the *Project Manager* aware (that's far too subjective and difficult to demonstrate) but to notify, remembering the provisions of clauses 13.1, 13.2 and 13.7. Legal commentators, better qualified than me, point to various uncertainties with this clause, particularly where it is used as a limit or exclusion of liability by the *Client*. I will avoid joining that discussion, but where Z clause amendments are being prepared, they need to be done by someone with the necessary knowledge of the wider legal issues involved. This clause has a constructive purpose, which is to encourage collaboration. If the time period is set so low as to be impractical, it may affect the legal enforceability of the clause, and it will certainly make the Parties' correct use of the contract more challenging. In both scenarios the creation of administrative difficulties is more likely. For example, a *Client* inserting clauses giving effect to short time bars is likely to encourage a barrage of correspondence for the *Project Manager* to receive, as the *Contractor* notifies every possible compensation event, however slight, in order to avoid losing entitlement.

My advice to those drafting notification provisions in contracts is

- If you want to alter the 8 weeks period, think carefully about the timescales needed for all to comply. Do not reduce it to a very low limit unless there is a good operational reason for doing so.
- If the 8 weeks period is to be altered, consideration should be given to how the revised period will work in practice and including the role of suppliers and Subcontractors.
- Don't try to improve the drafting around the notification periods (e.g. the reference to the *Contractor's* beliefs in clause 61.3 is often amended).
- As with all amendments, only appoint someone to draft these who has the necessary skills and qualifications to do so.

In general, my advice to those managing notifications in contracts is

- Understand the combined effect of the various compensation event clauses: core clauses, secondary Options and Z clauses.
- View the time bars as a maximum, and make your notifications as early as you can.
- Adhere to the formalities in clause 13 with respect to the format of communications.
- Later references to meeting minutes, 'that chat we had on site' and other vague recollections are unlikely to be contractually effective long after the event when they may be needed in adjudication or litigation.

The response by the *Project Manager* to a compensation event notification is one of the following

- Notify the *Contractor* that, for one or more of the reasons stated in clause 61.4, the Prices and dates will not be changed. This communication needs to state the *Project Manager's* reasons to comply with the contract, and possibly a verbal discussion would assist too.
- Notify an instruction to the *Contractor* to submit a quotation(s) for the event.

The final part of clause 61.4 is a time bar on the *Project Manager's* decision-making. If the *Project Manager* does not respond to the *Contractor's* notification within the week allowed, or agreed longer period, the *Contractor* may notify the *Project Manager* of that failure. This is a rare use of the word 'may' in the contract. If, 2 weeks after this reminder, the *Project Manager* still hasn't responded, then the *Contractor's* notification is treated as accepted and an instruction to submit a quotation. Any *Project Manager* that gets caught by these provisions is probably in the wrong job. Even without the optional notification, the *Project Manager* will be in difficulty because of the compensation event under clause 60.1(6) created by silence.

Clauses 61.5 and 61.6

When the *Project Manager* instructs the *Contractor* to submit a quotation, the following statements can be made by the *Project Manager*

- That the *Contractor* did not give an early warning of the event that an experienced contractor could have given (clause 61.5). I discuss this issue later in this book in Chapter 8. Remember that a notification of an early warning is different from the notification of a compensation event. The failure of the *Contractor* to notify the latter may lead to the time bar in clause 61.3 being relied upon by the *Client*.
- Assumptions as to the assessment of the compensation event where there is uncertainty (clause 61.6). Where those assumptions are subsequently corrected, a further compensation event will occur under clause 60.1(17). This opportunity to manage risk sensibly happens at the notification stage, which is often being driven by the *Contractor*, not the *Project Manager*. In that likely scenario the *Project Manager* needs to become proactive, quickly.
- The purpose of clause 61.6 is to reduce the risk faced by both Parties. Such an assumption might be that the *works* will be undertaken in daytime hours, or in summer. It might relate to a particular method or material. Perhaps the *Contractor* is uncertain that excavated material will be suitable for reuse, as opposed to landfill. Where uncertainties remain in the process, it is likely that the *Contractor* will allow for the impact in time and money when preparing the quotation. If the *Project Manager* states assumptions, then the uncertainty is removed, and the *Client* only

pays for the effects of these changes if and when they occur. The *Contractor* and the *Project Manager* should be aware that corrections to assumptions may lead to a reduction in the Prices (clause 63.4), so the initial assumptions need be neither optimistic nor pessimistic.

- Clause 61.6 benefits both Parties. The *Contractor* becomes more certain of the risks that it faces and can price that risk accordingly (clause 63.8). The *Client* benefits from lower prices (clause 63.8 again) and only pays for potentially expensive ways of Providing the Works if they are actually needed.

The contract requires those assumptions to be stated by the *Project Manager* in the instruction to submit a quotation, so possibly that is the only opportunity. If further assumptions become desirable, then perhaps a new instruction is needed, and the clock is reset for the *Contractor* for the time of its response.

Example – uncertain durations

A project had a credible threat of protestor action. The level of threat varied over time. At a particular point in the project, it was decided by the *Client* that it wanted to deploy 24/7 security to a particular point of access.

This was understood by the *Contractor* and the *Project Manager*, and they could easily work out that they would need certain facilities for the security staff with mobilisation and demobilisation costs. What they didn't know was how long these would be required for – the risk might reduce and was hard to predict. So, the *Project Manager* stated an assumption that the facilities would be required for 8 weeks, and included in the instruction that the overall duration was unknown at the point of instruction. This meant that the *Contractor* based the price on a 'per week' basis, and changing the price to reflect the actual duration was easy, by use of another compensation event. This is a fairly clear case of 'too uncertain to be forecast reasonably' – neither party controls the thing that dictates the duration.

Dealing with uncertain durations is one of the ways in which clause 61.6 is used. During the earlier stages of the COVID-19 pandemic, many arrangements were known to be temporary but with no real idea as to the likely duration, so assumptions from the *Project Manager* were common in compensation events.

Example – disposal of excavated fill material

An example of a sensible approach to the use of clause 61.6 was an assumption relating to disposal of excavated fill material that came about because of an instruction from the *Project Manager*. The *Contractor* was determined that it should be priced for offsite disposal 'because we can't carry the risk'. The *Client* was confident that a home could be found for the material on site. This went in circles for a while, and the final conclusion was that a *Project Manager* assumption was stated that offsite disposal would not be needed, which reduced the quotation by about £100 000. The *Client* was right this time, and the money was saved. Had it been wrong, it wouldn't have lost out. This was a convenient way of dealing with that scenario, and it gave the *Contractor* access to a further compensation event if the assumption had been shown to be wrong.

So, two examples demonstrating the use of clause 61.6. The first is maybe more 'correct' – filling in a factual gap that neither Party can control. The latter is a bit more creative, but this approach can be useful where the Parties have differing views and accept that both views are valid/reasonable/possible and the *Client* is willing to take a risk.

The system of *Project Manager* assumptions can work well, particularly where the *Contractor* is involved in proposing assumptions. Anything unilaterally proposed by the *Contractor* will not have any effect unless it is subsequently stated by the *Project Manager*. This doesn't stop *Contractors* trying to insert qualifications to quotations, often to the annoyance of *Project Managers* who know the contractual status of such comments. One, on my panel of consultees, says

> I am now assertive to the point of bluntness about *Project Manager* assumptions: only I (as the *Project Manager*) can make them – end of discussion. If you can't show me the correspondence where I agreed it, it doesn't exist. Having said that, I am happy to listen to suggestions about assumptions that might be mutually beneficial, but it is my call. Otherwise, the *Contractor* is welcome to price the risk.

A detail of clause 61.6, often missed by *Project Managers*, is that both actions of the *Project Manager* when read with clause 10.1 are mandatory: they must be done in the circumstances described. Many of my consultees report that *Project Managers* are too reticent to get involved in this type of activity, preferring instead to leave the quotation entirely to the *Contractor*. *Contractors* often state their own assumptions (which have no contractual effect) or demand that the *Project Manager* does so. As with many other areas of this contract, the *Project Manager* and *Contractor* should work together if they have potential ideas to share.

The final part of clause 61 states that a compensation event cannot be notified after the issue of the Defects Certificate. The Defects Certificate is issued by the *Supervisor* on or shortly after the *defects date*, and, coming long after Completion, is an action that is often delayed or even missed entirely as people move on and corporate memory loss is experienced. This is one of several connections to that clause that reinforce the need for it to be complied with. If the Defects Certificate is issued later, or not at all, the possibility for further compensation events being notified exists. From the *Client's* point of view, this won't be welcome, as such a notification may refer to a historic event that was missed by the *Contractor* at the time.

Quotations

Once the notification phase has concluded, and if the *Project Manager* agrees that a compensation event has occurred, the *Contractor* should (subject to the limitations in clause 64) prepare and submit a quotation. The happiest outcome of a submitted quotation is that it is accepted by the *Project Manager* and its contents are implemented, and that is the end of the matter. However, in most situations the quotation is merely the start of a process of to and fro, often unnecessarily prolonged. The task of assessing compensation events is one of many in the NEC suite that is enhanced by collaboration, here between the *Contractor* and the *Project Manager*. Such collaboration will reduce the time consumed by this particular element of contract administration.

The quotation must show 'proposed changes to the Prices and any delay to the Completion Date and Key Dates assessed by the *Contractor*' (clause 62.2).

Following the defined terms in the contract, we see that the financial element is the change to the Prices. Clause 63.1 sets out the rules for the change to the Prices, based largely on Defined Cost and the Fee. Each of the main Options includes its own definition of Prices and how the changed quantum is implemented. These must be the starting points for the financial part of the quotation. The definitions of Prices and the explanation of how the changes to the Prices are implemented are in the following clauses

- Main Option A – clause 11.2(32). The definition refers to the activities on the Activity Schedule. Clause 63.14 says, 'Assessments for changed Prices for compensation events are in the form of changes to the Activity Schedule.'
- Main Option B – clause 11.2(33). The definition refers to the lump sums and amounts from the Bill of Quantities. Clause 63.15 says, 'Assessments for changed Prices for compensation events are in the form of changes to the Bill of Quantities.'
- Main Option C – clause 11.2(32). The definition refers to the activities on the Activity Schedule, which, in main Option C, is the target. Clause 63.14 says, 'Assessments for changed Prices for compensation events are in the form of changes to the Activity Schedule.'
- Main Option D – clause 11.2(33). The definition refers to the lump sums and amounts from the Bill of Quantities, which, in main Option D, is the target. Clause 63.15 says, 'Assessments for changed Prices for compensation events are in the form of changes to the Bill of Quantities.'
- Main Option E – clause 11.2(34). The definition of Prices here reflects the cost-reimbursable nature of this Option, and refers to the forecast of the total Defined Cost plus the Fee for the whole of the *works*. In this Option, the assessment of a compensation event does not affect what the *Contractor* is paid for the work.
- Main Option F – clause 11.2(34). The definition of Prices here reflects the cost-reimbursable nature of this Option, and refers to the forecast of the total Defined Cost plus the Fee for the whole of the *works*. Clause 63.17 refers to a change to the **p**rice for the work but deliberately does not refer to the **P**rices (note the emphasis).

The *Contractor's* quotation for the financial impact of a compensation event eventually leads to Defined Cost, whichever main Option is used. It must follow several rules in the contract, not all of which are immediately apparent from clause 62. The simplification in NEC4 of the use of the Schedules of Cost Components has made life easier for contracting parties. Now only one will apply in any one main Option (A, B, C, D or E)

- for main Options A and B, the Short Schedule of Cost Components will apply
- for main Options C, D and E, the Schedule of Cost Components will apply
- for main Option F, neither schedule is used.

The relevant schedule is used to establish the Defined Cost, where actual and historic or forecast and future, as required by clause 63.1.

Clause 62.1 allows the *Project Manager*, following discussions with the *Contractor*, to instruct the submission of alternative quotations. The *Contractor* must comply with this instruction but may also provide further quotations based on alternative methods. For example, an instruction for additional work may be satisfied by the use of prefabricated components, or alternatively by in situ ones. The *Project Manager* could instruct the *Contractor* to provide a quotation for each method. Each will have different financial, quality and time considerations. The working of this clause sits well with clause 61.6, explained earlier. While the opening sentence of clause 62.1 suggests that discussion is optional, the importance of holding such a discussion cannot be overemphasised.

Such alternatives might include

- the sequence of working
- if/when possessions will be available (rail, highways, airports, etc.)
- the type of method or materials used, how long they take to be installed, and any drying/curing time before subsequent works
- daytime or night-time working
- using existing people, or bringing in additional personnel
- the technology to be deployed
- the training or certification of the people involved
- in situ works, or off-site manufacture
- adapting existing infrastructure or building new
- with or without delay to the Completion Date or Key Dates.

As with clause 61.6, while clause 62.1 relies upon an instruction from the *Project Manager*, it will operate more effectively if that instruction results from collaboration between the two participants.

Clause 62.1 suggests that the *Contractor* may not have to react instantly to a *Project Manager* instruction as clauses 27.3 and 63.9 might suggest. If, while going through the process of quoting and assessing the event, there are still alternatives under consideration, then the procurement of the necessary Plant and Materials, Equipment and Subcontractors can't take place until the decision-making is narrowed down, so, again, the Parties need to collaborate to do this. An immediate start on work may not be possible nor desirable.

This clause is often used to assist with value engineering. A further instruction may be needed from the *Project Manager* if the development of alternatives veers sufficiently far from the initial instruction or is ambiguous. For example, if the instruction causing the compensation event was for the construction of a pipeline across a highway and the *Project Manager* had instructed alternative quotations from either boring beneath the road or by the excavation of a trench, those works couldn't start until the method was selected. But, generally, a second instruction shouldn't be needed, as the alternative quotations are just different methods of achieving the same outcome.

Some users of the contract, particularly those that are the *Client* or *Project Manager*, report frustration with the paucity of *Contractor* proposals here, suggesting that there is little incentive for the *Contractor* to be creative. Speaking to second- and third-tier subcontractors, they report little appetite in their immediate customers to encourage or accept such suggestions.

What happens if one or more of the quotations is not accepted? Is the abortive work in preparing the quotations subject to the provisions of clause 60.1(20) (proposed instructions)? Probably not, but I can understand why *Contractors* may think that it should be.

Both clauses 61.6 and 62.1 benefit from collaboration and presumably, therefore, early warnings, early warning meetings and the proactive use of the Early Warning Register will assist.

> **Example – encountering rock when excavating**
>
> A *Contractor* is responsible for the design and construction of a substation adjacent to a wind farm. It encounters rock when excavating trenches to install cable ducts, and notifies a compensation event under clause 60.1(12). The *Project Manager*, after consultation with the *Contractor*, instructs the submission of two alternative quotations. The first was to maintain the current layout of ducts and break out the rock where necessary. The second was to construct longer duct runs that would avoid the localised rock. By doing this the *Project Manager* could see that the longer duct runs would cost less overall because the additional costs of doing so were considerably dwarfed by the rock-breaking costs.

The relatively simple use of clause 62.1 as in this example is unfortunately rare. I tend to see opportunities for this clause to be used that are missed. The clause needs collaboration between the *Project Manager* and the *Contractor* to achieve the clarity necessary to deliver value. Sometimes *Contractors* complain about the abortive cost of producing multiple alternative quotations when only one will be selected, but I think that misses the point. The Parties are obliged to do this, regardless of costs, and the *Contractor* will obtain additional profitable work as a consequence of collaborating properly. Where the Parties do this exercise alone in separate locations (as is often the case with the increase in remote working), neither will obtain the full value for their contribution.

Project Managers sometimes struggle to persuade the *Client* to allow the instruction of alternative quotations. *Clients* will sometimes cite governance or procurement issues that prevent or strongly advise towards such actions. Given that these procedures will hopefully contribute against achieving best value, it is difficult to see how good governance would allow the *Client* or *Project Manager* not to do this.

The conclusion of the clause 62.1 process is presumably the *Project Manager* accepting one of the quotations or making an assessment based on one of the alternatives. Whichever route is chosen, the *Project Manager* will need to identify which alternative has been selected, and, although the contract does not specify this, an instruction changing the Scope to that effect will be needed after implementation.

Clauses 62.2 and 62.3 require that a quotation should be submitted by the *Contractor* within 3 weeks of instruction, and must include

- proposed changes to the Prices
- any delay to the Completion Date
- any delay to the Key Date(s).

These terms are all defined and have a specific meaning in the contract. I routinely see quotations from *Contractors* (and, indeed, assessments prepared by *Project Managers*) that do not follow the contract. The term 'Prices' is specific to the main Option selected, as I discussed earlier. The cost and time impacts of a compensation event should be assessed in accordance with the provisions in clauses 63.1 and 63.5, respectively, and the terms in those clauses are also defined, and some of them are also main Option specific.

The quotations should contain enough explanation of the assessments, and should include any necessary alterations to the Accepted Programme too. Where the compensation event relates to the Information Execution Plan (clause X10.5), then any changes to that must also be provided in the quotation.

The default period of 3 weeks for the *Contractor* to prepare a quotation should not be viewed as absolute. If it can be done more quickly, then it should be. If the size and complexity of a quotation demands, then the period can be extended by agreement under clause 62.5, which appears to duplicate what has already been said in clause 13.5. Clause 62.5, and this advice, also applies to the *Project Manager's* response to a quotation.

I describe later what the *Project Manager* must do once a quotation is received. Differences of opinion are predictable in this type of arrangement, but those differences will be exacerbated if the quotation (and any response from the *Project Manager*) is not prepared in accordance with the contract. Where the quotation has been prepared in accordance with the contract, then any differences of opinion can be addressed much more easily.

The *Project Manager's* response to a quotation is one of

- Accept the quotation, in which case the compensation event is implemented on the terms in the quotation. I explain implementation in Chapter 8.
- Instruct the *Contractor* to submit a revised quotation, having explained the problem(s) with the previous quotation as required by clause 62.4.
- Tell the *Contractor* that the *Project Manager* will now assess the compensation event for one or more of the reasons in clause 64.

If the *Project Manager* elects to make an assessment, which is common, then the procedure is explained in clause 64, which I describe in Chapter 8.

Later chapters of this book look in detail at the financial assessment of compensation events and the use of the Schedules of Cost Components.

Clause 62.6 is another time bar on the *Project Manager's* decision-making. If the *Project Manager* does not respond to the *Contractor's* quotation within the 3 weeks allowed, or agreed longer period, the *Contractor* may notify the *Project Manager* of that failure. This is a rare use of the word 'may' in the contract. If, 2 weeks after this reminder, the *Project Manager* still hasn't responded, then the *Contractor's* quotation is treated as accepted. Even without the optional notification, the *Project Manager* will be in difficulty because of the compensation event under clause 60.1(6) created by silence.

Proposed instructions

The provisions for proposed instructions are included in the contract in clause 65 to allow a formal exploration by the *Project Manager* of the cost and time impact of a proposed instruction. This may be a change to the *works* or some additional work, or maybe a change to the constraints that must be complied with. This clause will only apply to instructions within the gift of the *Project Manager*, the primary one being the ability to change the Scope. Any wider change to the contract would need to be formalised through a change recognised in clause 12.3, and therefore this clause may not be of use. The provisions were broadened in the NEC4 suite, and are largely seen as being fairer by the people who have assisted me writing this book.

Sometimes a *Client* may obtain additional funding or budget to allow for increased expenditure on a project. Of course, the reverse also applies, and there is nothing in clause 65 to prevent it being used to identify how the cost of the project might be reduced by such an instruction. As the outcome of this clause is a compensation event, such a change would not be able to shorten the time for Completion, so a change to the total of the Prices is all that could be achieved. But I have seen such 'negative' changes in periods where the *Client* loses funding, for example the collapse of the residential market during the sub-prime problems of 2008 or the more-recent difficulties caused by the COVID-19 pandemic. *Clients* concerned that they needed to reduce expenditure could use the provisions of clause 65 to explore what reduction in cost could be achieved by a reduction in Scope.

In other forms of contract, and this includes the NEC4 short forms, such a provision is not included, and therefore the *Client* does not have a formal way of understanding the approximate cost of a proposed change without actually instructing it to happen.

I introduced the rationale behind clause 65 earlier, in my explanation on clause 60.1(20), which is linked to this clause. Where the *Project Manager* instructs the *Contractor* to submit a quotation, then the quotation must be submitted, but without undertaking the work in question. The normal period of 3 weeks for the *Contractor* to submit a quotation applies here. The *Project Manager* must state the period during which an instruction to proceed with the works will be given when instructing the quotation. The drafting of the instructions to proceed and the explanation of when the work is likely to take place are important considerations. The better that these instructions are drafted, the more likely it is that the *Contractor* will understand what is required and, at least in theory, the more compliant the quotation is likely to be. Where the *Project Manager's* instructions are vague or inconsistent, then the process is unlikely to start well. Discussion with *Contractors* suggests that less than 10% of compensation events occur through this route.

The usual provisions of compensation event assessments are available to the Parties here. Assumptions can be stated by the *Project Manager* (clause 61.6), and different ways of dealing with the compensation event can be instructed (clause 62.1), in an 'optioneering'-type approach. While not provided for in the contract, I often see contractors making their own assumptions in quotations. These do not have any contractual relevance, and won't lead to a further compensation event through clause 60.1(17) if they need correcting. But in a collaborative relationship any such assumptions should be discussed, and hopefully an understanding of where those risks lie, and what allowances should be made for them, can be achieved. Where appropriate, the *Project Manager* can state assumptions that were originally suggested by the *Contractor*.

Where a conventional compensation event is being quoted by a *Contractor*, it is almost certain that the works in question will be happening and the timescales are predictable too. With proposed instructions, it is often unclear when the works will take place in the event a firm instruction is eventually given, despite the requirement in clause 65.1 for the *Project Manager* to say so. Even where such a timescale is provided, it is often too far in the future as to be helpful. Some *Contractors* prefer to place a time limit on such quotations, particularly where a quotation is supported by time-limited quotations from suppliers and Subcontractors. The contract doesn't provide for any such limit. This is a risk that the *Contractor* is exposed to, and therefore should provide an allowance under clause 63.8 in assessments. This risk isn't just faced by the additional works that cause the compensation event but also to subsequent operations that are pushed back to a later Completion. A clear and unambiguous date by which the instruction will be given is a useful assumption for the *Project Manager* to state, and, by doing so, this complies with clause 65.1.

The *Project Manager* has some familiar choices when making a response to the quotation received from the *Contractor*

- Instruct the *Contractor* to submit a revised quotation, presumably having explained the non-compliance in the previous quotation.
- Accept the quotation, instruct the works and notify a compensation event. There are three communications here, so the *Project Manager* should issue them separately to comply with clause 13.7.
- Notify the *Contractor* that the quotation is not accepted.

The final bullet then triggers a compensation event under clause 60.1(20), discussed earlier in Chapter 5.

Interestingly, in the event that several different quotations have been submitted for the same proposed instruction, the *Project Manager* is not required (by clause 65) to state which one is being accepted. Clearly, it is hoped that the *Project Manager* would do so anyway.

Clause 65.3 allows the *Project Manager*, if an acceptable quotation cannot be obtained through this route, to instruct the change (presumably to the Scope) through the other routes in the contract, notify a compensation event and instruct the *Contractor* to submit a further quotation. That then allows the *Project Manager* to assess the compensation event if the next quotation from the *Contractor* is still unacceptable. This process is unduly burdensome, and justifies the need for the *Project Manager* and the *Contractor* to meet and discuss these issues before committing to a process that potentially could take many weeks to conclude.

What happens if the *Contractor* submits a quotation for a proposed instruction that is then not accepted, but the additional work happens anyway after the *Project Manager* instructs it through the conventional route? The contract says that the *Contractor's* costs of preparing the unaccepted quotation will be paid by the *Client* as a compensation event, and the *Contractor* then benefits from being paid for the additional work anyway. So, the *Contractor* gets paid both for the costs of preparing a quotation and for the work – probably not the original intention of the NEC's drafters.

Contractors may be comforted by the compensation event in clause 60.1(20), but it is unlikely to placate those who complain of being used as a free estimating service. It is unlikely that the consequence of this process will cause any impact on the Completion Date or Key Dates, so the likely discussion area will be that of Defined Cost. Where the unaccepted quotation has been prepared by a member of the *Contractor's* project team, then it might be difficult to demonstrate any impact on Defined Cost, particularly in an environment where the person in question is paid a fixed salary with no payments for overtime. The *Project Manager* in this scenario may argue that no additional cost has been incurred by the *Contractor*. Some *Contractors* now outsource this work to external providers as a way of demonstrating and recovering the costs involved.

Even where these costs are recovered, *Contractors* still report concerns about being led to believe that an instruction will be given, and preparing for that instruction, only to be told at the last minute that the additional works are not now needed. As one *Contractor* told me, ‘there is a good moral argument for additional payment here, but morals don’t pay the bills’. While this may generate accusations of being contractual (for some of us, that is a compliment), I advise *Contractors* not to dedicate resources to the proposed instruction until it is actually given.

Where unaccepted quotations involve design and build work, the costs may be more significant than with build-only projects. Keeping records of the costs of, say, designers, planners and estimators is vital. Compensation events under clause 60.1(20) are likely to involve the assessment of the actual Defined Cost of work already done, rather than the forecast of work to be done. Even with good records there are likely to be areas for discussion as to the time and cost commitment made by the people involved. In main Option C, D, E and F contracts the *Project Manager* can rely on the drafting in clause 52.2 or 52.3 for verifying information, but there are no such provisions to rely on in contracts formed with main Options A or B. In the priced contracts, the *Project Manager* can only rely on the requirements of clause 10.2 when requesting evidence of costs incurred. This process may elongate if the *Contractor* has worked with Subcontractors also employed under the same provisions, which will likewise wish to recover their own costs.

There follow two examples from NEC3 contracts that contain the provisions for proposed instructions but do not provide for a compensation event if the instruction is not given.

Example – the missing link

A local authority appointed a contractor to design and construct a new highway under the NEC3 ECC. Crucially, unlike the NEC4 ECC, this did not provide for a compensation event for the preparation of quotations for proposed instructions that did not progress. One aspect of the project was that it included a junction arrangement for the future connection of another major road that was being planned by another, neighbouring, local authority.

Eighteen months into the construction of the first road project the other project got the go ahead after a public inquiry. Both local authorities decided that it would be beneficial to road users that approximately 100 m of the second project’s highway, which connected into a roundabout junction, was constructed by the contractor of the first project; however, the second local authority needed cost certainty.

An instruction pursuant to clause 61.2 was issued. The *Contractor*, which was under some time and cost pressure, decided to inflate the quotation to recover some of its losses. Under the NEC3 provisions for proposed instructions, the *Project Manager* can only accept or not accept the quotation. Thus, it was not accepted as not being value for money.

An instruction to change the Works Information leading to a compensation event under clause 61.1 could have been issued, but this would not have provided cost certainty.

Example – linking old with new

The Works Information in a highways-widening contract using the NEC3 ECC required the *Contractor* to install new drainage for the widened road and link it into existing old drainage. There was a problem: the existing drainage had not been surveyed by the *Employer*, and when the *Contractor* tried to connect the new drainage to the existing drainage it found the existing drainage to be blocked and damaged beyond repair. The existing drainage had a significant length before it connected to a serviceable access chamber. The *Employer* had not budgeted for repairing or replacing the existing drainage, but had no choice in having the work done.

The *Employer* asked the *Project Manager* to instruct the *Contractor* to provide a quotation for a proposed instruction to replace the existing drainage. The *Contractor* duly obliged, but provided a rushed quotation because it did not have the time, resources or will to produce a proper quotation. The quotation was for £370 000 but the true cost was less than £150 000. The *Contractor* included several weeks of time-related site overheads because it claimed the additional work would be on the critical path. The result was that the *Project Manager* did not instruct the work through this *Contractor*.

I imagine that if the *Project Manager* had not instructed under the proposed instruction route, the *Contractor* may have produced a more realistic quotation, knowing that if the quotation was not accepted, then the *Project Manager* could self-assess the impact and the *Contractor* would be paid anyway.

Under NEC 4 the proposed instruction is included as a separate clause (65), but the mechanism is no different from NEC3, and, therefore, even with the additional compensation event, the mechanisms may not encourage the openness needed to make it work.

It remains to be seen if the incentive of a compensation event for an uninstructed change will affect the dynamics of a situation like those in the two examples to produce a different outcome. If the *Contractor* does not want the work, or sees a commercial opportunity to unreasonably profit, then the NEC4 provisions are unlikely to work effectively. If the *Project Manager* does not accept the quotation but then proceeds to instruct the change anyway and eventually make an assessment itself, the outcome may well be a dispute.

These examples support circumstantial evidence from some NEC practitioners who tell me that *Contractors* tend to pay less attention to quotations for proposed instructions than they do to actual ones.

Problems may arise in the process of proposed instructions when

- *Project Managers* make verbal requests for quotations and do not follow the communications requirements of the contract. I have come across this situation many times, and have heard of *Project Managers* who are ‘characters’ and avoid formalities wherever possible. This type of conduct makes subsequent compensation events difficult to process.
- *Project Managers* aren’t clear with their correspondence. Loose wording may make it easy to misinterpret a proposed instruction as an actual instruction. Both the *Project Manager* and the *Contractor* must be aware that a quotation is wanted for a proposed instruction, and what the consequences will be.

- Costs are incurred by suppliers, designers or Subcontractors, and are then more difficult to verify.
- Subcontractors are involved, which is often at the last minute in the process so any 'quotation' is very loose and may turn out to be inaccurate. Involving the wider supply chain is often necessary if the quotation is to be meaningful, but where those companies are engaged under NEC contracts, they too will be entitled to recover their costs in the event that the instruction is not given.
- The age-old subject of design development rears its ugly head. *Contractors* dedicate resources to a proposed instruction, but the instruction ultimately isn't given, and the *Project Manager* claims that the effort would have been needed in any event and was only design development. Clear words are needed in the original instruction from the *Project Manager* if this is indeed the expectation.
- *Project Managers* request quotations for political reasons in order to get a guide price for something that is unlikely to happen. Political decision-makers may not understand that their requests are likely to cost money in these scenarios. *Project Managers* must keep *Clients* alert to these provisions.

Example – differing views on cost

A project to refurbish five floors of a hospital was procured under the NEC4 ECC. The *Project Manager* instructed the *Contractor* to submit a quotation for a proposed instruction to replace the roof. The *Contractor's* quotation was for £110 000 to replace the roof, and it spent £9000 on a structural engineer to survey the existing roof and calculate loadings, etc. The *Project Manager* did not accept the quotation. The *Contractor* sought to recover the £9000 engineer's fee in the subsequent compensation event. The *Project Manager* had not appreciated that the *Contractor* had spent as much as that. This identifies the need for the *Project Manager* and the *Contractor* to discuss what the abortive costs might be before committing to them. That is the sensible approach.

This example demonstrates that the costs will not always be viewed in the same way by the *Project Manager* and the *Contractor*. These need to be better understood: the *Project Manager* needs to understand what things cost, and the *Contractor* needs to understand what the task is worth to the *Client*. Early discussion on these points will help. Despite the NEC4 provisions, there are still many in the industry who think that the costs of preparing quotations should be absorbed by the *Contractor* as part of overheads that are already allowed for. The contract does not see things that way, and, as part of the wider bargain agreed by the Parties, the *Contractor* is entitled to its abortive costs if the proposed instruction does not proceed. However, these provisions have reduced the number of requests for quotations issued by *Project Managers* who have little serious intention of proceeding with the works in question.

ice Publishing

Patrick Waterhouse
ISBN 978-0-7277-6560-4
https://doi.org/10.1680/necdcce.65604.059

Chapter 8
Assessing and implementing compensation events

The assessment of a compensation event can happen in one of two ways, or frequently in both. It can be done either by the *Contractor* in a quotation or in a subsequent *Project Manager's* assessment, each of which must comply with the contract. A compliant structure to the quotation or assessment will make the resolution of any differences between the *Project Manager* and the *Contractor* much easier.

Clause 63 sets out the rules for assessing compensation events, in terms of both time and money. Many of the subclauses link to other parts of the contract, particularly with the main Option clauses, which have a direct bearing on the financial assessment. All assessments of compensation events should follow the rules of this clause if they are to comply with the contract and stand scrutiny.

The two most important subclauses in clause 63 are 63.1 and 63.5, as they are the governing provisions for the cost and time impacts, respectively, of compensation events. They are assessed simultaneously: the contract does not recognise the separation of these two issues, although I often see Parties seeking to generate discrete compensation events in that manner. Particularly in subcontracts, it is common for the receiving party to deal with a compensation event promptly, to 'get the money in' quickly without dealing with any adjustment to Completion Dates or Key Dates. Parties acting in this way often then try to deal with the time impact later, only to be told that the earlier compensation event, since implemented, cannot be revised (clause 66.3), and therefore any time entitlement is lost. In such a situation the *Subcontractor* could find itself having delay damages deducted for an event that was not at its risk.

The default method for assessing the financial impact is in clause 63.1, requiring the Defined Cost and Fee to be assessed.

> Clause 63.1
>
> The change to the Prices is assessed as the effect of the compensation event upon
>
> - the actual Defined Cost of the work done by the dividing date,
> - the forecast Defined Cost of the work not done by the dividing date and
> - the resulting Fee.
>
> For a compensation event that arises from the *Project Manager* or the *Supervisor* giving an instruction or notification, issuing a certificate or changing an earlier decision, the dividing date is the date of that communication.
>
> For other compensation events, the dividing date is the date of the notification of the compensation event.

The dividing date is stated here, and it applies to the assessment of time impact too, which I explain in Chapter 9. It is also used in clause X1.5. The aim of providing a dividing date, which for some reason the drafters chose not to define, is to establish the point at which the assessment of Defined Cost changes from actual records to a forecast. It sets out that date to avoid any entitlement being lost because of late assessment of a compensation event, possibly long after the *works* have been completed. It is still common to see compensation events assessed entirely retrospectively due to delays in the assessment process. Sometimes the *Project Manager* may deliberately delay the assessment so as to ensure that the assessment is retrospective and effectively ignores the dividing date provisions. Sometimes, too, the *Contractor* will do likewise. The preference for assessing actual costs after the event is usually driven by a fear of the subjective forecasting of future costs and the perceived accuracy of assessing past costs. In my experience, neither method is free of disagreement. Adopting such an approach leaves the Parties with the risk allowances still to deal with, as these will not be accommodated by such an approach. Subcontractors complain that they suffer from prevarication by the (main) *Contractor* in these situations, and tactics often include repeated demands for further details when they are not actually needed.

Regardless of the assessment methods used, collaboration in the process between the *Project Manager* and the *Contractor* will improve the speed of assessment and its accuracy, and should help the Parties' relationship. This should ease the conclusion of final assessments too at the end of the project if the amounts concerned have been arrived at by agreement.

Calculation of the Fee is straightforward once the Defined Cost has been established. The term 'Defined Cost' is a defined term, and its meaning is particular to each main Option. In main Options A and B, the definition sends you to the Short Schedule of Cost Components, and in main Options C, D and E it sends you to the Schedule of Cost Components. So, an immediate test of the compliance of a quotation or assessment in main Options A to E is whether its structure matches the eight headings in the schedules. If so, read on. If not, ask the originator to start again. I often see well-intentioned attempts at preparing quotations that are based on a starting template that bears no resemblance to the ECC. In that scenario, the final number will be wrong, quite possibly to the *Contractor's* detriment.

In main Option F the definition of Defined Cost refers to the *Contractor's* own costs and those of Subcontractors, but neither of the schedules of cost components is used.

A common area of difficulty in assessing compensation events is the difference between the first and second bullets of clause 63.1. Many people are uncomfortable with the subjectivity of forecasting future costs, and prefer to delay the assessment, monitor actual costs and apply a wholly retrospective assessment. Not only does that go against what the contract states but it potentially skews the payments in favour of one of the Parties. There is case law in Northern Ireland involving an NEC3 contract that supports the fully retrospective approach – and to be frank I don't agree with the decision of the court on that occasion. Abiding by the contract's provisions is not difficult, and that should always be the default approach. But where the courts have decided on an issue, the court's approach probably becomes binding on future similar cases and therefore on commercial practice in general. The decision of a Northern Ireland court will be binding in Northern Ireland contracts and may be persuasive elsewhere.

The *Project Manager* and the *Contractor* may agree to use 'rates or lump sums' instead of this methodology (clause 63.2), and the contract is not specific about where those rates and lump sums come from. One possibility is the existing Bill of Quantities or Activity Schedule (as appropriate), another might be industry publications. This route requires agreement, and therefore neither Party should be in a position where it is forced to accept rates that it isn't comfortable with. Clause 63.2 provides a short-cut away from the default Defined Cost assessment provisions in section 6 of the ECC. Assessing low-value or repeat activities in this way is probably preferable to the alternative, as it will save time and effort while still producing a figure that each Party is content with. I see many *Contractors* and *Project Managers* going down this route for all compensation event assessments as a way of avoiding what is perceived to be the more-difficult default methodology. In time that leads to at least one of the Parties reflecting ruefully on this choice. Clause 63.2 should be reserved for specific situations where it is of practical use.

Some, but not all, compensation events lead to a reduction in the Prices, and this is expressly stated in the relevant clause. Clauses 63.3 and 63.4 provide for this process.

Clause 63.3

If the effect of a compensation event is to reduce the total Defined Cost, the Prices are not reduced unless otherwise stated in these *conditions of contract.*

Clause 63.4

If the effect of a compensation event is to reduce the total Defined Cost and the event is

- a change to the Scope other than a change to the Scope provided by the *Client* which the *Contractor* proposed and the *Project Manager* accepted or
- a correction to an assumption stated by the *Project Manager* for assessing an earlier compensation event

the Prices are reduced.

Clause 63.3 sets out the overriding principle that, in most cases, the Prices are not reduced by a compensation event. For a reduction to occur there must be a statement in the contract to that effect. This is an occasional area for Z clauses, where *Clients* want to take advantage of any reduction in Defined Cost. The contract is clear as to which may lead to reduced Prices; some apply in all circumstances, while some apply just in certain Options. These are

- Changes to the Scope in each of the main Options, by virtue of the first part of clause 63.4.
- Corrections to the *Project Manager's* previously stated assumptions in all main Options under clause 61.6. I explained the process of assumptions in the previous chapter. Remember that this provision only applies to assumptions previously stated by the *Project Manager*, not to any that were proposed by the *Contractor.*
- Changes to the Scope provided by the *Client* that were proposed by the *Contractor* and accepted by the *Project Manager.* In this scenario, specific rules apply in each of the main Options which I explain later in the relevant chapters. In main Options A and B, the two priced Options, clause 63.12 links to clause 16.1, where the *Contractor* may propose that the Scope provided by the *Client* is changed in order to reduce the amount paid by the *Client*. Clause 16.1 doesn't refer to the Prices, but clause 63.12 does. The financial effect of a compensation event under this clause is assessed in the usual manner, but not all of the saving is realised by the *Client*, as the *Contractor* receives a proportion calculated using the *value engineering percentage.* In main Options C and D, the target contracts, the acceptance of such a proposal does not lead to a

reduction in the Prices (clause 63.13), and hence the share will improve for both Parties. Therefore, in each of main Options A, B, C and D the *Contractor* benefits from the proposal(s) made under clause 16. I explain this further in Chapters 11, 13 and 14.

- Main Options B and D, and Clauses 60.4 and 60.6. These relate to problems with the Bill of Quantities involving, respectively, changed quantities and errors in the bill. Clause 60.4 states that the rates are reduced. By virtue of the role of the rates in the definition of the Prices in clause 11.2(33), a reduced rate will lead to reduced Prices. In clause 60.6, errors in the Bill of Quantities, if corrected, are designed to be neutral. The corrections can work in either direction, to the advantage or disadvantage of either Party.

Two of the secondary Options also create compensation events that can lead to reduced Prices. These are

- Secondary Option X2 (changes in the law). A change in the law can add to, or take away from, Defined Cost, depending on the law in question. For example, additional environmental mitigation measures may lead to increased costs, whereas a new trade deal could lead to reduced import duties. This provision is neutral, and is designed to avoid the *Contractor* allowing for the risk. The *Client* only pays for, or benefits from, such an event if it happens.
- Multiparty collaboration in clauses X12.3(6) and X12.3(7). The changes in these clauses are (*a*) to the Partnering Information and (*b*) to the programme caused by changes to the timetable. The partnering arrangements must by their very nature be flexible to change to meet the Partners' needs. In a partnering relationship no one should unreasonably benefit from changed requirements, so the clause allows increases to and reductions from the Prices.

I mentioned the importance of clause 63.5 earlier. This clause provides for the assessment of the time-related impact of a compensation event. The impact on the Completion Date, sectional Completion (clause X5.1) and Key Dates is established via this rule. Although this book is primarily aimed at the financial assessment of compensation events, Chapter 9 includes a brief description of the assessment of time in compensation events.

The failure of the *Contractor* not giving an early warning that could have been given is mentioned in clauses 61.5 and 63.7. If the *Project Manager* has stated that this is the case, then the event will be assessed as if an early warning had been given. For clause 63.7 to apply and for the assessment to be impacted, the *Project Manager* must have made the statement required by clause 61.5. This subject also features in the issue of Disallowed Cost in clauses 11.2(26) and 11.2(27), although the two scenarios are treated slightly differently. Here, in clauses 61.5 and 63.7, the failure is of the *Contractor* to notify an early warning that **could** have been given. In the definition of Disallowed Cost, which I explain in Chapters 12 and 14, the failure is to notify an early warning that the contract **required** the *Contractor* to give.

Therefore, in respect of compensation events, the assessment will be affected by the failure of the *Contractor* to give an early warning that could have been given by an experienced contractor. This applies to all of the requirements of clause 15.1. Depending on the secondary Options selected, this would also extend to clause X10.3 (information modelling) and clause X12.3 (multiparty collaboration).

The aim of clause 63.7 is to reflect the missed opportunity(ies) to mitigate the effect of something that created a compensation event. It is an example of a contractual obligation to collaborate.

Example – communications problems

A *Contractor* required access to a number of cellular telecoms transmission sites to upgrade and replace apparatus. Access to one such site was blocked by a landowner who controlled the track between the public highway and the transmission site. The landowner complained that payments due to her by the *Client* telecoms company had not been made, and that access would be denied until such time as the payments were made in full.

The *Contractor* was denied access for 3 days in succession before being allowed entry on day 4. Seven weeks later it notified a compensation event, seeking delay costs for the three people involved for 3 days. The *Project Manager* relied on clauses 61.5 and 63.7, and notified the *Contractor* to base the quotation on half a day's delay. The *Project Manager* said that if an early warning had been given on day 1, then access to this site, or another one nearby, could have been facilitated, with the loss of progress limited to no more than half a day. In the absence of an early warning, the *Project Manager* did not know of this delay and therefore could not mitigate it. The compensation event was assessed as if an early warning had been given.

Clause 63.6 is a sole remedy clause, limiting the Parties' entitlement to that established by the rules in clause 63. This clause presumably prevents either Party seeking to recover other costs that it claims to have incurred and that were not dealt with by the assessment rules.

Clause 63.8 provides a challenge for those quoting and assessing compensation events.

Clause 63.8

The assessment of the effect of a compensation event includes risk allowances for cost and time for matters which have a significant chance of occurring and are not compensation events.

The implication of clause 63.8 is that there must be a risk to the *Contractor*, so the allowances must be for a risk that isn't borne by the *Client*. This clause is subjective in its application, so tends to generate some debate between the Parties. It only applies to matters that have a 'significant' chance of occurring. Significant isn't defined, nor does the contract state how the *Contractor* should allow for risks with an insignificant chance of occurring (presumably not at all). Hence, the addition of allowances, both financial and time, cause difficulties for the Parties. While the addition of risk allowances alone would not likely cause a dispute, this clause features regularly in NEC adjudications. Not all participants apply it to time issues, seemingly unaware that it expressly includes time.

Where allowances are made, it is preferable to base them on accurate data if it is available, but there will always be subjectivity involved, and therefore differences of opinion. Careful documentation of decision-making becomes important in these situations. A broad-brush allowance across all activities is not correct: each risk allowance should be applied to the activity that may be affected.

There is a sensible restriction on the assessment of time and money in clause 63.9: anything assessed must be reasonably incurred, and not incurred due to the *Contractor's* delayed or incompetent response to an instruction. *Contractors* 'dragging their heels' to try and exert pressure on the assessment process will not be compensated for the time nor the cost of such tactics.

Clause 63.10 concerns the assessment of compensation events where the event results from an ambiguity or inconsistency that caused an instruction to change the Scope. It says that the assessment will be made in favour of the Party that did not provide the Scope in question. Clause 63.10 reflects the position in law in several jurisdictions. Responsibility, and hence liability, for 'an ambiguity or inconsistency' rests with the Party that provided the Scope. The wording is odd in one respect in that the ambiguity or inconsistency is not expressly stated as being in the Scope, but the clause only applies when there is a change to the Scope.

These events arise out of

- clause 17.1 – ambiguities and inconsistencies in or between documents that are part of the contract
- clause 60.6 – a correction to a mistake in the Bill of Quantities caused by an ambiguity or inconsistency.

In each of these situations there may be a delay to the dates, and therefore the consistency and clarity of the original Scope will be scrutinised. The contract says that the Party that prepared the Scope will be liable for the consequences of the compensation event. In most situations this will be the *Client*, but where the original error arises from a problem with the *Contractor's* Scope for its design, the *Contractor* will be liable.

Clause 63.10 wouldn't apply to clause 60.3, which refers to ambiguities and inconsistencies within the Site Information, not the Scope.

Clause 63.11 allows changes to the description of a Condition for a Key Date to be corrected by the *Project Manager*. This presumably needs to be notified as part of the instruction changing the Scope that affects the Key Date and Condition so that the *Contractor* may allow for the change in its quotation.

Where assessments of compensation events are undertaken in a contract that includes secondary Option X1 (price adjustment for inflation), there are additional assessment rules in clause X1.5 when considering Defined Cost, which I explained in chapter 6. This is straightforward arithmetic, and should not cause undue difficulty. Once again, the dividing date from clause 63.1 is used.

The *Project Manager's* assessments

I explained in Chapter 7 what the *Project Manager* must do once a quotation has been received from the *Contractor*. In summary, clause 62.3 says that the *Project Manager* must

- accept the quotation or
- instruct the *Contractor* to provide a revised quotation or
- state that the *Project Manager* will now make the assessment.

As with everything concerned with compensation events, the *Project Manager* must respond within a defined timescale, in this case 2 weeks.

If the quotation received from the *Contractor* is accepted by the *Project Manager*, then there is no need for an assessment by the *Project Manager*. Presumably the *Project Manager* will have made a check of the *Contractor's* quotation prior to accepting it. But what are the *Project Manager's* obligations in the event that the *Contractor* does not submit a quotation at all, or on time? Or it's plain wrong? Or there isn't a decent programme to base a time assessment on?

Clause 64 states the situations in which the *Project Manager* makes an assessment and the timescales involved. These aren't all in response to the receipt of a quotation from the *Contractor*. Where the *Contractor* has breached its obligations in some way, the *Project Manager* will make an assessment of the compensation event without the *Contractor* having the opportunity to submit a quotation.

The references to the *Project Manager's* obligations in clause 62.3 are added to by clauses 64.1 and 64.2.

In clause 64.1 the *Project Manager's* role in assessing compensation events is set out for the situation where

- The *Contractor* has not submitted the quotation within the time allowed. The starting point is 3 weeks for the *Contractor*, although this can be lengthened by clause 62.5. So, the *Project Manager* can make the assessment from day 22 onwards in the absence of a quotation from the *Contractor*. Clearly, if the *Contractor* is struggling to comply, then an extended timescale can be agreed, for example when prices from proposed suppliers and Subcontractors are late in being provided. In such a scenario it's hard to see how the *Project Manager* would fare any better preparing an assessment.
- The *Project Manager* decides that the quotation has not been prepared correctly. This is possibly the most common reason for a *Project Manager's* assessment. To some extent the *Project Manager* has a difficulty here. To say that the *Contractor's* quotation is incorrect requires the *Project Manager* to have made some sort of assessment already. I see a good number of compensation event quotations where the wrong structure has been used, there is no correlation with the contract's provisions or where 'say' allowances have been used. For a quotation to stand any chance of being accepted as compliant with the contract, it must follow the rules of Defined Cost and the Fee set out in the contract.
- The quotation did not include the programme information required by the contract. It seems illogical to me that a quotation would contain a request to extend the time available without the supporting analysis. But this often happens, and the *Project Manager* is confronted with a difficult task. If the *Contractor's* quotation asks for the Completion Date or a Key Date to be delayed, then that request should be supported by analysis. Clause 63.5 establishes the delay to dates being analysed from the Accepted Programme. So, its role is paramount in assessing the time impact.
- At the time of submitting the quotation, the *Contractor's* latest programme has not been accepted for a reason stated in the contract. This provision only applies in the event that a programme has been submitted by the *Contractor* and that the *Project Manager* has notified the non-acceptance pursuant to clause 31.3. Sometimes, Z clauses (particularly in subcontracts) add to the list in clause 31.3, so they should be checked too.

Clause 64.2 adds to the *Project Manager's* authority in this area by requiring the programme to be assessed by the *Project Manager* for remaining work and then used in the *Project Manager's* assessment of the compensation event where

- There is no Accepted Programme. This might be very early in the project or, unfortunately common, where the Parties have never created an Accepted Programme. *Contractors* need to understand the sanctions in this clause for not having a programme in place: they lose the right to produce the quotation and thereby get their point(s) across as to how the compensation event should be assessed.
- The *Contractor* has not submitted a programme or alterations to the programme. The information required by the contract includes the list in clause 31.2 and the Scope. Note that this clause only requires the *Contractor* to have submitted these details, not for them to have been accepted.
- The *Project Manager* has not accepted the *Contractor's* latest programme for one of the reasons in the contract. This bullet refers to the routine programme submissions required by clause 32.1. The *Project Manager's* decision not to accept (or silence perhaps?) must be for a reason stated in the contract, stated in clause 31.3 for this provision to apply.

All seven of these situations lead to the *Contractor* losing some or all input into the assessment process. Each clause reflects the apparent failure of the *Contractor* to comply with the programme provisions in the contract, and therefore these are matters that the *Contractor* should dedicate attention and resources to. But several of these situations must be assessed by the *Project Manager*, and it is common to hear of difficulties about those judgements even before the assessment begins. Where the *Project Manager* decides to accept or not accept something, then the implications of that must be properly considered and communicated (clause 13.4). Consider the first bullet in clause 64.1, which is a matter of fact: the *Contractor* has either responded within the time period or not. But the second bullet, by way of example, can be subjective.

Many *Contractors* report *Project Managers* making their own assessments as a matter of routine and never accepting a quotation. It is far better for the two Parties to work together to achieve a single common assessment that can be submitted as a quotation by the *Contractor* and (presumably) accepted by the *Project Manager* at speed. This would seem to be an efficient way of working.

Where the *Project Manager's* obligation to assess a compensation event becomes 'apparent', the *Contractor* must be notified, and the *Project Manager* has the same time period that the *Contractor* had (clause 64.3). Normally that will be 3 weeks (clause 62.3), but that may have been lengthened by agreement (clause 62.5).

As with other compensation event provisions, the *Project Manager* can be caught out by the treated acceptance provisions in clause 64.4, so it must plan and track each step carefully. Quotations or notifications treated as accepted may only be unpicked either by the Parties making an agreement to that effect (clause 12.3) or through the dispute resolution provisions. Neither route is desirable, so *Project Managers* should avoid being placed in that situation.

Implementing compensation events

References in NEC contracts to implementing compensation events have sometimes caused confusion in their everyday use. The term has often been mistaken for referring to the implementation of the physical works that are the subject of the event in question. But that has never been, and is not, the intention of the drafting. A compensation event is implemented when the assessment process has been concluded, either by agreement or by the *Project Manager's* assessment, and the revised Prices, Key Dates and Completion Date(s) are 'changed accordingly'.

Compensation events are implemented at the conclusion of one of the processes in the contract

- When the *Project Manager* accepts the *Contractor's* quotation (clause 62.3). This, incidentally, is the line of least resistance, and is recommended.
- The *Project Manager* notifies the *Contractor* of an assessment made by the *Project Manager* (clause 64.3). In other words, where the *Contractor* has not complied for some reason, and the *Project Manager* has consequently made an assessment.
- The *Contractor's* quotation is treated as having been accepted (clauses 62.6 and 64.4). In other words, where the *Project Manager* has not dealt with correspondence on time.

So, what does implementation look like, and who should do it? The contract answers neither of these questions in clause 66, and I am of the view that each implementation should be recorded in accordance with the usual communication rules in clause 13. Main Options A, B, C and D contain a statement explaining the output of the assessment process (clauses 63.14 and 63.15). In these Options either the Bill of Quantities or the Activity Schedule is changed to reflect the financial assessment. In main Options E and F the only impact of the financial assessment is to change the forecast of the total Defined Cost plus the Fee for the whole of the *works*. For all six main Options there are also changes to the Completion Date, sectional Completion Date(s) and Key Date(s) to consider. A simple, short statement saying what these changes are is very helpful, including copies (where appropriate) of the changed Bill of Quantities or Activity Schedule.

Clause 66.3 suggests that, once implemented, a compensation event cannot be revised, 'except as stated in these conditions of contract'. So, where does that arise? Look at the dispute resolution process. Clauses W1.3(5) and W2.3(4) each allows the *Adjudicator* to 'review and revise any action or inaction of the *Project Manager* … and alter a matter which has been treated as accepted'. Therefore, even where the *Project Manager* has failed to deal with the notification and/or quotation, the *Client* has a final opportunity to recover its position, if the *Adjudicator* can be persuaded.

If assumptions had previously been stated by the *Project Manager* under clause 61.6, then any correction to these under clause 60.1(17) will not revisit the original compensation event, but will require a further compensation event to be processed in order to address the correction. Where one of the Parties is unhappy with the implementation terms, then it needs to establish what it wishes to do. Its options are limited: try to negotiate with the other Party to agree a change under clause 12.3 or refer to the selected dispute resolution process. There really isn't an alternative that avoids a prolonged exchange of communications going over old ground for months to come.

Clause 66 does not expressly state that the *Project Manager* should notify the *Contractor* and *Client* of the final implemented terms, but, as explained earlier, I think it is good practice for this to happen to assist with later audit and verification activities. If, although rare, the compensation event is implemented by the third bullet of clause 66.1, it may be left to the *Contractor* to record the implementation.

ICE Publishing

Patrick Waterhouse
ISBN 978-0-7277-6560-4
https://doi.org/10.1680/necdcce.65604.069

Chapter 9
Time assessments of compensation events

Time assessments in this book

This book is primarily about the financial impact of compensation events. The assessment of delay and disruption in construction contracts generally, and certainly in NEC contracts, deserves at least a book of its own. I cannot hope to do the subject justice in a book aimed at a different topic. But the subjects of time and money are inextricably linked. Some contracts deal with the two subjects separately and with a logic that has stood the test of time. NEC contracts do not, and therefore this book cannot, completely ignore the subject of time. When assessing compensation events, the *Contractor* and *Project Manager* must consider the issue of time and the many ways that it is linked to money. Therefore, this chapter describes sufficient of the principles of assessing the impact on Completion Dates and Key Dates to inform assessments of Defined Cost.

Time obligations in contracts generally

The subject of time in construction projects is a complex one. In most situations where a contractor is given a task with a fixed date for completion, that obligation is linked to the payment of damages for the failure to do so. Typically in construction, parties prefer to agree to liquidated damages as the sanction for late completion, but we also see damages at large without an advanced agreement as to the quantum.

So, with significant financial consequences for each party in the event of late completion, it is important that contracts contain provisions for dealing with time. The client in a contract with a fixed completion date cannot hold the contractor to that date, nor demand damages, if it is responsible for any of the delay itself. Therefore, contracts with such requirements must contain provisions to extend the time allowed for the contractor to achieve completion.

In a simple example, if the contractor finishes a project 10 weeks late and is only responsible for 8 weeks of that delay, with the client being responsible for the remaining 2 weeks, then the contract needs a mechanism that extends the time allowed for completion by 2 weeks so that the contractor is liable for damages for the 8 weeks it caused itself. Without such a clause, time would be at large, and the sanctions of failing to achieve completion on time would possibly not be available to the client.

So, all contracts with provisions for completion on specified dates need a mechanism for adjusting the required date of completion in the event that a delay is suffered either through an action/inaction of the client, or from an event that is as the client's risk.

Time obligations in the ECC

The ECC contains a number of obligations whereby the *Contractor* is required to achieve something by a specified date. These are

- The Completion Date. The requirement is to complete all of the *works* by the specified Completion Date in the contract. The *Client* is obliged to take over the *works* within 2 weeks of the date when Completion is achieved. Where secondary Option X7 is included in the contract, delay damages will be deducted for the *Contractor's* failure to achieve Completion by the Completion Date.
- Section Completion. Sectional Completion dates can be established in the contract to allow for individually identified sections to be completed by specific dates. The *Client* is obliged to take over the section within 2 weeks of when sectional Completion was achieved. Where secondary Option X7 is included in the contract, delay damages will be deducted for the *Contractor's* failure to achieve sectional Completion by the sectional Completion Date(s).
- Key Dates. Key Dates can be set in the Contract, by which the *Contractor* must achieve a defined Condition. A noticeable difference between Key Dates and the sectional Completion provisions is that with Key Dates the *Client* does not take over any part of the *works* after the Condition is achieved. Key Dates are usually used to facilitate access for Others. Damages for the *Contractor's* failure to achieve the Condition by the Key Date are not agreed in advance: they are set out in clause 25.3 with a number of limitations.

How are dates adjusted?

The ECC allows Completion Dates and Key Dates to be adjusted, but in specific ways.

The compensation event provisions specifically refer to '*delay* to the Completion Date and Key Dates' in clause 62.2, and these words are also used in clause 63.5. In other words, the impact of a compensation event cannot be to reduce the time available for Completion, it can only add to it. To some *Clients* that seems unfair. And watch out for Z clauses that try to reduce time when a compensation event results from a reduction in the Scope. The contract allows a reduction in the Prices in these circumstances, but not a reduction in time.

The compensation event provisions deal with time and money at the same time. There are links between the two. The time provisions extend the time for Completion and for Key Dates. One of the effects of clause 63.5 is to allow the *Contractor* to retain the terminal float in the programme, whether positive or negative. A delay of *x* weeks to the Completion Date does not of itself translate into *x* weeks of additional time-related overheads for the *Contractor*. Any impact on costs for the *Contractor* must be assessed in accordance with clause 63.1 and be based on the effect of the compensation event upon Defined Cost.

Key Dates, unlike Completion Dates, can be moved both ways by the *Project Manager* by virtue of clause 14.3.

As with most of the provisions in NEC contracts, the adherence to the contract will make assessment of time much easier. The Parties need to understand the terminology and the rules. The rules need to be followed in terms of the routine programme updates (clause 32.2) and compensation event quotations (clause 62.2).

Shared principles in the assessment of time and money

By allowing the simultaneous assessment of time and money, the contract can share some of the principles in each area. For example, in clause 63.8, risk allowances for cost **and** time for matters that have a significant chance of occurring can be included in the assessment of a compensation event.

How is the delay calculated?

Clause 63.5 is the primary clause to consider when assessing additional time from compensation events. It sets out how the assessment should be undertaken, by reference to the Accepted Programme. The clause requires the Accepted Programme to be brought up to date before the effect of the compensation event is then superimposed.

> Clause 63.5
>
> A delay to the Completion Date is assessed as the length of time that, due to the compensation event, planned Completion is later than planned Completion is later than planned Completion as shown on the Accepted Programme current at the dividing date.
>
> A delay to a Key Date is assessed as the length of time that, due to the compensation event, the planned date when the Condition stated for a Key Date will be met is later than the date shown on the Accepted Programme current at the dividing date.
>
> The assessment takes into account
>
> - any delay caused by the compensation event already in the Accepted Programme and
> - events which have happened between the date of the Accepted Programme and the dividing date.

Clause 63.1 sets out the financial assessment of compensation events that I describe elsewhere in this book. But one detail that affects the time impact of compensation events is worthy of comment here. This is the dividing date. It is not defined here as it isn't, strictly speaking, a defined term in the contract. But it is used elsewhere in the contract, not just with financial assessments. One of those uses is in clause 63.5

The dividing date is used as the point at which we stop using the **actual** Defined Cost and start forecasting the **future** Defined Cost.

The dividing date was introduced in clause 63.1.

> Clause 63.1 (excerpt)
>
> For a compensation event that arises from the *Project Manager* or the *Supervisor* giving an instruction or notification, issuing a certificate or changing an earlier decision, the dividing date is the date of that communication.
>
> For other compensation events, the dividing date is the date of the notification of the compensation event.

The importance of the Accepted Programme can be seen from clause 63.5. The *Contractor's* time entitlement in a compensation event always refers back to the Accepted Programme. If the Accepted Programme has been properly prepared and maintained, then the task of establishing time impact should be easier than the opposite scenario. Quotations and assessments need to contain an explanation of how they have been prepared. Clause 62.2 requires a quotation to contain any alterations to the Accepted Programme.

The issue of establishing the additional time in any form of construction contract can be difficult whatever form of contract is used. The NEC processes depend on the programme actions being kept up to date and used as a management tool. Too often I adjudicate disputes in NEC contracts where, for various reasons, the programme has not been kept up to date, and that generates problems where no or fewer actions should exist. I have sometimes encountered *Contractors* that 'don't do programmes' and *Project Managers* that avoid accepting programmes. Both approaches will disrupt the compensation event process. Anyone who avoids their own programme obligations is fooling themself if they expect anything other than difficulty when compensation events are assessed. Even where the programme is maintained properly, the assessment of the time impact of the compensation event in accordance with clause 63.5 can be difficult, and is a routine part of dispute resolution.

One of the important components of a programme is the date of planned Completion: this must be shown on each programme by the *Contractor* in order to comply with clause 31.2. The *Contractor* shows planned Completion as the date when it expects to achieve Completion in advance of actually reaching it. The same applies for sectional Completion and Key Dates too. The forecast of planned Completion is an important date for all involved with a project, not least of all the *Client*, which must take over within the 2 weeks after Completion is certified by the *Project Manager*.

The added importance of planned Completion is in the time assessment of compensation events. Essentially, the *Contractor* is entitled to the additional time caused by the compensation event's impact on planned Completion. The terminal float, whether positive or negative, is maintained by the event. There is no analysis of whether the *Contractor* 'needs' the additional time, the time is due by contractual entitlement.

The assessment of the delay is made with respect to an updated Accepted Programme. The third and final paragraph of clause 63.5 requires the Accepted Programme to be brought up to date before the impact of the compensation event is assessed. Typically in ECC contracts, the programme is updated monthly by the *Contractor*, potentially more frequently with *Project Manager* instructions. So, in a well-run contract, the Accepted Programme could be 29 days out of date before it is used for assessing a compensation event. This is why the contract requires the updating of the Accepted Programme first.

The additional clauses that link to clause 63.5

Earlier, I described clause 63.5 as the primary clause to consider for time assessments. But it cannot be viewed in isolation: there are several others that are also relevant.

Clause 61.6 – *Project Manager* assumptions

Clause 61.6, explained earlier in Chapter 7, requires the *Project Manager* to state assumptions to be used in a compensation event quotation when it would be otherwise difficult to forecast the effect reasonably –

a very rare NEC use of the word 'reasonably'. That applies to the time assessment of a compensation event as much as it does to the financial assessment.

Users of the ECC on both sides of the contract report that this clause is rarely used to its maximum effect. One experienced *Project Manager* says that this clause is often used as a 'cop-out' where the parties are trying to steer the problem into a cost reimbursement scenario. He suggests the submission of two quotations: one that provides minimum cost, the other providing minimum time. Then the *Client*, through the *Project Manager*, can choose which it most desires. An interesting suggestion and one worthy of experiment.

Example – unhealthy problems

A *Contractor* appointed under the ECC was refurbishing parts of a multi-building mental health hospital. The Scope required that construction operations in areas where vulnerable patients were present could only be carried out by construction operatives who had clearance to do so and who were accompanied by mental health nurses acting as chaperones. This had three effects. Firstly, there were fewer subcontract operatives available locally who had the appropriate clearance, so they were more expensive and worked on a longer lead time. Secondly, the chaperones represented a cost to the *Contractor* and took time to arrange. Thirdly, working around patients was much slower than doing the work in a vacated environment.

A series of instructions under clause 14.3 was instructed by the *Project Manager* for additional work in a unit within the hospital where patients might be present. The *Project Manager* notified a compensation event and instructed the *Contractor* to submit a quotation.

The *Contractor* explained the potential problems and likely longer duration of the *works* if patients were present in the unit while the *works* took place. A proposal was made to the *Project Manager* suggesting that assumption(s) should be stated.

The *Project Manager* subsequently stated under clause 61.6 that the quotation should be prepared on the assumption that the *works* would be undertaken in an environment without patients and therefore without the need for cleared operatives and chaperones. The *Contractor* submitted the quotation based on that assumption. Consequently, the *Contractor* did not make any risk allowances for the possible disruption, and the cost of the *works* was lower than it might have been. Had the actual conditions included the delay and disruption caused by the presence of patients, then the *Project Manager* would have had to notify a correction to the initial assumption. There would then therefore have been a compensation event to reflect the additional time and costs of the correction under clause 60.1(17). Here the risk did not materialise, so the *Client* did not have to pay for the additional precautions.

Clause 62.1 – alternative quotations

Clause 62.1 works in a similar way to clause 61.6, and potentially the two clauses could be used together. The *Project Manager* may instruct the *Contractor* to submit quotations based on alternative ways of dealing with the compensation event. Frequently the alternatives considered look at the time impact, enabling the Parties to select an option that minimises either the time impact or the financial impact. I have explained clause 62.1 earlier in Chapter 7.

Clause 62.2 – quotation contents

Clause 62.2 establishes what a quotation must consist of. In terms of the delay to the Completion Date, sectional Completion or Key Date(s), the *Contractor* must include a programme.

> Clause 62.2 (excerpts)
>
> The *Contractor* submits details of the assessment with each quotation.
>
> If the programme for remaining work is altered by the compensation event, the *Contractor* includes the alterations to the Accepted Programme in the quotation

So, the *Contractor* has two tasks here in respect of the impact on time

- State and justify the delay (if any) to the various dates.
- Show the alterations to the programme. Even where a particular alteration doesn't directly impact on a delay to one of the important dates (i.e. it isn't on the critical path for that date), it still needs to be shown to the *Project Manager* in the quotation. This is quite a demand in some circumstances, and may impact upon the *Contractor's* ability to submit a quotation within 3 weeks of being instructed to do so.

Clause 63.8 – risk allowances

Clause 63.8 presents a challenge to many users of the ECC: the inclusion of risk allowances for cost *and* time for matters that have a significant chance of occurring and are not compensation events. This clause is popular, if that is the right word, when dealing with the Defined Cost of the event, but isn't always thought of when assessing the time impact.

Take, for example, the possible impact of bad weather. The *Contractor* is responsible for the effects of bad weather up to the threshold described in clause 60.1(13). Depending what the activity is and what time of year it's taking place, there will be a risk of delay due to bad weather. The *Contractor* needs to be specific. Work taking place inside and not reliant on craneage is unlikely to be affected by high winds. Work in the summer in the UK is unlikely to be disrupted by temperatures below 3°C, which would prevent concreting, brickwork and plastering from happening. So, in each of the two scenarios described no risk allowance would be appropriate.

Looking now at physical conditions, a risk allowance would be appropriate if it was feared that difficult ground conditions might be encountered that would slow down works. The *Contractor* is responsible for the effect of physical conditions up to the threshold set out in clause 60.1(12), and therefore the risk in the conditions in question may be allowed for. This may be for encountering rock that requires specialist Equipment to remove it, a high water table requiring the installation of a pumping main or contaminated material such as asbestos needing specialist treatment. In each case the *Contractor* is liable for the costs of dealing with the problems until the threshold in clause 60.1(12) is reached, and therefore may allow for the risk in assessing the time impact.

Subcontractors particularly report that (main) *Contractors* often refuse to accept the additional time added to quotations either in full or at all. Then, when delays inevitably occur, the Subcontractor becomes liable for the consequences of late Completion or missing Key Dates.

Clause 63.9 – competently and promptly

Aside from the proposed instructions provisions in clause 65, all compensation events require the *Contractor* to proceed with whatever the matter is that created the compensation event. *Contractors* that refuse to proceed with, say, a changed Scope until the effects are agreed are in breach of their obligations. Clause 27.3 requires the *Contractor* to obey instructions, so this would seem to suggest prompt response to instructions from the *Project Manager* or *Supervisor*, leading to compensation events and to other issues such as the effects of physical conditions or weather.

While clause 63.9 doesn't create an obligation for the *Contractor*, it does say that compensation events will be assessed on the assumption that the *Contractor* responded competently and promptly to the event. *Contractors* that delay works by their refusal to procure the necessary resources to respond to an instruction from the *Project Manager* will not be able to include that delay in a compensation event assessment, even if they have done so pending agreement on the assessment. Agreement of compensation event assessments is desirable, although not necessary.

Clause 64 – the *Project Manager's* assessments

I described the contents of clause 64 more fully in Chapter 8. Some of its contents affect the way that time assessments are made, and by whom. Essentially, this clause says that the *Contractor* loses its opportunity to prepare a quotation when it has defaulted in some way, either with a previously submitted quotation or with its broader programme obligations. The provisions of this clause act as an incentive for the *Contractor* to comply with its programming obligations.

Clause 66.2 – implementation of a compensation event

I have explained elsewhere in this book that the implementation of a compensation event should really be recognised by a communication that states what has been implemented. The implementation happens when one of the three bullets in clause 66.1 has occurred and clause 66.2 says that the Completion Date and the Key Dates are changed. The much-discussed clause 66.3 says that the assessment (including that of the delays to the dates) will not be revised except in certain circumstances.

I have warned *Contractors* particularly that dealing with the time impact of compensation events is vital to protect themselves from the sanctions elsewhere in the contract and, in some situations, to protect entitlement. So, at this point, the dates will change, and the revised dates will feed into other consequential matters such as

- delay damages (secondary Option X7)
- Key Dates costs (clause 25.3)
- the *defects date*
- retention (secondary Option X16)
- a bonus for early completion (secondary Option X6).

ICE Publishing

Patrick Waterhouse
ISBN 978-0-7277-6560-4
https://doi.org/10.1680/necdcce.65604.077

Chapter 10
What is Defined Cost?

The concept of Defined Cost is a necessary component for cost reimbursement contracts and for those contracts that include elements of cost reimbursement, for example with the change process.

In the ECC, Defined Cost is used to establish

- the change to the Prices caused by compensation events in all main Options
- the Price for Work Done to Date in main Options C, D, E and F
- certain amounts due on termination.

'Prices' is a defined term that differs by the main Option selected

- in main Options A and B, the Prices are established from either the Activity Schedule or the Bill of Quantities, and are the amounts paid by the *Client*
- in main Options C and D, the Prices are also established from either the Activity Schedule or the Bill of Quantities, but are used as the target from which the *Contractor's* share is calculated
- in main Options E and F the Prices are the forecast of the total outturn cost for the works.

The ECC contains two priced main Options (A and B) that allow the Parties to agree what something costs before the work is undertaken. That allows certainty (more so with main Option A than with main Option B) for each Party, and can provide a large profit or loss for the *Contractor*, depending on how things go. For the *Client* there is cost certainty, and many client organisations are willing to pay a premium for that perceived certainty.

The routine monthly payments in the remaining main Options (C, D, E and F), and compensation events in all six, rely upon cost reimbursement. *Contractors*' costs for delivering work are incurred in various locations: at the Site, in the remainder of the Working Areas, at head office, in regional offices and potentially at many other locations such as fabrication factories. Some of these may be at a considerable distance from the Site. So there has to be a set of rules that assesses what is due for each type of activity. Those rules must be fair to both Parties, recognising that full visibility and therefore verification will not always be available for each cost.

So, any contract relying upon the reimbursement of one Party's costs needs to have rules to define what those reimbursable costs are, and the provisions for verification. Unsurprisingly, this is an area of contracts, and not just NEC contracts, that creates considerable disagreement and dispute.

The 80/20 rule probably applies here, meaning that 80% of the costs of a project will be generated from 20% of the transactions.

Imagine a large construction project. A small number of supply contracts and subcontracts will command significant sums towards the overall expenditure. But tens or hundreds of thousands or possibly millions of transactions with local suppliers and others will also litter the accounting system. These will deal with the many other aspects of expenditure, the small tools, catering supplies, toilet rolls, stationery, ancillaries, etc. But the contract's rules need to be equally capable of application for the £10 million steel supply and the £1.50 parking charge claimed by the site engineer when she was visiting the designer's offices. Of course, the same should be said of those administering the payments system and those auditing on behalf of the *Client*. The people applying the rules need to apply them sensibly. The presence of several millions of pounds of structural steel at the Site should be relatively easy to identify. Where *Contractors* import thousands of lines of transaction data from company charge cards, expense claims and the like, there will always be discrepancies and missing documents. But if we know that the site engineer visited the designer's office on a certain date, we should pay for her car parking nearby even if she has mislaid her ticket or smartphone record. Strictly speaking, if any cost is not 'justified' by accounts and records, it should be disallowed. But I think that the justification should be flexible, reflecting the standard of proof in civil matters of the balance of probabilities.

The use of technology can make the verification of expenditure much easier. In the last example we would once have expected to see a small piece of paper with the date, times and cost of parking. Of late, we have become accustomed to paying for such things with smartphone technology, and perhaps having an account with the parking provider where past transactions are stored. Such technology helps, as does, for example, vehicle tracker technology. But in the background we may have a challenge with how the data from such processes is captured, stored and processed. This is an important consideration, but, alas, one that falls outside the remit of this book.

Technology equally helps with the larger-value transactions with automatic processing of orders, invoices and payments between suppliers and contractors. Again, this creates an audit trail that is easy to trace if required.

Of course, we potentially face some problems with the larger-value transactions such as the structural steelwork. But the quantity of work required to verify £1 million of structural steel products will probably be dwarfed by that required for £1 million of personal expenses unless the people administering those systems and the systems themselves are managed accordingly and allocate their time sensibly.

I have used the examples of expensive steelwork and inexpensive personal expenses as opposite ends of the spectrum when dealing with the reimbursement of costs. In both cases we probably have something tangible to use in verification ('accounts and records', clause 52.4): an invoice for the first item and a ticket or emailed invoice for the second.

Perhaps more complex in terms of value and verification is the subject of people costs. Subject to data rules it is straightforward to prove that the site engineer was paid £*x* last month and that additional payroll costs of £*y* were paid in addition in respect of taxes, healthcare, pension, etc. But what did she do? Do we judge her contribution by presenteeism; that is, how often was she at the Site? Or do we want to understand what she did, and with what outcome? This is a perennially difficult judgement call for all involved in such processes.

Example - reimbursable people costs

A *Client* on an NEC4 main Option E contract was concerned about the people costs it was paying to the *Contractor*. Claiming to be concerned about Site security, it installed new fencing, turnstiles and gate houses around the Site. Each person working on the Site was issued with a smart card that was necessary to allow access and egress through the turnstiles.

Without notifying any of the people involved, the *Client* started monitoring the movements of people in and out of the Site. It discovered that many people entered the fenced part of the Site up to half an hour late each morning, departed up to 15 min early and seemed to enjoy a lunch break of an hour when only 30 min should have been allowed. Therefore, it concluded, overcharging was occurring for up to 1.25 h per day.

The *Contractor* was understandably surprised to learn of the monitoring. It argued that the Site's car parks, fabrication workshops, canteen and offices were all outside the fenced area, and therefore some of the time outside the gated area could not be assumed to be unproductive.

Security checks on personnel entering in the morning and again after lunch created delays. This is a common problem in secure premises. So, in conclusion, the *Contractor* said that the turnstile data could not be relied upon to establish what payments were due.

The *Client's* claims for unproductive time failed in an adjudication because they couldn't show what was happening when people were outside the fenced area. Also, the contract did not recognise the role of the turnstiles. Given the significant data, privacy and payment issues concerned with the use of control equipment such as turnstiles, it is imperative that the Parties agree to their usage and to the various protocols surrounding their operation.

Nothing in this example has yet assessed whether the people in question did anything of value – the argument was largely about their presence in a specified location at specified times.

So far in this chapter I have spoken about the generic processes of reimbursing costs. The set of rules I mentioned earlier revolve, in NEC contracts, around Defined Cost. Defined Cost always has a definition in each of the main Options. In the four main Options C, D, E and F, Defined Cost represents almost all of the *Contractor's* income through the Price for Work Done to Date and the financial impact of compensation events.

The contract by necessity has to define:

- What Defined Cost is
  - main Options A and B (clause 11.2(23))
  - main Options C, D and E (clause 11.2(24))
  - main Option F (clause 11.2(25))
- What the Fee is (clause 11.2(10))
- How to separate Defined Cost and the Fee (clause 52.1)
- What isn't included at all: Disallowed Cost (clauses 11.2(26) and 11.2(27)).

Defined Cost is used for assessing

- compensation events in all six main Options (clause 63.1)
- the Price for Work Done to Date in main Options C, D, E and F (clause 11.2(31))
- amounts due on termination (clause 93).

Defined Cost is typically assessed

- for each compensation event
- typically monthly, for routine assessments of the Price for Work Done to Date (main Options C, D, E and F)
- During the project finalising Defined Cost for 'a part of the works' (clause 50.9, main Options C, D, E and F; this phrase is the amended wording in this clause from January 2019)
- After the issue of the Defects Certificate (clause 53.1)
- After termination (clauses 53.1 and 93).

Each of the definitions of Defined Cost in main Options A, B, C, D and E points you to either the Schedule of Cost Components or the Short Schedule of Cost Components. Main Option F has a different approach and does not use either of the schedules.

Clause 52.1 applies to each of the main Options.

> Clause 52.1
>
> All the *Contractor's* costs which are not included in the Defined Cost are treated as included in the Fee. Defined Cost includes only amounts calculated using rates and percentages stated in the Contract Data and other amounts at open market or competitively tendered prices with deductions for all discounts, rebates and taxes which can be recovered

From a starting point of defining Defined Cost the contract gets increasingly more involved when considering how to assess it

- Clause 52.1 separates the Fee from Defined Cost, essentially cementing the importance of the schedules.
- Clause 52.1 requires amounts not otherwise stated in the contract to
  - be at open market prices or
  - be competitively tendered, and
  - to include discounts and rebates obtained by the *Contractor*.
- The introductory paragraphs to the Schedule of Cost Components and the Short Schedule of Cost Components limit amounts due to those 'incurred in order to Provide the Works'. I discuss this restriction later.
- Disallowed Cost in main Options C, D and E (clause 11.2(26)) and in main Option F (clause 11.2(27)). This lists the circumstances in which costs, even if incurred, will not be payable by the *Client*.

I look at the Schedule of Cost Components in Chapter 12 and at the Short Schedule of Cost Components in Chapter 11. The substance of Defined Cost is in these documents; the issues in the seven bulleted points above are important too, but secondary overall. I explain Disallowed Cost in Chapters 12 and 14.

The introductory statement to each of the Schedules of Cost Components seems straightforward on first reading but can create problems: 'only if it is incurred in order to Provide the Works'. Remember that to Provide the Works is a defined term in clause 11.2(15), and therefore must be included in any assessment of a cost for its payment as Defined Cost.

> Clause 11.2(15)
>
> To Provide the Works means to do the work necessary to complete the works in accordance with the contract and all incidental work, services and actions which the contract requires.

This definition uses the word 'necessary'. So, if we are judging whether a cost should be included in Defined Cost, we have to decide if it was necessary, if it was done in order to Provide the Works.

Plant and Materials delivered to the Working Areas will qualify under this requirement if they match the needs set out in the Scope, for example on drawings or in other design documents. So, costs for the delivery of palleted bricks or ready-mixed concrete will be easy to verify.

The steel beams mentioned earlier are clearly necessary. But what if the *Contractor's* design required a bridge with larger beams than strictly necessary merely to fit in with a significant structural steel order that the *Contractor* was making on another project? Can the *Contractor* prove any economy of scale?

A trivial example has been used to demonstrate the wider point in one of the NEC's project manager accreditation assessment papers. It asked a straightforward question about how a capsule-based quality coffee machine might be paid for in the event that the *Contractor* had one in the site office. Many respondents commented on the perceived luxury of such an item and how people with such tastes should pay for their own coffee. Perhaps, they opined, the site kitchen could use the cheapest mass market brand of instant coffee from the local catering supplier or supermarket? But in the grand scheme of things, the machine would cost about £250 and need the ongoing purchase of relatively inexpensive capsules. *Contractors*, as with other organisations who employ people, have a legal obligation to provide facilities for food and drink, so is such a machine to be paid for under Defined Cost, or just the costs of a kettle and cheap instant coffee? I'd happily allow such provision, allocating the cost to section 2 of the Schedule of Cost Components. Others, I know, would be vehemently against such apparent decadence.

I came across a contractor working in the water treatment industry. It has a closely selected supply chain of material suppliers, installers and subcontractors that it uses from project to project. Water treatment plants use a seemingly never-ending list of specialist components, many of which must pass industry-accredited testing if being used in potable water supply systems, to reduce the risk of contamination. Some of the products the *Contractor* purchases are noticeably more expensive than those that could be obtained elsewhere, a point not missed by costs' auditors and quantity surveyors assessing Defined Cost on behalf of the *Project Manager*. The *Contractor* justified its costs on the basis of familiarity, learning curve and proven collaboration. It said that to introduce admittedly cheaper products may jeopardise the overall costs, speed of construction and quality of the finished product. These are persuasive arguments, but the benefits can be difficult to quantify and demonstrate. We come back to the necessity argument, and hopefully realise that we must consider the whole of the *Contractor's* offering and not just individual constituents.

The assessment of Defined Cost typically involves good people and good technology. The assessment process should give each Party confidence that the sums assessed, certified and paid are correct and in accordance with the contract.

Patrick Waterhouse
ISBN 978-0-7277-6560-4
https://doi.org/10.1680/necdcce.65604.083

Chapter 11
Defined Cost and assessing compensation events in main Option A and B contracts and the Short Schedule of Cost Components

Defined Cost in main Option A and B contracts

The only roles for Defined Cost in main Option A and B contracts is in the assessment of compensation events and the payments due on termination. I explain the latter in Chapter 19.

There is no role for Defined Cost in establishing the Price for Work Done to Date in main Option A and B contracts.

Assessment of compensation events in main Option A and B contracts

How do we establish how much money is due for a compensation event?

A reminder about the assessment of compensation events, from the core clauses follows.

> Clause 63.1 (excerpt)
>
> The change to the Prices is assessed as the effect of the compensation event upon
>
> - the actual Defined Cost of the work done by the dividing date,
> - the forecast Defined Cost of the work not done by the dividing date and
> - the resulting Fee.

So, in any main Option we need to establish the effect of the event on Defined Cost, and then add the Fee to it, based on the percentage in Contract Data part two. The Defined Cost is defined in each of the main Options.

In main Options A and B the contract has clause 11.2(23).

> Clause 11.2(23)
>
> Defined Cost is the cost of the components in the Short Schedule of Cost Components.

The Short Schedule of Cost Components is explained later in this chapter. It contains eight cost headings. When any of the components is incurred as a result of the compensation event, it can be included in the assessment of Defined Cost, subject to the other rules in the contract.

Don't we just use the rates in the contract to assess compensation events?

The assessment of compensation events in these two main Options recognises that the original basis of paying the *Contractor* is on prices agreed in the contract between the *Client* and the *Contractor*. Unlike other forms of commercial contract, the ECC does not default to the existing price data in the contract for assessing the financial impact of changed work or other events that lead to an entitlement.

In each of these two Options the Parties have agreed a series or prices and/or rates to be used in deciding what to pay the *Contractor* for the works that were known about at the beginning. Particularly with a Bill of Quantities, it is tempting to use the rates and lump sums in the bill to assess the financial impact of a compensation event. The use of existing prices is entirely possible in the ECC, but requires the express agreement of the *Contractor* and the *Project Manager* to do so.

Clause 63.2, which, as part of the core clauses, applies to each of the main Options, allows this use.

> Clause 63.2
>
> The *Project Manager* and the *Contractor* may agree rates or lump sums to assess the change to the Prices.

So why, in a contract with detailed pricing information (such as a main Option A or main Option B contract), does it not default to that data? The answer is that we expect the Parties to benefit from their original agreement, but, for future changes to the *works* or the manner in which they are provided, neither Party should be required to continue a financial arrangement that is disadvantageous to them. For example, if the *Contractor* has entered into the contract with a series of loss-making rates, then it will be required to complete the *works* known about at the Contract Date at the loss-making rates. But, without an agreement between the *Contractor* and *Project Manager*, additional work will not have to be provided at a loss by using the original rates. The new works will be paid for on the basis of Defined Cost. The reverse holds too: the *Client* will not have to continue paying excessively profitable rates either.

Where the Parties do agree to use rates and lump sums, the contract is silent about where they may be found. In main Options A and B the costs data in the Activity Schedule or the Bill of Quantities is likely to be very helpful, and may therefore be used. Equally, data from elsewhere could also be used. Problems are encountered when one Party, unilaterally, decides that it will default to rates and prices from either the Activity Schedule or the Bill of Quantities.

Can we reduce the Prices?

A reminder about the effect of compensation events on the possible reduction of the Prices follows. The starting point is Clause 63.3, which is in the core clauses and so applies to each main Option.

Clause 63.3

If the effect of a compensation event is to reduce the total Defined Cost, the Prices are not reduced unless otherwise stated in these *conditions of contract*.

I explained the contract's approach to reduced Prices in Chapter 8. Main Option A and main Option B contracts allow for the reduction in Prices through the core clauses (63.3 and 63.4) and specific compensation events that expressly allow for the reduction in Prices.

Clause 63.4

If the effect of a compensation event is to reduce the total Defined Cost and the event is

- a change to the Scope other than a change to the Scope provided by the *Client*, which the *Contractor* proposed and the *Project Manager* accepted or
- a correction to an assumption stated by the *Project Manager* for assessing an earlier compensation event

the Prices are reduced.

In clause 63.4 the first bullet refers to Scope changes, except those resulting from clause 16.1. The second bullet refers to the *Project Manager's* actions under clause 61.6. These are two examples of where the contract expressly allows compensation events to lead to a reduction in the Prices.

The route for amending the Prices in main Option A and B contracts is through clause 63.14 (main Option A) and 63.15 (main Option B), which I describe in more detail later in this chapter.

Clause 63.14

Assessments for changed Prices for compensation events are in the form of changes to the Activity Schedule.

Clause 63.15

Assessments for changed Prices for compensation events are in the form of changes to the Bill of Quantities.

Clauses 63.14 and 63.15 allow for the reduction in Prices, and indeed their increase, because they refer to 'changes' to the respective pricing document.

Value engineering assessments in main Options A and B

Clauses 16.1 and 16.2 allow the *Contractor* to propose changes to the Scope provided by the *Client* in order to reduce the Prices. In main Option A and B contracts, their effect on the assessment of compensation events differs from the other main Options.

Clause 16.1

The *Contractor* may propose to the *Project Manager* that the Scope provided by the *Client* is changed in order to reduce the amount the *Client* pays to the *Contractor* for Providing the Works. The *Project Manager* consults with the *Client* and the *Contractor* about the change.

Clause 16.2

Within four weeks of the *Contractor* making the proposal the *Project Manager*

- accepts the *Contractor's* proposal and issues an instruction changing the Scope,
- informs the *Contractor* that the *Client* is considering the proposal and instructs the *Contractor* to submit a quotation for a proposed instruction to change the Scope or
- informs the *Contractor* that the proposal is not accepted.

The *Project Manager* may give any reason for not accepting the proposal.

When assessing compensation events that result from a proposal under clause 16.1, we need to look at clause 63.12 and the use of the *value engineering percentage*. This is designed to encourage the *Contractor* to propose value engineering ideas and share in the savings generated. Clause 63.12 dovetails with clause 16, which uses the same terminology. To qualify, the compensation event has to be

- a change to the Scope provided by the *Client*
- proposed by the *Contractor* (clause 16.1)
- accepted by the *Project Manager* (clause 16.2).

Clause 16 only refers to the reduction in Prices. The percentage allows the *Contractor* to share in the benefits of its own proposal. Without this provision the *Contractor* would face a financial disincentive when proposing changes. Here, provided the *value engineering percentage* exceeds the *fee percentage*, the *Contractor* will profit from any proposals that are accepted.

Clause 63.12 allows for the reduction of the Prices for value engineering in main Option A and B contracts.

Example – reduced Prices from a *Contractor* proposal to change the Scope

Here is how clauses 16 and 63.14/15 should work

(*a*) The *Contractor* proposes to the *Project Manager* that the Scope is changed to accommodate permanent formwork in some of the foundation base slabs of a building. This will reduce the time for construction, reduce the amount spent on Equipment and improve safety, but will also marginally increase the cost of Plant and Materials. Overall, there will be a saving.

(*b*) The *Project Manager*, after consulting the *Client*, accepts the proposal and issues an instruction changing the Scope, which clause 14.3 provides for.

(*c*) Clause 60.1(1) says that this instruction is a compensation event, and therefore the remaining provisions of section 6 will now apply in terms of quotation, assessment and implementation.

(*d*) The reduction in the Prices is £600 000 and the *value engineering percentage* is 40%. Therefore, in accordance with clause 63.12, the net reduction in the Prices is £360 000, and the *Contractor* is rewarded for the initiative with £240 000.

(*e*) The Prices' revision of £360 000 would then be entered into either the Activity Schedule (main Option A, clause 63.14) or the Bill of Quantities (main Option B, clause 63.15).

Main Option A Contracts

The specific clauses that apply to main Option A contracts reflect its use of the Activity Schedule for establishing the Prices. The Activity Schedule is typically created by the *Contractor* during the tender or negotiation period. On the Contract Date it is the *activity schedule* and, as it says in clause 11.2(21), that remains the case until later changed in accordance with the contract. It likely changes and develops through the project due to the effect of changes to the programme and compensation events.

> Clause 11.2(21) – main Options A and C
>
> The Activity Schedule is the *activity schedule* unless later changed in accordance with these *conditions of contract*.

So, how can the Activity Schedule change in accordance with the contract? There are six possibilities

- a compensation event (clause 63.1)
- accepting a Defect (clause 45.2)
- agreeing acceleration (clause 36.3)
- to align with the programme (clauses 31.4 and 55.3)
- to align with the Scope (clauses 55.1 and 55.3)
- an agreed change to the contract (clause 12.3).

The Prices in a main Option A contract are defined in clause 11.2(32).

> Clause 11.2(32) – main Options A and C
>
> The Prices are the lump sum prices for each of the activities on the Activity Schedule unless later changed in accordance with the Contract.

The reference to 'in accordance with the Contract' is to the six possibilities listed above. In a priced contract, the Prices are what the *Client* pays for the *works*.

Once implemented, the effect of the compensation event is to change the Activity Schedule (clause 63.14). So, the Activity Schedule will be changed by one or more of the following

- a new item – description and price
- a revised description
- a revised price
- the removal of an item and its price entirely
- the amendment of a grouping, moving an activity to change the sequence of payment.

Once the compensation event has been implemented, it leads (eventually) to an obligation for the payment. The Price for Work Done to Date is the amount that forms most, if not all, of the routine payments from the *Client* to the *Contractor*.

The Price for Work Done to Date is defined in clause 11.2(29).

> **Clause 11.2(29) – main Option A**
>
> The Price for Work Done to Date is the total of the Prices for
>
> - each group of completed activities and
> - each completed activity which is not in a group.
>
> A completed activity is one without notified Defects the correction of which will delay following work.

Contractors often complain of the time it can take to get paid for compensation events in main Option A or B contracts. There is an obligation to obey an instruction in clause 27.3, and any assessment will assume that there was a competent and prompt response to the event (clause 63.9). Yet the payment process rumbles along in parallel, and typically takes several weeks.

No payment is due in a main Option A contract until

- the compensation event is implemented (in other words, the Activity Schedule now contains the revised prices)
- the work in question is done and an activity is completed.

Main Option B Contracts

The specific clauses that apply to main Option B contracts reflect its use of the Bill of Quantities for establishing the Prices. The Bill of Quantities is typically created by the *Client* during the tender or negotiation period, and completed by the *Contractor* in its tender. On the Contract Date it is the *bill of quantities* and, as it says in clause 11.2(22), that remains the case until later changed in accordance with the contract. It likely changes and develops through the project due to the effect of changes to the programme and compensation events.

The use of bills in construction contracts has reduced considerably in the lifetime of NEC contracts, and perhaps NEC's alternatives are partly to blame. Bills do carry a greater workload in contract administration and require people who are trained in their use.

As fellow NEC author Jon Broome has said of bills of quantities in his book[i]

> Take my word for it that it is confusing and heinously hard to operate. Consequently, when I have recommended the use of bills of quantities under the ECC, regrettably I have also recommended the redrafting of these clauses. Perhaps this is also one of the reasons why Option A has proved far more popular in use than Option B.

> **Clause 11.2(22) – main Options B and D**
>
> The Bill of Quantities is the *bill of quantities* unless later changed in accordance with these *conditions of contract*.

---

[i] Broome J (2021) *NEC4: A User's Guide*. ICE, London, UK.

So, how can the Bill of Quantities change in accordance with the contract? There are seven possibilities

- a compensation event (clause 63.1)
- accepting a Defect (clause 45.2)
- agreeing acceleration (clause 36.3)
- a significant change to a quantity (clause 60.4)
- a change to correct an error in item descriptions where they do not comply with the *method of measurement* (clause 60.6)
- a change to correct an ambiguity or inconsistency (clause 60.6)
- an agreed change to the contract (clause 12.3).

The Prices in a main Option B contract are defined in clause 11.2(33).

> Clause 11.2(33) – main Options B and D
>
> The Prices are the lump sums and the amounts obtained by multiplying the rates by the quantities for the items in the Bill of Quantities.

This definition makes the assessment of changed work relatively simple once the compensation event has been implemented and the revised entries are in the Bill of Quantities. In a priced ECC contract, the Prices are what the *Client* pays for the work: the actual quantities of work multiplied by the relevant rates in the Bill of Quantities.

Once implemented, the effect of the compensation event is to change the Bill of Quantities (clause 63.15). So, the Bill of Quantities will be changed by one or more of the following

- a new item – description and rate or lump sum
- a revised description
- a revised quantity
- a revised rate or lump sum
- the removal of an item and its price entirely.

There are three compensation events added to main Option B in clauses 60.4, 60.5 and 60.6. These were described earlier in Chapter 6.

Clause 60.4 refers to major changes in quantity, and allows for the consequential change in unit rates. The change in quantity must not come from a change to the Scope, in other words the quantity of work for an item in the Scope has changed by 0.5% of the original contract value in financial terms. A common example is in earthworks, particularly where difficult ground conditions are encountered. If the level of excavation increases significantly, then its unit rate is likely to reduce.

Clause 60.5 refers to any change in quantities, and there is no 0.5% limit here. There is a compensation event for the effect of delays to Key Dates or Completion Dates.

Clause 60.6 refers to technical errors in the Bill of Quantities and any ambiguities and inconsistencies. Where the Bill of Quantities has been inconsistent with another contract document, the Bill of Quantities has precedence. The contract assumes that the *Contractor* has taken the Bill of Quantities to be correct.

Once the compensation event has been implemented, it leads to an obligation for the payment. The Price for Work Done to Date is the amount that forms most, if not all, of the routine payments from the *Client* to the *Contractor*.

The Price for Work Done to Date is defined in clause 11.2(30).

> Clause 11.2(30) – main Option B
>
> The Price for Work Done to Date is the total of
>
> - the quantity of the work which the *Contractor* has completed for each item in the Bill o Quantities multiplied by the rate and
> - a proportion of each lump sum which is the proportion of the work covered by the item which the *Contractor* has completed.
>
> A completed activity is one without notified Defects the correction of which will delay following work.

No payment is due in a main Option B contract until

- the compensation event is implemented (in other words, the Bill of Quantities now contains the revised rates or quantities)
- the work in question is done either in part or in whole.

The Short Schedule of Cost Components

Some parts of the Short Schedule of Cost Components are identical to parts of the Schedule of Cost Components (which I will refer to as the 'Full Schedule'). I explain the use of the Full Schedule in Chapter 12. I have provided a complete guide to each schedule in the respective chapters, and there is some unavoidable repetition, which is deliberate.

Introduction to the Short Schedule of Cost Components

The Short Schedule has only one role in the ECC: the assessment of Defined Cost in compensation events in main Option A and B contracts. While its eight headings are identical to the Full Schedule, their contents are different. Clearly, from the name, the Short Schedule has fewer components. To make up for the lack of detail in some of them, they use different mechanisms for assessing the cost of some components.

The Short Schedule starts with the same two introductory statements as the Full Schedule.

> Short Schedule of Cost Components
>
> This schedule is part of these *conditions of contract* only when Option A or B is used. An amount is included
>
> - only in one cost component
> - only if it is incurred in order to Provide the Works

The first bullet is easy enough to understand. There can be no double counting. If a rate for an item of Equipment in section 2, for example a tower crane, includes for its operator, then there will be no separate cost allowed in section 1 for that person.

The second bullet needs to be read in conjunction with the definition of Provide the Works in clause 11.2(15).

> Clause 11.2(15)
>
> To Provide the Works means to do the work necessary to complete the *works* in accordance with the contract and all incidental work, services and actions which the contract requires.

Reading the introduction from the Short Schedule with clause 11.2(15), we can see that anything done to complete the *works* or any of the incidental things mentioned will qualify for payment.

While not part of the Short Schedule, clause 52.1 is also relevant here because it

- separates Defined Cost from the Fee
- requires use of agreed rates and percentages, in Contract Data part two
- requires transparent and effective purchasing where rates and percentages are not available in the contract
- entitles the *Client* to benefit from specified deductions.

Therefore, when considering the cost attributed to each of the components in the Short Schedule, the *Project Manager* and *Contractor* must consider all of these restrictions and requirements set out in the introduction, clause 52.1 and Contract Data part two.

People

People are the mainstay of construction projects. Their productivity and the quality of what they produce will be enhanced by the use of Equipment and Plant and Materials. But the cost of people will always form a major constituent of projects.

What does the Short Schedule say about People costs?

> Short Schedule of Cost Components – 1
>
> 1 The following components of the cost of
>
> - people who are directly employed by the *Contractor* and whose normal place of working is within the Working Areas,
> - people who are directly employed by the *Contractor* and whose normal place of working is not within the Working Areas but who are in the Working Areas, proportionate to the time they spend working in the Working Areas and
> - people who are not directly employed by the *Contractor* but are paid for by it according to the time worked while they are within the Working Areas.
>
> 11 Amounts calculated by multiplying each of the People Rates by the total time appropriate to that rate spent within the Working Areas.

The Short Schedule has attempted to simplify dealing with people costs by the use of People Rates compared with the much longer list of components in the Full Schedule.

People Rates only exist in contracts formed using either main Option A or B. They are defined in clause 11.2(28).

> Clause 11.2(28) – main Options A and B
>
> The People Rates are the *people rates* unless later changed in accordance with the contract.

This clause links to the *people rates* in Contract Data part two agreed at the Contract Date. There isn't an obvious place to see where an existing People Rate would be changed, other than through clause 12.3. Where additional people become relevant to the contract, additional rates might be added or existing ones amended in accordance with clause 63.16, explained below.

While the Parties are free to adjust the format of the Contract Data, in its default form it lists the following headings for *people rates*

- category of person (this needs careful thought, see below)
- unit (e.g. per hour, per day, per week)
- rate (in currency).

I have mentioned the careful thought needed when categorising people. This is important in any form of contract where the categories impact on the amount paid for the respective people. *Clients* sometimes question whether the person they're getting is worth the amount charged. The industry is too fragmented for there to be a common definition or understanding of terms such as 'principal engineer', 'project director' or 'site manager'. When categorising people, description needs to be provided as to what that person will do and what level of experience, qualification or experience they will need. This will reduce disagreements later as to what category of person has been deployed.

What happens if we want to add new People Rates? Clause 63.16 provides some suggestion of a loose process.

> Clause 63.16 – main Options A and B
>
> If, when assessing a compensation event the People Rates do not include a rate for a category of person required, the *Project Manager* and *Contractor* may agree a new rate. If they do not agree the *Project Manager* assesses the rate based on the People Rates. The agreed or assessed rate becomes the People Rate for that category of person.

Effectively, this gives the *Project Manager* the opportunity to decide new People Rates, and there is little that the *Contractor* may do to change the decision other than to negotiate or adjudicate. While there isn't an express obligation to do so (other than clause 10.2), it would be advisable for the *Project Manager* and the *Contractor* to collaborate and try to agree a rate here, recognising that the existing *people rates* are a reference and possible starting point for the new rate(s).

The calculation of the amount due also relies upon the 'total time appropriate to the rate spent within the Working Areas'. So, do we charge just for presenteeism (i.e. being there)? Or does each hour/day/week worked have to be productive? I think it has to be productive time, based on the introductory paragraph to the Short Schedule and the requirement that something was incurred in order to Provide the Works. In addition to recording the hours (i.e. the first bullet of clause 63.1), we should also document what that person did. Likewise, when forecasting future commitments (i.e. the second bullet of clause 63.1), we should explain what that person will be doing.

The simple drafting of the people components does not differentiate between people who are employed, self-employed, provided through a service company or agency, etc. Each is assessed based on time within the Working Areas and the relevant rate. I expect to see this clause varied on a frequent basis to match the change in working patterns experienced during the COVID-19 pandemic. Working at home or other remote venues is likely to increase, and Parties will need to find ways of gaining comfort as to the right way to monitor someone's contribution. It is possible that a simple measure of time committed may not, on its own, be sufficient in the future.

Equipment

The assessment of Equipment should, in theory, be relatively simple. Most equipment of any significant cost in the industry comes with a time charge – by the hour, day, week, etc. But the more you look at the details, the more exceptions arise. The Full Schedule deals with some of those exceptions, but the Short Schedule, in its drive for brevity, has simplified things somewhat.

The Short Schedule allows for the payment of Equipment costs where that Equipment is used within the Working Areas. So, not just the Site. But Equipment used elsewhere will be assumed to be included in the Fee (clause 52.1). *Contractors* need to consider the impact of their choice of *working areas* that they include in Contract Data part two at tender. Following the introductory statement in component 2, there are seven paragraphs that state the categories of Equipment that qualify as a component and an explanation of how each is assessed.

> **Short Schedule of Cost Components – 21**
>
> Amounts for Equipment which is in the published list stated in the Contract Data. These amounts are calculated by applying the percentage adjustment for listed Equipment stated in the Contract Data to the rates in the published list and by multiplying the resulting rate by the time for which Equipment is required.

This is probably the simplest way of assessing the cost of Equipment. Contract Data part two contains an entry for the *Contractor* to state a published list of Equipment, for example that published by the Civil Engineering Contractors' Association.[ii] Other organisations also publish similar lists. The list contains items of commonly used Equipment with a rate for its use. The percentage adjustment is also included by the *Contractor* in Contract Data part two. The adjustment can be positive or negative, and allows the *Contractor* to apply the published prices to the specific situation and time where the stated rate may

[ii] Civil Engineering Contractors' Association (CECA) (2019) *Volume 1: Schedules of Dayworks Carried out Incidental to Contract Work including Rail Equipment Items*. CECA, London, UK.

either be too low to make a profit or too high to remain competitive. The calculation needed here is to multiply the adjusted rate by the time commitment. As with any time-related calculation, the *Contractor* must keep good records of actual Defined Cost where this is the basis for assessment. Contract Data part two requires the use of 'the edition current at the Contract Date' of the list.

> **Short Schedule of Cost Components – 22**
>
> Amounts for Equipment listed in the Contract Data which is not in the published list stated in the Contract Data. These amounts are the rates stated in the Contract Data multiplied by the time for which the Equipment is required.

The published lists do not contain all of the items used by *Contractors* as Equipment. There are several reasons for this, which include

- items that are so rare that there is not a clear market rate
- items such as large mobile cranes where the costs of transport, assembly and disassembly are disproportionate and bespoke
- low-value items such as hand tools, or information and communications technology (ICT) equipment, for which there is no established market for rental
- bespoke equipment manufactured for the installation of proprietary products.

Where one or more of these reasons is relevant, the *Contractor* can include rates in Contract Data part two at the tender stage, and when the contract is formed those rates become applicable as part of the contract agreement.

> **Short Schedule of Cost Components – 23**
>
> The time required is expressed in hours, days, weeks or months consistent with the list of items of Equipment in the Contract Data or with the published list stated in the Contract Data.

Paragraph 23 is short, and is really a statement of the obvious but provided nonetheless to avoid misunderstandings later. Each published list states the time unit relied upon, so paragraph 23 requires this to be adhered to. The rates in Contract Data part two allow the Parties to use whatever time interval they wish.

> **Short Schedule of Cost Components – 24**
>
> Unless the item is in the published list and the rate includes the cost component, payments for
>
> - transporting Equipment to and from the Working Areas other than for repair and maintenance,
> - erecting and dismantling equipment and
> - constructing, fabricating or modifying Equipment as a result of a compensation event.

Cost component 24 recognises that not all Equipment is available to provide on a simple hourly or daily rate. Some Equipment will need to be delivered and assembled before its use, and then the reverse activities at the end of the project, for example

- an onsite concrete batching plant
- the site electricity supply network
- a short-term use of a very large mobile crane
- 'normal' construction equipment where the Site is remote and transport costs are high.

These can be significant costs for the *Contractor*, and trying to blend them into a hire rate, when the total duration isn't known, would not be sensible.

Where a rate is in the published list and that rate includes for these costs, nothing further will be paid.

> Short Schedule of Cost Components – 25
>
> Unless the item is in the published list and the rate includes the cost component, the purchase price of Equipment which is consumed.

This component can apply to a huge range of items. At the expensive end of the spectrum, this could include

- Permanent formwork manufactured in steel to provide repeat shapes for a concrete structure. The formwork will be designed to meet the shape of the permanent structure and will be bespoke. After use it will only have scrap value, and therefore the amount consumed will be the difference in value between the manufacture cost and the amount realised for scrap.
- The site electricity network, as mentioned in the previous example, which will probably be provided with a combination of new and used items. Each of those items will have a lesser value when no longer needed after Completion.
- Large items of Equipment that are purchased by the *Contractor* solely for the *works* in the contract, which are then sold after Completion. Sometimes, *Contractors* will do this when a particular item, for example tower cranes, are in short supply in the rental market and purchasing them guarantees their availability.
- Site infrastructure such as hardstandings and car parks, provision of utilities, etc., all of which will be removed at the end of the project.

But the definition of Equipment is sufficiently broad to include much smaller items. Examples are

- Small hand tools such as screwdrivers, saws and hammers. Rarely will any of these survive a project and be available for reuse or sale after Completion.
- Electrically powered hand tools, for example drills and saws.
- Computer equipment in Site offices, and on the Site. Sites are notorious places for the loss of cameras, phones, tablets and the like either through theft, carelessness or damage.

Equipment that is consumed may therefore include

- batteries for ICT equipment, surveying apparatus, radios, etc.
- stationery for offices such as paper and toner cartridges
- sanitary supplies for welfare facilities – a cost incurred by the *Contractor* to comply with the law
- catering to include the catering equipment and food and drink.

Short Schedule of Cost Components – 26

Unless included in the rate in the published list, the cost of operatives is included in the cost of people.

Component 26 prevents 'double counting' of people costs. Some items of Equipment are charged at a rate that includes the operator. This is common for items such as excavators and cranes where the operator needs specific skills and probably certification to use the item. It would be wrong to charge for that person's costs of employment in addition to the hire rate if the rate already included for the operative. For simplicity of auditing, *Contractors* should ensure that their accounts and records include correspondence with the Equipment provider with a clear statement that an operator is or is not included in the hire rate.

Where an additional cost of the Equipment operative(s) is needed, then this component requires it to be included in the cost of people – in other words in section 1 of the Short Schedule. While this seems to contradict the opening statement in the Short Schedule about including an amount only in one component, it does make sense.

Short Schedule of Cost Components – 27

Amounts for Equipment which is neither in the published list stated in the Contract Data nor listed in the Contract Data, at competitively tendered or open market rates, multiplied by the time for which Equipment is required.

This final component of section 2 refers to possibly the most difficult aspect of pricing the provision of Equipment, where there is nothing in the contract already for its costs. The *Contractor* and the *Project Manager* need to establish an appropriate rate for the item in question. This situation is often complicated by the use by the *Contractor* of its own in-house Equipment provider, which often leads to suspicions from *Clients* and *Project Managers* that excessive rates are paid for Equipment.

How should the *Contractor* competitively tender the provision of Equipment? We probably all have views on that. Should we use prequalification? How many potential suppliers should we approach? Can the *Contractor* use its framework supplier from which it receives outstanding service, but which is not necessarily as cheap as alternatives? How long do we give each supplier to respond? Should the *Contractor* be required to use one of the *Client's* framework suppliers? Which form of contract should be used? What should the payment terms be? What liability and insurances should be required? No two people or companies will see these things in the same way, so the *Client* should include a procurement procedure in the Scope for such items.

Establishing an open market rate can be challenging. Such a rate will need to reflect any unique requirements for the Equipment and also the locality where it will be needed. Good records are needed to demonstrate the market rate charged at the time and, where necessary later on with auditing. Obtaining comparative rates isn't always easy, particularly where a supplier suspects it is merely being used for this purpose. An alternative is to use advice from an external quantity surveyor with access to cost databases and/or market knowledge.

Plant and Materials

Plant and Materials, generally speaking, need to be purchased. The cost component here is therefore based on payments for purchasing, and the associated activities.

> Short Schedule of Cost Components – 3
>
> **31** Payments for
>
> - purchasing Plant and Materials
> - delivery to and removal from the Working Areas
> - providing and removing packaging and
> - samples and tests
>
> **32** Cost is credited with payments received for disposal of Plant and Materials unless the cost is disallowed.

Few words are expended by the NEC drafters here, reflecting what should be relatively straightforward purchasing. As ever, the detail requires some further analysis.

Contract users need to remember the requirements of clause 52.1

- Use rates and percentages stated in the Contract Data (if any).
- Other amounts are at open-market or competitively tendered prices. My earlier comments in this chapter about the procurement of Equipment are relevant here too. There should be some procedure in the Scope to explain how amounts should be assessed if tendering or open-market prices are needed.

The introductory paragraph of the Short Schedule is also relevant

- an amount is only included if it is incurred to Provide the Works.

Amounts assessed for Plant and Materials therefore have a few tests to pass. Components 31 and 32 add a few more, largely obvious, reasons for payment. Delivery, packaging and testing are all important parts of providing Plant and Materials. Component 32 reflects the ability of the *Contractor* to dispose of over-ordered materials. For example, where bricks are supplied in multiples of thousands, and you need to procure 7500 bricks, you will have some left over if you purchased 8000. In some situations, these might be suitable for reselling, in which case the amount obtained should be offset against the original purchase price.

Subcontractors

Clause 26 requires all Subcontractors to be accepted by the *Project Manager* prior to their appointment, so the identity of organisations whose costs are being assessed here should not come as a surprise to the *Project Manager*.

Subcontractor is a defined term: see clause 11.2(19).

> Clause 11.2(19)
>
> A Subcontractor is a person or organisation who has a contract with the *Contractor* to
>
> - construct or install part of the *works*
> - design all or part of the *works*, except the design of Plant and Materials carried out by the supplier
> - provide a service in the Working Areas which is necessary to Provide the Works, except for the
>   - hire of Equipment
>   - supply of people paid for by the *Contractor* according to the time they work.

Component 4 refers to the costs of work done by Subcontractors.

> Short Schedule of Cost Components – 41
>
> Payments to Subcontractors for work which is subcontracted.

This component does not apply to those suppliers that may typically be referred to as subcontractors to the *Contractor* but that don't satisfy the definition. The costs of any subcontractors engaged by the *Contractor* that are not Subcontractors (note the use of 's' and 'S') will fall to be assessed under other components.

In clause 26 the *Project Manager* has a limited role in accepting the appointment and the conditions of contract of Subcontractors. The core clauses expressly exempt the pricing information from the submission that the *Contractor* must make to the *Project Manager* when seeking acceptance of the subcontract documents. So, there may be some work for the *Contractor* to do to demonstrate the veracity of these costs. Clause 52.1 and the introduction to the Short Schedule will be relevant in this analysis.

Charges

The list of charges provided in this section cover most of the unavoidable costs faced by *Contractors* when operating a construction or engineering operation. Interestingly, this component also covers charges received by the *Contractor*. The only component that expressly refers to payments received is 54, for the sale of materials from excavation and demolition.

> Short Schedule of Cost Components – 51
>
> Payments for the provision and use in the Working Areas of
>
> - water,
> - gas,
> - electricity,
> - telephone and
> - internet.

Cost component 51 is relatively straightforward, paying for the provision of utilities to the Working Areas. Dependent upon the location of the Working Areas (these aren't confined to the Site) there may be some choice in supplier, and it is possible that wider arrangements between the *Contractor* and its utilities suppliers may lead to advantageous terms being used here. Remember that in clause 52.1 the *Contractor* is required to share discounts and rebates with the *Client*.

> Short Schedule of Cost Components – 52
>
> Payments to public authorities and other properly constituted authorities of charges which they are authorised to make in respect of the *works*.

The first part of this component is easy to understand and to apply. But the second part is more open to interpretation. What is a 'properly constituted authority'? Presumably it isn't a public authority, as that is mentioned in the first part of the sentence.

The public authorities in question will include planning authorities, health and safety authorities, payments for business rates and the like. Properly constituted authorities will be those bodies that are likely appointed or licensed by the government to do specified activities on its behalf.

> Short Schedule of Cost Components – 53
>
> Payments for
>
> (*a*) cancellation charges arising from a compensation event
> (*b*) buying or leasing land or buildings within the Working Areas
> (*c*) compensation for loss of crops or buildings
> (*d*) royalties
> (*e*) inspection certificates
> (*f*) charges for access to the Working Areas
> (*g*) facilities for visits to the Working Areas by Others
> (*h*) consumables and equipment provided by the *Contractor* for the *Project Manager's* and *Supervisor's* offices.

Most of these components are easy to understand, but some are worthy of comment.

Cancellation charges may be incurred when a compensation event occurs, for example when work is removed or changed and the *Contractor* has made contractual commitments based on the previous Scope.

Occasionally, compensation will be payable to third parties for the use of their property or the impact that the construction works have on that property. Typically, these costs will be incurred temporarily, otherwise, if permanent interference is likely, the adjacent property would most likely be purchased by the *Client*.

Charges for access to the Working Areas may be payable when third-party access is needed, for example through somebody else's land or maybe a tolled bridge. In the UK I have seen several cases of the London congestion charge being recovered through this component for delivery vehicles.

Most projects will receive visits from Others. Some of these will be necessary for the *works*, such as visits from government bodies or statutory undertakers. Some will be for communications reasons, and visits by local residents and professional bodies. Typically, reception facilities are needed, a stock of suitable personal protective equipment (PPE) and so on.

Many contracts use the *Contractor* to equip the site offices of the *Project Manager*, *Supervisor* and *Client*. Although this component does not limit such provision to the Site offices, I think that is its aim. Typical provisions will include furniture, PPE, catering, office equipment, office consumables, sanitary consumables and maintenance.

> Short Schedule of Cost Components – 54
>
> Payments made and received by the *Contractor* for the removal from Site and disposal or sale of materials from excavation and demolition.

The final component in section 5 is for the removal from the Site (note, not the Working Areas) of excavation and demolition materials. Where the materials are contaminated and unsuitable for use on the Site, they will need to be removed, and costs will be payable to a waste handler for doing so. Sometimes such materials, where not contaminated, will be sold, and the receipts for this need to be credited to any calculation of Defined Cost. This component should be read in conjunction with clause 73.2, which allows the *Contractor* title to such materials. If the materials are retained within the *works*, then no payment would be due from the *Contractor*: it is only where a payment is received that it must be credited to Defined Cost.

Sometimes the amounts realised can be significant, for example the replacement of high-voltage transmission cables will produce considerable quantities of the life-expired cables, which will have a high recycling value.

Manufacture and fabrication

Manufacture and fabrication have become more important in the construction industry, with developments in offsite manufacture, information modelling and improvements in quality in factories. Significant improvements can be made to the speed of construction and to quality by adopting offsite manufacture.

The NEC's Practice Note 4[iii] says

> The benefits that offsite construction can bring are largely related to the creation of the components in a factory setting, protected from the weather and using manufacturing techniques such as assembly lines with dedicated and specialist equipment and the use of technology to
>
> - increase the speed of construction by increasing the speed of manufacture of the component parts,
> - reduce waste,
> - increase economies of scale,
> - improve quality leading to reduction in the whole life costs of assets,
> - reduce environmental impact such as dust and noise and
> - reduce accidents and ill health by reducing the amount of construction work taking place at site.
>
> All of these should lead to greater efficiency and a reduction in the cost of construction.

[iii] NEC (2018) *Practice Note 4: Offsite Modular Construction*. ICE, London, UK. https://www.neccontract.com/getmedia/234a23f1-6736-4785-8aab-a07af58789e1/Practice-Note-4_finalweb (accessed 20/06/21).

The Practice Note explains how NEC's drafters intend the NEC contracts to be used in the procurement of offsite manufactured items. Given this recognition by the drafters of the importance of offsite manufacture, it is surprising that neither the Short Schedule nor the Full Schedule contain much detail in respect of offsite manufacture, assuming that the only components needed are (*a*) Plant and Materials and (*b*) people. The Short Schedule allows the identification of rates for people, which presumably need to be considerably loaded with overheads to allow the manufacturing facility to recover its costs.

The two components are as follows.

> Short Schedule of Cost Components – 6
>
> 6 The following components of the cost of manufacture and fabrication of Plant and Materials by the *Contractor* which are
>
> - wholly or partly designed specifically for the *works* and
> - manufactured or fabricated outside the Working Areas.
>
> 61 Amounts calculated by multiplying each of the rates for people in the Contract Data by the total time appropriate to that rate spent on manufacture and fabrication of Plant and Materials outside the Working Areas.

I have worked with technology suppliers in road traffic signals, railway signalling, internet facilities and medical buildings. Each faces considerable costs in intellectual property rights (IPR) when manufacturing and supplying items assembled away from the Working Areas. Each complains that there is not a suitable place in either Schedule of Cost Components for IPR. Typically, such IPR is licensed with a combination of fixed and variable (per/unit) fees. It is difficult to recover such fees by a crude x% overhead charge on the people time committed. One client of mine, a global technology provider, tells me that it cannot obtain visibility of people hours from its own manufacturing plants internally, let alone release that information to external organisations.

Typically, this leads to tender queries and proposals for Z clause amendments to the Schedules. Given the costs of IPR and the legal consequences for breaching licence terms, it is important that all aspects are properly considered in the contract, not just payment.

The Short Schedule will only be used for the assessment of compensation events in main Option A and B contracts. Once the costs have been assessed, they should be inserted into the Activity Schedule (main Option A) or Bill of Quantities (main Option B). The nature of payments under main Option A (see Price for Work Done to Date – clause 11.2(29)) requires activities to be completed before money can be paid, so the *Contractor's* quotation should make clear what change, addition or omission to the Activity Schedule is proposed, so that, once implemented, the revised Prices can drive payment on a regular basis. Payments under main Option B do not require completion to any predefined level.

Under both main Options the issue of title may arise if, as usual, the offsite manufacturer will require ongoing monthly payments and will not wish to await Site delivery before being paid. There are a number of ways of protecting the *Client* from supply chain insolvency risk in this scenario, and the ECC provides some of the provisions for the marking of Plant and Materials in clauses 70.1 and 71.1.

Clause 70.1

Whatever title the *Contractor* has to Plant and Materials which are outside the Working Areas passes to the *Client* if the *Supervisor* has marked them as for the contract.

Clause 71.1

The *Supervisor* marks Equipment, Plant and Materials which are outside the Working Areas if

- the contract identifies them for payment and
- the *Contractor* has prepared them for marking as the Scope requires.

The physical marking of completed items outside the Working Areas, for example in a storage warehouse, or part-completed items still in the manufacturing facility, is part of a process of being able to demonstrate ownership in the event of insolvency. The ECC allocates this task to the *Supervisor*, which, in addition to marking, is well advised to take copious notes, photos and videos of what has been marked. Further drafting is needed in the Scope to provide the detail that satisfies the two bullet points in clause 71.1 and to establish the action that leads to an obligation to make payment as part of the Price for Work Done to Date. As with many issues in NEC contracts, this one relies on several clauses in different places in the contract, but without the assistance of cross-referencing.

Before leaving the subject of payment for offsite manufacture and fabrication, it is worth recognising that the provisions of this section do not apply to standard components, in other words those that have not been designed for the *works*. The first part of component 6 states that limitation. So, where designers specify off-the-shelf items, their costs can be assessed on the purchase price. The structure of cost component 6 is designed to achieve a cost-effective assessment for the *Client* when the project demands bespoke components that do not have a 'market' rate but need pricing individually.

Design

The *Contractor's* obligations for the design of permanent works should be set out in the Scope, according to clause 21.1. Not all contracts will contain obligations for permanent works design but, where they do, the design will usually take place outside the Working Areas. Cost component 7 covers the design of both permanent works and temporary works. So, it will be relevant even in contracts that aren't described as design and build, because the *Contractor* will always be responsible for temporary works design.

Design work, permanent and temporary, has to be undertaken in conjunction with the *Project Manager* to whom it is submitted in compliance with clauses 21.2 and 23.1, respectively.

Short Schedule of Cost Components – 7

7 The following components of the cost of design of the *works* and Equipment done outside the Working Areas.

71 Amounts calculated by multiplying each of the rates for people in the Contract Data by the total time appropriate to that rate spent on design of the *works* and Equipment outside the Working Areas.

72 The cost of travel to and from the Working Areas for the categories of design people listed in the Contract Data.

The opening paragraph explains that this component refers to both elements of design.

Component 71 sets out the simple way of calculating the amount due for design. The rates for people in the Contract Data are set out with

- the category of person
- the rate
- which category of design people whose travel expenses to and from the Working Areas are to be included in Defined Cost.

The use of a time-based assessment calculation calls for good record keeping. The designers must keep records of the hours spent on design for the *works* or Equipment and a narrative explaining what was done in those hours. Where the schedule is being used to forecast Defined Cost, then each estimate of the hours included in a quotation should be accompanied by an explanation of what will be achieved in the hours proposed.

The rates will be inserted into Contract Data part two by the *Contractor*, either at the tender stage or during pre-contract negotiations. To a certain extent, without a competitive process, there is no urgency for them to be at market rates – this is something that the *Client's* tender processes and appraisals should consider. After the Contract Date, the rates will apply regardless of whether they are at market rates; the restrictions of clause 52.1, for example, will not apply.

Travelling expenses are allowed as part of Defined Cost for those categories of designers identified in the Contract Data. This reflects the need for designers to visit the Site for meetings, inspections, audits and so on. The contract requires those people to be identified by their category, which is probably unnecessary in most projects. If the visit to the Site is necessary, then the cost should really be included. Occasionally I see this entry left blank, in which case no travel expenses will be recoverable.

Component 72 only refers to the travelling expenses, and is silent about the time incurred travelling. If a designer spends a total of 3 days travelling to and from a remote site for 1 day of productive work, who should pay for that person's time? Most people are capable of doing some productive work while travelling, but the 2 days of travel time here will not be fully productive. Is such travel time, 'time … spent on design'? Should this be included in the Fee, or should the *Client* pay for such time as Defined Cost? *Contractors* argue that the costs of this time are incurred in order to Provide the Works, so this should be payable. I have no definitive answer to the question, having seen both approaches used. But where the Site is remote and requires significant time for travel, the *Client* should consider, when drafting tender documents, how it expects travel time to be paid for.

The contract is also silent about the travel expenses and time for other business travel of designers, for example meetings with other designers or Subcontractors or visits to offsite manufacturers. Presumably these costs will not form part of Defined Cost at all, as component 72 only refers to travel to and from the Working Areas for designers.

Insurance

The insurance entry reflects any insurance proceeds resulting from an insurance claim. The contract requires the *Contractor* to have specified insurances in place that are not chargeable in Defined Cost (they are paid for out of the Fee).

Component 8 avoids the *Client* being required to pay amounts to the *Contractor* that have already been paid, or are likely to be paid, by insurers.

> Short Schedule of Cost Components – 8
>
> The following are deducted from cost
>
> - the cost of events for which the contract requires the *Contractor* to insure and
> - other costs paid to the *Contractor* by insurers.

Typical insurance claims will be from theft, accidental fires, arson and vandalism. The component only refers to events that the *Contractor* is required to insure, and the deduction would apply even if the *Contractor* was not insured.

Patrick Waterhouse
ISBN 978-0-7277-6560-4
https://doi.org/10.1680/necdcce.65604.105
ICE Publishing:

Chapter 12
Defined Cost in main Option C, D and E contracts, Disallowed Cost and the Schedule of Cost Components

Defined cost in main Option C, D and E contracts

Defined Cost is used, with the Fee, for the payment of the *Contractor* for all of the work undertaken, whether known about at the Contract Date, or arising subsequently as compensation events.

The Price for Work Done to Date is based on the *Project Manager's* forecast of the future payment of Defined Cost. Defined Cost is also used for the assessment of compensation events. The details of the forecasting process and the assessment of compensation events are explained in Chapter 13.

The Price for Work Done to Date is the amount of the payment that the *Contractor* receives from the *Client* after each assessment. The contract is flexible on how often this is done, but typically it is monthly. The assessment of compensation events adjusts the total of the Prices that is the target (in main Options C and D) or adjusts the forecast of the total (in main Option E).

How do we establish how much money is due for a compensation event?

A reminder about the assessment of compensation events, from the core clauses follows.

> Clause 63.1 (excerpt)
>
> The change to the Prices is assessed as the effect of the compensation event upon
>
> - the actual Defined Cost of the work done by the dividing date,
> - the forecast Defined Cost of the work not done by the dividing date and
> - the resulting Fee.

So, in any main Option we need to establish the effect of the event on Defined Cost and then add the Fee to it, based on the percentage in Contract Data part two. I explain the specifics of how compensation events are assessed in main Option C, D and E contracts in the next chapter.

Defined Cost

Defined Cost is defined in each of the main Options.

In main Options C, D and E the contract has clause 11.2(24).

> Clause 11.2(24)
>
> Defined Cost is the cost of components in the Schedule of Cost Components less Disallowed Cost.

The Schedule of Cost Components is explained later in this chapter. It contains eight cost headings. When any of the components is incurred as a result of the compensation event, it can be included in the assessment of Defined Cost, subject to the other rules in the contract.

Disallowed Cost acts as a further regulator (together with clause 52.1 and the introductory paragraph to the Schedule of Cost Components) on what the *Contractor* is paid.

Disallowed Cost

Disallowed Cost is a simple name for a simple concept that, when explored further, becomes more complicated when the detail is understood. The role for Disallowed Cost is to govern the costs paid to the *Contractor* and to ensure that these have been properly incurred and do not result from the *Contractor's* breach of other obligations or its inefficient working. The *Contractor* may have costs disallowed that it can demonstrate through accounts and records, but that were incurred inefficiently or in breach of other obligations and therefore will not fall for the *Client* to pay. Equally, it may incur costs legitimately but not be able to provide accounts and records, and will similarly struggle to obtain payment.

The provisions of clause 11.2(26) need to be considered by *Contractors* when establishing costs management systems. Some flexibility in reporting functionality is possible in accounting systems, but manual human intervention is usually needed to identify which of the *Contractor's* costs fall within Defined Cost and which, by exception, are in the Fee. Where wrongly categorised costs are reported to the *Project Manager* in payment applications, they should be disallowed either for the fact they are not Defined Cost or for the fact that they fall within the definition of Disallowed Cost.

Disallowed Cost is defined, for main Option C, D and E contracts, in clause 11.2(26).

Clause 11.2(26)

Disallowed Cost is cost which

- is not justified by the *Contractor's* accounts and records [DC1],
- should not have been paid to a Subcontractor or supplier in accordance with its contract (DC2),
- was incurred only because the *Contractor* did not
  - follow an acceptance or procurement procedure stated in the Scope [DC3],
  - give an early warning which the contract required it to give [DC4] or
  - give notification to the *Project Manager* of the preparation for and conduct of an adjudication or proceedings of a tribunal between the *Contractor* and a Subcontractor or supplier [DC5].

and the cost of

- correcting Defects after Completion [DC6],
- correcting Defects caused by the *Contractor* not complying with a constraint on how it is to Provide the Works stated in the Scope [DC7],
- Plant and Materials not used to Provide the Works (after allowing for reasonable wastage) unless resulting from a change to the Scope [DC8],
- resources not used to Provide the Works (after allowing for reasonable availability and utilisation) or not taken away from the Working Areas when the *Project Manager* requested [DC9] and
- preparation for and conduct of an adjudication, payments to a member of the Dispute Avoidance Board or proceedings of the *tribunal* between the Parties [DC10].

[I have added Disallowed Cost (DC) references to the definition for ease of explanation in this book. They do not feature in the ECC.]

The reference to accounts and records in the first bullet of clause 11.2(26) links to clauses 52.2 and 52.4. Those latter clauses require the *Contractor* to keep certain records, largely about payments of costs, and to allow access to them for the *Project Manager*. There is the ability to state additional requirements in the Scope, and this is also a common topic for Z clauses. Accounting systems should maintain records of amounts paid, for example linking a payment made to a supplier with that supplier's invoice. The item or service in question needs to be capable of being discretely identified.

The first five elements of Disallowed Cost, numbered DC1 to DC5 by me, refer to failures in the *Contractor's* administration. Elements DC6 to DC9 refer to failures in the construction process.

DC1 requires a cost to be 'justified' by accounts and records. Accounts systems are rarely 100% effective, so there may not always be a perfect trail of documents to justify Defined Cost. But something should always be available. Typically, it is the smaller amounts of expenditure that cause difficulties in audit. The *Project Manager* and *Contractor* should remain flexible in how costs are demonstrated. The *Project Manager* should only use this restriction when the records do not justify the payment of a cost.

DC2 guards against payments to Subcontractors or suppliers that may not be contractually required in respect of the *works*. It should be relatively easy to show that a payment was in accordance with a subcontract or supply agreement. If the Subcontractor was properly appointed in accordance with clauses 26.2, 26.3 and 26.4, then the *Project Manager* will already have a copy of the subcontract documents. If the costs relate to a supplier, then the *Contractor* will need to provide a copy of the supply contract to the *Project Manager* if requested. *Contractors* should consider this issue when concluding final account or settlement agreements with Subcontractors where the terms fall outside the ECC.

DC3 relies on the Scope containing an acceptance or procurement procedure. Where large sums of the *Client's* money are expected to be reimbursed through the contract, the *Client* has a justified expectation that the money will be spent effectively. Procedures for procurement and acceptance are part of the contract, if included in the Scope, to ensure that items or services are provided to the right quality and price. Such requirements are much easier to enforce where they are written objectively and with clear wording. The *Contractor* will need to show that it has followed the procedures in question. Acceptance procedures may apply to accepting the type or quality of specification, and subsequently to the quality of finished work, for example dovetailing with clause 42.1. Procurement procedures will specify how proposed suppliers are selected, how many should be approached and the rules for tendering. These should be consistent with clause 52.1 and the Schedule of Cost Components.

DC4 refers to the failure to give an early warning that was required. This is a similar provision to clauses 61.5 and 63.7 in the core clauses, but it is not identical. Those clauses refer to an early warning that **could** have been given. Here, the reference is to early warnings that were **required**. I interpret this restriction as referring to

- the first part of clause 15.1 (i.e. something affecting one or more of the four bullets, but not something that only affects the *Contractor's* total costs)
- clause X10.3 – creation or use of the Information Model
- clause X12.3(3) – achievement of another Partner's objectives

The aim of this provision is to encourage the *Contractor* to give early warnings where they are required, and to avoid the *Client* paying for the additional costs that have been incurred as a result of that failure to warn.

DC5 recognises that the *Project Manager*, *Supervisor* or *Client* may have a role to play in disputes between the *Contractor* and its supply chain members. Sometimes the disputes will involve both the main contract and a subcontract, for example over the quality of work or whether Completion was achieved on a certain date. In such situations the *Project Manager* may be able to help with resolving the dispute. The considerable expense of adjudication, arbitration or litigation often exceeds the costs of a sensible compromise. By requiring a notification, the contract allows the intervention of the *Client* and its appointees. Where such a notification has not been given, the *Client* will not be required to pay costs that could have been avoided if it had known of the proceedings. The worst-case scenario could be if the first that the *Client* knew of the dispute was when it received a notice of adjudication itself under the main contract pursuant to clause W1.3(4) or W2.3(3).

DC6 disallows the cost of correcting Defects after Completion. For many contract users the thought of paying for Defects correction before Completion is confusing. But that is a necessary part of the risk sharing in contracts formed using main Option C, D or E. Costs incurred by the *Contractor* after Completion still, in general, are due to be paid by the *Client*. Therefore, any costs that are incurred when correcting Defects should be separated from other costs after Completion.

DC7 refers to specific types of Defect: those that occurred because the *Contractor* failed to comply with a constraint in the Scope. All Defects, by definition, result from a failure to comply with the Scope, so cost cannot be disallowed merely because it has been incurred correcting Defects. The constraint in question might be about the selection of materials, the use of licensed people or the methodology used. The *Project Manager*, if disallowing cost under this element, must be able to identify the constraint relied upon. It is wrong to disallow cost merely because it was incurred dealing with Defects, however incompetent it was to have created them.

DC8 and DC9 refer to inefficiencies in the *Contractor's* working methods. Each allows for reasonable wastage or loss, and therein lies a subjective decision for the *Project Manager* to make. These elements resonate with the requirements for Plant and Materials and other resources in the Schedules of Cost Components. There is an interesting reference to an instruction from the *Project Manager* for the *Contractor* to remove resources away from the Working Areas: this is consistent with clause 72.1. If the *Contractor* does not remove the resources in question, then they will no longer be paid for by the *Client* as Defined Cost. Disputes often occur when the Parties argue about the efficiencies involved – the subjective argument explained earlier. What is reasonable wastage or utilisation? As ever, good records are absolutely necessary for the *Contractor* to obtain payment without Disallowed Cost. What should happen if the *works* are required to pause for several weeks? Should the Contractor remove Equipment and redeploy people? What if it cannot? These issues often challenge the Parties.

DC10 is an obvious requirement, but not so obvious that it can be omitted. No *Client* will want to find itself paying for the costs of legal action taken against itself. Additional rules apply to the payment of the other Party's costs in adjudication in the UK that would make any contrary position unenforceable anyway. Payments to the Dispute Avoidance Board's members are shared equally in the NEC4 Dispute Resolution Service Contract (clause 3.9), so these should not be charged back to the *Client* by the *Contractor*.

Schedule of Cost Components

Some parts of the Schedule of Cost Components (referred to as the 'Full Schedule' below) are identical to parts of the Short Schedule of Cost Components. I have explained the use of the Short Schedule in Chapter 11. I have provided a complete guide to each schedule in the respective chapters, and there is some unavoidable repetition, which is deliberate.

The Schedule of Cost Components only forms part of the contract when main Option C, D or E is used.

Introduction to the Schedule of Cost Components

Ostensibly, the Full Schedule has only one role in the ECC: the assessment of Defined Cost in main Options C, D and E. In reality, this branches out into three uses

(*a*) assessment of amounts due for the work known about at the Contract Date
(*b*) assessment of the financial impact of compensation events
(*c*) assessment of amounts due on termination (I look at these in Chapter 19).

The assessment of items (*a*) and (*b*) occur as one task in the routine assessment of the Price for Work Done to Date.

While the eight headings of the Full Schedule are identical to the Short Schedule, their contents are different. Clearly, from the name, the Short Schedule has fewer components. The two schedules use different mechanisms for assessing the cost of some components.

The Full Schedule starts with the same two introductory statements as the Short Schedule.

> Schedule of Cost Components
>
> This schedule is part of these *conditions of contract* only when Option C, D or E is used. An amount is included
>
> - only in one cost component
> - only if it is incurred in order to Provide the Works

The first bullet is easy enough to understand. There can be no double counting. If a rate for an item of Equipment in section 2, for example a safety boat on marine works, includes for its operator, then there will be no separate cost allowed in section 1 for that person.

The second bullet needs to be read in conjunction with the definition of Provide the Works in clause 11.2(15).

> Clause 11.2(15)
>
> To Provide the Works means to do the work necessary to complete the *works* in accordance with the contract and all incidental work, services and actions which the contract requires.

Reading the introduction from the Full Schedule with clause 11.2(15), we can see that anything done to complete the *works* or any of the incidental things mentioned will qualify for payment.

While not part of the Full Schedule, clause 52.1 is also relevant here because it:

- separates Defined Cost from the Fee
- requires use of agreed rates and percentages, in Contract Data part two
- requires transparent and effective purchasing where rates and percentages are not available in the contract
- entitles the *Client* to benefit from specified deductions

Therefore, when considering the cost attributed to each of the components in the Full Schedule, the *Project Manager* and *Contractor* must consider all of these restrictions and requirements set out in the introduction, clause 52.1 and Contract Data part two.

People

People are the mainstay of construction projects. Their productivity and the quality of what they produce will be enhanced by the use of Equipment and Plant and Materials. But the cost of people will always form a major constituent of projects.

What does the Full Schedule say about People costs? The answer is, quite a lot. Section 1 differs significantly from the Short Schedule.

Schedule of Cost Components – 1

1 The following components of the cost of

- people who are directly employed by the *Contractor* and whose normal place of working is within the Working Areas,
- people who are directly employed by the *Contractor* and whose normal place of working is not within the Working Areas but who are in the Working Areas, proportionate to the time they spend working in the Working Areas.

11 Wages, salaries and amounts paid by the *Contractor* for people paid according to the time worked on the contract.

12 Payments related to work on the contract and made to people for

(*a*) bonuses and incentives
(*b*) overtime
(*c*) working in special circumstances
(*d*) special allowances
(*e*) absence due to sickness and holidays
(*f*) severance

13 Payments made in relation to people in accordance with their employment contract for

(*a*) travel
(*b*) subsistence and lodging
(*c*) relocation
(*d*) medical examinations
(*e*) passports and visas
(*f*) travel insurance
(*g*) items (a) to (f) for dependents
(*h*) protective clothing
(*i*) contributions, levies or taxes imposed by law
(*j*) pensions and life assurance
(*k*) death benefit
(*l*) occupational accident benefits
(*m*) medical aid and health insurance
(*n*) a vehicle
(*o*) safety training

14 The following components of the cost of people who are not directly employed by the *Contractor* but are paid for by the *Contractor* according to the time worked while they are within the Working Areas.

Amounts paid by the *Contractor*.

The payment of costs for people is necessarily lengthy in the Full Schedule due to the many costs, and different ways, that businesses have to pay their staff. The differentiation between (in simple terms) those who are 'directly employed' by the *Contractor* and those who are not allows more detail for those who are employed. An additional differentiation is applied, whether people are based in the Working Areas, or not.

People whose normal place of work is in the Working Areas can be paid for wherever they work, for example when they split their time between the Working Areas and home. People who aren't based in the Working Areas can only be paid for when inside the Working Areas. The *Contractor* may request a change to the Working Areas at any time under clause 16.3, so should do so when necessary, rather than risk doing work elsewhere that does not subsequently lead to an entitlement for payment.

I expect to see these provisions varied on a frequent basis to match the change in working patterns experienced during the COVID-19 pandemic. Working at home or at other remote venues is likely to increase, and Parties will need to find ways of gaining comfort as to the right way to monitor someone's contribution and how the costs of home working such as heating, lighting, broadband, office equipment, etc., are paid for. It is possible that a simple measure of time committed may not, on its own, be sufficient in the future.

Employees who are based in the Working Areas have their costs of employment reimbursed under the Full Schedule, provided that those costs fall within component 11, 12 or 13. When assessing these costs the Parties need to remember the overriding restriction of the Schedules: that something has to be necessary to Provide the Works. It is a regular consideration of cost assessors whether an amount is necessary. A *Contractor* can usually demonstrate that a person is necessary, but what if the associated salary and benefits package is greater than would usually be paid to someone in the role? This is a particularly relevant consideration when component 12(a), 12(c) or 12(d) is used.

Component 11 covers what the *Contractor* pays **for** people who work on the contract, either full time, or proportionate to the time spent in the Working Areas. Note that the component does not say amounts paid **to** people. This should be relatively easy to establish through payroll records, subject to suitable data protection provisions.

Component 12 considers some of the additional payments that are made to people, but is qualified by the reference to 'work on the contract', and here the reference is to payments made **to** people. The lettering of the list below corresponds to that in component 12.

(*a*) Bonuses and incentives are frequently paid by companies to their employees, and are often based partly on the project where a person is deployed and partly on the company's overall performance. In such a scenario, only the first element would be due as Defined cost, not the second. The incentives made to the employee and the reward must be related to Providing the Works.

(*b*) Overtime is easy to identify and to audit. Occasionally I see differences of opinion between Parties about enhanced rates for overtime, for example working at night, on weekends and on public holidays.

(*c*) Payments for working in special circumstances offers little explanation, and is no doubt intended to be broad so that it can be applied in any situation. Such allowances might be paid while people are working away from home for prolonged periods, working offshore or working in unpleasant conditions. Sometimes *Contractors* pay such allowances separately from salaries, to avoid those amounts permanently inflating the payroll and also to avoid those costs adding to pension liabilities.

(*d*) Special allowances is another term that is broad. This has been listed separately to the previous component, which is for special circumstances, so it must have been intended to be different.
(*e*) Absence due to sickness and holidays costs *Contractors* money – typically, the obligation to pay people continues in full while they are absent. Long-term absences due to sickness can present challenges to contract administrators about the extent of payments and the *Client's* obligation to pay them.
(*f*) Severance payments must be linked to work on the contract. Sometimes, people are recruited solely for a particular project and released at its conclusion. Severance pay in these circumstances is straightforward. But what if someone leaves a company after 10 years' service, the last 2 years of which were on the current contract? The full payments associated with that severance must not all fall for the *Client* to pay. What if the *Contractor* chose to pay enhanced severance terms, in excess of the legal minimum? These are challenges faced by those assessing and (hopefully) agreeing such matters.

Component 13 lists 15 costs that, if incurred in order to Provide the Works, will be reimbursed. Here, the costs are those made **in relation to people**, not necessarily **to** people. But these costs must be in relation to the person's employment contract.

Payments for travel, subsistence and lodging are straightforward. The mobile nature of construction and the need for contractors to move their people to the places where the work happens means that costs will be incurred for travel and subsistence.

Sometimes relocation is necessary, most probably temporary, to move people close to the Working Areas. This may involve that person's family too, so the costs of their relocation are also included by virtue of component 13(g).

The provision of medical examinations, passports/visas and travel insurance are all a feature of travel and relocation, so are allowed. Medical examinations may relate to the *works*, for example someone working in a water treatment works or a hospital. Or they may relate to travel to or from an infected area. In the recent COVID-19 pandemic, medical examinations in the form of viral tests were common and were frequently paid for through this component.

Protective clothing is usually a legal requirement for employers and is therefore necessary to Provide the Works. I sometimes see claims from *Contractors* for the reimbursement of costs for purchasing branded workwear that is not necessarily provided for safety but to assist with the corporate image. These costs are usually disallowed. But what if the office staff on the Site need fleeces to stay warm inside? These are all low-value, high-frequency items that need to be decided and dealt with.

Component 13(i) refers to 'contributions, levies or taxes imposed by law'. The nature of these costs will vary by legal jurisdiction in the place where the Working Areas are situated. Such charges must be imposed by law, so they cannot be made voluntarily by the *Contractor*, for example to a trade body. This component needs to be read in conjunction with clause 52.1, which requires any reductions in taxes that can be recovered to be included in Defined Cost.

Component 13(j) presents a challenge, particularly to the *Project Manager* whose task it is to assess Defined Cost. The *Client* for a particular project will presumably be content to contribute to the pensions of the people working on that project. But how much should that contribution be? This component restricts payments to those that are in accordance with an employment contract. That is simple where a person's contract requires the *Contractor* to pay, say, 8% of the gross salary to a pension. But what if that person is a member of a defined benefit scheme, as distinct from the previous defined contribution scheme? It is not uncommon for defined benefit schemes to be in deficit and for employers' contributions to include an element for reducing the deficit as well as an element for the present employment. How does your average *Project Manager* assess the relevant element for Providing the Works? Remember that your average *Project Manager* will not have had much training in actuarial science. Clearly, the *Project Manager* will need assistance here, and the *Client* should become involved.

Death benefit, life assurance, occupational accident benefits and health insurance can all be purchased from policy providers, so demonstrating their cost is relatively straightforward.

Component 13(m) refers to 'medical aid and health insurance'. It's not clear whether this means (*a*) medical aid and (*b*) health insurance or (*a*) medical aid insurance and (*b*) health insurance. Either way, the costs will be capable of demonstration. Whether medical aid is paid at cost or as an insurance premium, it will be capable of being assessed under the rules of the contract.

The provision of a vehicle forms part of some people's employment contract, and therefore falls to be paid for under this component. Whether the vehicle is needed for the person to do the role is immaterial. If it forms part of that person's employment contract, it can be reimbursed as Defined Cost.

Safety training is allowed to be reclaimed as Defined Cost. Remember that any employer has a duty to its employees to keep them safe at work. But also consider the requirement in the schedules for all costs to have been incurred in order to Provide the Works. Safety inductions, toolbox talks and the like that are relevant to the *works* will all be suitable for reimbursement. But the cost of a member of the site management studying part time at university for a degree in health and safety would not be reimbursable.

Component 14 refers to people who are self-employed, provided through an agency or who work through a service company. The amount paid by the *Contractor* for such people is usually inclusive of those costs listed in component 13, so, by separating the costs of non-employed people from employed people, the contract ensures that those 'on-costs' are not paid twice. The definition of Subcontractor in 11.2(19) expressly excludes the 'supply of people paid for by the Contractor according to the time they work'. Therefore, the costs of such people definitely fall in component 14, not component 4.

Equipment

The assessment of Equipment should, in theory, be relatively simple. Most equipment of any significant cost in the industry comes with a time charge – by the hour, day, week, etc. But the more you look at the details, the more exceptions arise. The Full Schedule deals with some of those exceptions.

The Full Schedule allows for the payment of Equipment costs where that Equipment is used within the Working Areas. So, not just the Site. But Equipment used elsewhere will be assumed to be included in the Fee (clause 52.1), with the exception of Manufacture and Fabrication (see later in this chapter). *Contractors* need to consider the impact of their choice of *working areas* that they include in Contract Data part two at tender. Following the introductory statement in component 2 there are eight paragraphs that state the categories of Equipment that qualify as a component and how each is assessed.

Schedule of Cost Components – 21

Payments for the hire or rent of Equipment not owned by

- the *Contractor*
- the *Contractor's* ultimate holding company or
- a company with the same ultimate holding company

at the hire or rental rate multiplied by the time for which the Equipment is required.

This first component addresses the hire of Equipment from external providers, as distinct from component 22 below, when the *Contractor* uses its own Equipment. As with several other components relating to Equipment, this refers to the time that the Equipment is **required**, not used. In other words, it needs to reflect an efficient way of working, and any superfluous hours will not be paid for.

Schedule of Cost Components – 22

Payments for Equipment which is not listed in the Contract Data but is

- owned by the *Contractor*,
- purchased by the *Contractor* under a hire purchase or lease agreement or
- hired by the *Contractor* from the *Contractor's* ultimate holding company or from a company with the same ultimate holding company

at open market rates, multiplied by the time for which the Equipment is required.

This component addresses the often-thorny issue of Equipment provided to the *Contractor* by a related company. Many contractors use Equipment provided by group companies, and there is frequently fear among *Clients* that uncompetitive rates are charged by the *Contractor* for that Equipment. The *Project Manager* may need access to market information to establish if rates are at open-market levels. The second bullet addresses the issue of title in some finance agreements where, in a legal sense, the *Contractor* does not actually own the item in question until the end of the agreement.

Schedule of Cost Components – 23

Payments for Equipment purchased for work included in the contract listed with a time-related on cost charge, in the Contract Data, of

- the change in value over the period for which the Equipment is required and
- the time-related on cost charge stated in the Contract Data for the period for which the Equipment is required.

The change in value is the difference between the purchase price and either the sale price or the open market sale price at the end of the period for which the Equipment is required. Interim payments of the change in value are made at each assessment date. A final payment is made in the next assessment after the change in value has been determined.

If the *Project Manager* agrees, an additional item of Equipment may be assessed as if it had been listed in the Contract Data.

This component reflects the purchase of Equipment for the project. At the expensive end of the scale, this might be tower cranes or specialist excavation or piling equipment. Items that require an operator may include the cost of that person in the on-costs. Less-expensive items might include proprietary edge protection systems, steel formwork and catering equipment in welfare facilities. The provision of site facilities such as hardstandings, car parks and drainage will also qualify as Equipment, and are likely to be purchased.

At the lower end of the scale this might include computer equipment such as desktop PCs, tablets, printers, cameras and servers. These will all carry a purchase price and an ongoing cost to operate and maintain. Earlier editions of the ECC including an item for the provision of high-volume, low-cost items that was calculated as a percentage of people costs. That was removed, unfortunately in my view, when the NEC4 suite was published. Every item of Equipment is now due to be assessed individually – screwdrivers, hammers, brushes and so on. The *Contractor* and the *Project Manager* are well advised to agree a sensible way of assessing such things; the final sentence of this component allows such sensible agreements. Anyone who has worked on a construction site will know how electronic devices magically disappear at the end of the project, and this increases the difficulty of establishing resale prices.

With the more-expensive items, such as a crane or excavator, these will command a resale value once they are no longer needed for the contract.

Consideration of component 25, consumption of Equipment, needs to be made here to avoid double counting.

> Schedule of Cost Components – 24
>
> Payments for special Equipment listed in the Contract Data. These amounts are the rates stated in the Contract Data multiplied by the time for which the Equipment is required.
>
> If the *Project Manager* agrees, an additional item of special Equipment may be assessed as if it had been listed in the Contract Data.

Component 24 refers to the types of Equipment that aren't likely to feature on standard lists or have a market rate. These may include

- items that are so rare that there is not a clear market rate
- items such as large mobile cranes where the costs of transport, assembly and disassembly are disproportionate and bespoke
- bespoke equipment manufactured for the installation of proprietary products.

Where one or more of these reasons is relevant, the *Contractor* can include rates in Contract Data part two at the tender stage, and when the contract is formed those rates become applicable as part of the contract agreement. Again, the final sentence allows sensible agreements to be made between the *Contractor* and the *Project Manager* where there isn't a rate in the Contract Data.

> Schedule of Cost Components – 25
>
> Payments for the purchase price of Equipment which is consumed.

This component can apply to a huge range of items. There is a potential for an overlap with component 23, given the lack of a definition for 'consumed', and my suggestions here do overlap with my earlier ones.

The definition of Equipment is sufficiently broad to include much smaller items. These may include

- Small hand tools such as screwdrivers, saws and hammers. Rarely will any of these survive a project and be available for reuse or sale after Completion.
- Electrically powered hand tools, for example drills and saws. These seem to miraculously disappear at the end of contracts.
- Computer equipment in Site offices, and on the Site. Sites are notorious places for the loss of cameras, phones, tablets and the like either through theft, carelessness or damage.
- The provision of diesel or fuel oil is probably included elsewhere within the rates for the Equipment it powers. If not, this would be the place to include it.

Equipment that is consumed will include

- batteries for installation equipment, information and communications technology equipment, surveying apparatus, radios, etc.
- stationery for offices such as paper and toner cartridges
- sanitary supplies for welfare facilities – a cost incurred by the *Contractor* to comply with the law.
- catering to include catering equipment and food and drink.

Schedule of Cost Components – 26

Unless included in the hire or rental rates, payments for

- transporting Equipment to and from the Working Areas other than for repair and maintenance,
- erecting and dismantling equipment and
- constructing, fabricating or modifying Equipment as a result of a compensation event.

Cost component 26 recognises that not all Equipment is available to provide on a simple hourly or daily rate. Some Equipment will need to be delivered and assembled before its use, and then the reverse activities at the end of the project, for example

- an onsite concrete batching plant
- the site electricity supply network
- a short-term use of a very large mobile crane
- 'normal' construction equipment where the Site is remote and transport costs are high.

These can be significant costs for the *Contractor*, and trying to blend them into a hire rate, when the total duration isn't known, would not be sensible.

Where a hire or rental rate includes for these costs, nothing further will be paid.

Schedule of Cost Components – 27

Payments for purchase of materials used to construct or fabricate Equipment.

Component 27 is linked to component 26. Where materials are needed for the provision of Equipment, the purchase prices will be assessed here. As these refer to temporary works, the word 'materials' is used, as distinct from Plant and Materials, which only relate to permanent works.

> Schedule of Cost Components – 28
>
> Unless included in the hire rates, the cost of operatives is included in the cost of people.

Component 28 prevents 'double counting' of people costs. Some items of Equipment are charged at a rate that includes the operator. This is common for items such as excavators and cranes where the operator needs specific skills and probably certification to use the item. It would be wrong to charge for that person's costs of employment in addition to the hire rate if the rate already included for the operative. For simplicity of auditing, *Contractors* should ensure that their accounts and records, include correspondence with the Equipment provider and includes a clear statement that an operator is or is not included in the hire rate.

Where an additional cost of the Equipment operative(s) is needed, then this component requires it to be included in the cost of people – in other words in section 1 of the Full Schedule. While this seems to contradict the opening statement in the Full Schedule about including an amount only in one component, it does make sense.

Plant and Materials

Plant and Materials, generally speaking, need to be purchased. The cost component here is therefore based on payments for purchasing and associated activities.

> Schedule of Cost Components – 3
>
> 31 Payments for
>
> - purchasing Plant and Materials,
> - delivery to and removal from the Working Areas,
> - providing and removing packaging and
> - samples and tests.
>
> 32 Cost is credited with payments received for disposal of Plant and Materials unless the cost is disallowed.

Few words are expended here, reflecting what should be relatively straightforward purchasing. As ever, the detail requires some further analysis.

Contract users need to remember the requirements of clause 52.1

- Use rates and percentages stated in the Contract Data (if any)
- Other amounts are at open-market or competitively tendered prices. My earlier comments about the procurement of Equipment are relevant here too. There should be a procedure in the Scope to explain how amounts should be assessed if tendering or open-market prices are needed.

The introductory paragraph of the Full Schedule is also relevant

- an amount is only included if it is incurred to Provide the Works.

Amounts assessed for Plant and Materials therefore have a few tests to pass. Components 31 and 32 add a few more, largely obvious, reasons for payment. Delivery, packaging and testing are all important parts of providing Plant and Materials. Component 32 reflects the ability of the *Contractor* to dispose of over-ordered materials. For example, where bricks are supplied in multiples of thousands, so if you need to procure 7500 bricks, you will have some left over if you have purchased 8000. In some places, these might be suitable for reselling, in which case the amount obtained should be offset against the original purchase price.

Subcontractors

Clause 26 requires all Subcontractors to be accepted by the *Project Manager* prior to their appointment, so the identity of organisations whose costs are being assessed here should not come as a surprise to the *Project Manager*.

Subcontractor is a defined term: see clause 11.2(19).

> Clause 11.2(19)
>
> A Subcontractor is a person or organisation who has a contract with the *Contractor* to
>
> - construct or install part of the *works*
> - design all or part of the *works*, except the design of Plant and Materials carried out by the supplier
> - provide a service in the Working Areas which is necessary to Provide the Works, except for the
>   - hire of Equipment
>   - supply of people paid for by the *Contractor* according to the time they work.

Component 4 refers to the costs of work done by Subcontractors.

> Schedule of Cost Components – 41
>
> Payments to Subcontractors for work which is subcontracted without taking into account any amounts paid to or retained from the Subcontractor by the *Contractor*, which would result in the *Client* paying or retaining the amount twice.

This component does not apply to those suppliers that may typically be referred to as subcontractors to the *Contractor* but that don't satisfy the definition. The costs of any subcontractors engaged by the *Contractor* that are not Subcontractors (note the use of 's' and 'S') will fall to be assessed under other components.

In clause 26 the *Project Manager* has a role in accepting the appointment and the conditions of contract of Subcontractors. The clauses for main Options C, D and E include clause 26.4, which requires the

Contractor to submit pricing information to the *Project Manager* when seeking acceptance of the Subcontractor's appointment and of the subcontract documents. So, the *Contractor* may fall back on the original acceptance when having to demonstrate the veracity of these costs. Clause 52.1 and the introduction to the Short Schedule will be relevant in this analysis.

The second part of the sentence in component 41 is self-explanatory. Such deductions, depending on the terms of the subcontract, might include retention, delay damages and amounts relating to Key Dates. Payments to Subcontractors in this regard might include advanced payments or a bonus for early Completion.

Charges

The list of charges provided in this section cover most of the unavoidable costs faced by *Contractors* when operating a construction or engineering operation. Interestingly, this component also covers charges received by the *Contractor*. The only component that expressly refers to payments received is 54, for the sale of materials from excavation and demolition.

Schedule of Cost Components – 51

Payments for the provision and use in the Working Areas of

- water,
- gas,
- electricity,
- telephone and
- internet.

Cost component 51 is relatively straightforward, paying for the provision of utilities to the Working Areas. Dependent upon the location of the Working Areas (these aren't confined to the Site) there may be some choice in supplier, and it is possible that wider arrangements between the *Contractor* and its utilities' suppliers may lead to advantageous terms being used here. Remember that in clause 52.1 the *Contractor* is required to share discounts and rebates with the *Client*.

Schedule of Cost Components – 52

Payments to public authorities and other properly constituted authorities of charges which they are authorised to make in respect of the *works*

The first part of this component is easy to understand and to apply. But the second part is more open to interpretation. What is a 'properly constituted authority'? Presumably it isn't a public authority, as that is mentioned in the first part of the sentence.

The public authorities in question will include planning authorities, health and safety authorities, payments for business rates and the like. Properly constituted authorities will be those bodies that are likely appointed or licensed by the government to do specified activities on its behalf.

> **Schedule of Cost Components – 53**
>
> Payments for
>
> (*a*) cancellation charges arising from a compensation event
> (*b*) buying or leasing land or buildings within the Working Areas
> (*c*) compensation for loss of crops or buildings
> (*d*) royalties
> (*e*) inspection certificates
> (*f*) charges for access to the Working Areas
> (*g*) facilities for visits to the Working Areas by Others
> (*h*) consumables and equipment provided by the *Contractor* for the *Project Manager's* and *Supervisor's* offices.

Most of these components are easy to understand, but some are worthy of comment.

Cancellation charges may be incurred when a compensation event occurs, for example when work is removed or changed and the *Contractor* has made contractual commitments based on the previous Scope.

Occasionally, compensation will be payable to third parties for the use of their property or the impact that the construction works have on that property. Typically, these costs will be incurred temporarily, otherwise, if permanent interference is likely then, the adjacent property would most likely be purchased by the *Client*.

Charges for access to the Working Areas may be payable when third-party access is needed, for example through somebody else's land or maybe a tolled bridge or tunnel. In the UK, I have seen several cases of the London congestion charge being recovered through this component for delivery vehicles.

Most projects will receive visits from Others. Some of these will be necessary for the *works*, such as visits from government bodies or statutory undertakers. Some will be for communications reasons, and visits by local residents and professional bodies. Typically, reception facilities are needed, a stock of suitable personal protective equipment (PPE) and so on.

Many contracts use the *Contractor* to equip the site offices of the *Project Manager*, *Supervisor* and *Client*. Although this component does not limit such provision to the Site offices, I think that is its aim. Typical provisions will include furniture, PPE, catering, office equipment, office consumables, sanitary consumables and maintenance.

> **Schedule of Cost Components – 54**
>
> Payments made and received by the *Contractor* for the removal from Site and disposal or sale of materials from excavation and demolition.

The final component in section 5 is for the removal of excavation and demolition materials. Where the materials are contaminated and unsuitable for use on the Site, they will need to be removed, and costs will be payable to a waste handler for doing so. Sometimes such materials, where not contaminated, will be sold, and the receipts for this need to be credited to any calculation of Defined Cost. This component should be read in conjunction with clause 73.2, which allows the *Contractor* title to such materials. If the materials are retained within the *works*, then no payment would be due from the *Contractor*: it is only where a payment is received that it must be credited to Defined Cost.

Sometimes the amounts realised can be significant, for example the removal of photovoltaic (solar) panels from the roof of a building set to be demolished, which will have a high recycling or reuse value.

Manufacture and fabrication

Manufacture and fabrication have become more important in the construction industry, with developments in offsite manufacture, information modelling and improvements in quality in factories. Significant improvements can be made to the speed of construction and to quality by adopting offsite manufacture. The NEC's Practice Note 4, explained in Chapter 11, sets out some of the benefits.

The Full Schedule allows the identification of rates for people, which presumably need to be considerably loaded with overheads to allow the manufacturing facility to recover its costs.

The two components are as follows.

> Schedule of Cost Components – 6
>
> 6 The following components of the cost of manufacture and fabrication of Plant and Materials by the *Contractor* which are
>
> - wholly or partly designed specifically for the *works* and
> - manufactured or fabricated outside the Working Areas.
>
> 61 Amounts calculated by multiplying each of the rates for people in the Contract Data by the total time appropriate to that rate spent on manufacture and fabrication of Plant and Materials outside the Working Areas.

I have worked with technology suppliers in road traffic signals, railway signalling, internet facilities and medical buildings. Each faces considerable costs in intellectual property rights (IPR) when manufacturing and supplying items assembled away from the Working Areas. Each complains that there is not a suitable place in either Schedule of Cost Components for IPR. Typically, such IPR is licensed with a combination of fixed and variable (per/unit) fees. It is difficult to recover such fees by a crude x% overhead charge on the people time committed. One client of mine, a global technology provider, tells me that it cannot obtain visibility of people hours from its own manufacturing plants internally, let alone release that information to external organisations.

Typically, this leads to tender queries and proposals for Z clause amendments to the Schedules. Given the costs of IPR and the legal consequences for breaching licence terms it is important that all aspects are properly considered in the contract, not just payment.

Under the three main Options the issue of title may arise if, as usual, the offsite manufacturer will require ongoing monthly payments and will not wish to await Site delivery before being paid. There are a number of ways of protecting the *Client* from supply chain insolvency risk in this scenario, and the ECC provides some of the provisions for the marking of Plant and Materials in clauses 70.1 and 71.1.

Clause 70.1

Whatever title the *Contractor* has to Plant and Materials which are outside the Working Areas passes to the *Client* if the *Supervisor* has marked them as for the contract.

Clause 71.1

The *Supervisor* marks Equipment, Plant and Materials which are outside the Working Areas if

- the contract identifies them for payment and
- the *Contractor* has prepared them for marking as the Scope requires.

The physical marking of completed items outside the Working Areas, for example in a storage warehouse, or part-completed items still in the manufacturing facility is part of a process of being able to demonstrate ownership in the event of insolvency. The ECC allocates this task to the *Supervisor*, which, in addition to marking, is well advised to take copious notes, photos and videos of what has been marked. Further drafting is needed in the Scope to provide the detail that satisfies the two bullet points in clause 71.1 and to establish the action that leads to an obligation to make payment as part of the Price for Work Done to Date. As with many issues in NEC contracts, this one relies on several clauses in different places in the contract, but without the assistance of cross-referencing.

Before leaving the subject of payment for offsite manufacture and fabrication it is worth recognising that the provisions of this section do not apply to standard components, in other words those that have not been designed for the *works*. The first part of component 6 states that limitation. So, where designers specify off-the-shelf items, their costs can be assessed on the purchase price. The structure of cost component 6 are designed to achieve a cost-effective assessment for the *Client* when the project demands bespoke components that do not have a 'market' rate but need pricing individually.

Design

The *Contractor's* obligations for the design of permanent works should be set out in the Scope, according to clause 21.1. Not all contracts will contain obligations for permanent works design but, where they do, the design will usually take place outside the Working Areas. Cost component 7 covers the design of both permanent works and temporary works. So, it will be relevant even in contracts that aren't described as design and build, because the *Contractor* will always be responsible for temporary works design.

Design work, permanent and temporary, has to be undertaken in conjunction with the *Project Manager* to whom it is submitted for acceptance in compliance with clauses 21.2 and 23.1 respectively.

Schedule of Cost Components – 7

7 The following components of the cost of design of the *works* and Equipment done outside the Working Areas.

71 Amounts calculated by multiplying each of the rates for people in the Contract Data by the total time appropriate to that rate spent on design of the *works* and Equipment outside the Working Areas.

72 The cost of travel to and from the Working Areas for the categories of design people listed in the Contract Data.

The opening paragraph explains that this component refers to both elements of design.

Component 71 sets out the simple way of calculating the amount due for design. The rates for people in the Contract Data are set out with

- the category of person
- the rate
- which category of design people whose travel expenses to and from the Working Areas are to be included in Defined Cost.

The use of a time-based assessment calculation calls for good record keeping. The designers must keep records of the hours spent on design for the *works* or Equipment and a narrative explaining what was done in those hours. Where the Schedule is being used to forecast Defined Cost, then each estimate of the hours included in a quotation should be accompanied by an explanation of what will be achieved in the hours proposed.

The rates will be inserted into Contract Data part two by the *Contractor*, either at the tender stage or during pre-contract negotiations. To a certain extent, without a competitive process, there is no urgency for them to be at market rates – this is something that the *Client's* tender processes and appraisals should consider. After the Contract Date, the rates will apply regardless of whether they are at market rates; the restrictions of clause 52.1, for example, will not apply.

Travelling expenses are allowed as part of Defined Cost for those categories of designers identified in the Contract Data. This reflects the need for designers to visit the Site for meetings, inspections, audits and so on. The contract requires those people to be identified by their category, which is probably unnecessary in most projects. If the visit to the Site is necessary, then the cost should really be included. Occasionally I see this entry left blank, in which case no travel expenses will be recoverable.

Component 72 only refers to the designers' travelling expenses, and is silent about the time incurred travelling. If a designer spends a total of 3 days travelling to and from a remote site for 1 day of productive work, who should pay for that person's time? Most people are capable of doing some productive work while travelling, but the 2 days of travel time here will not be fully productive. Is such travel time, 'time … spent on design'? Should this be included in the Fee, or should the *Client* pay for such time as

Defined Cost? *Contractors* argue that the costs of this time are incurred in order to Provide the Works, so this should be payable. I have no definitive answer to the question, having seen both approaches used. But where the Site is remote and requires significant time for travel, the *Client* should consider, when drafting tender documents, how it expects travel time to be paid for.

The contract is also silent about the travel expenses and time for other business travel for designers, for example meetings with other designers or Subcontractors or visits to offsite manufacturers. Presumably these costs will not form part of Defined Cost at all, as component 72 only refers to travel to and from the Working Areas.

Insurance

The insurance entry reflects any insurance proceeds resulting from an insurance claim. The contract requires the *Contractor* to have specified insurances in place that are not chargeable in Defined Cost (they are paid for out of the Fee).

Component 8 avoids the *Client* being required to pay amounts to the *Contractor* that have already been paid, or are likely to be paid, by insurers.

Schedule of Cost Components – 8

The following are deducted from cost

- the cost of events for which the contract requires the *Contractor* to insure and
- other costs paid to the *Contractor* by insurers.

Typical insurance claims will be from theft, accidental fires, arson and vandalism. The component only refers to events that the *Contractor* is required to insure and the deduction would apply even if the *Contractor* was not insured.

ICE Publishing

Patrick Waterhouse
ISBN 978-0-7277-6560-4
https://doi.org/10.1680/necdcce.65604.125

Chapter 13
Main Option C, D and E contracts: assessment of Price for Work Done to Date and assessment of compensation events

Assessment of Price for Work Done to Date

The Price for Work Done to Date is typically assessed monthly in NEC contracts. It is important because it represents the majority of the *Contractor's* income in an ECC contract by virtue of clause 50.3. After assessment by the *Project Manager*, the amount is then due for payment by the *Client* within the timescales set out in clause 51.2, possibly amended in a Y or Z clause and the Contract Data.

In main Option C, D and E contracts the amount is assessed as follows.

> Clause 11.2(31)
>
> The Price for Work Done to Date is the total Defined Cost which the *Project Manager* forecasts will have been paid by the *Contractor* before the next assessment date plus the Fee.

I said earlier that typically these assessments and the associated payments occur monthly. The contract is flexible on this frequency, setting the *assessment interval* in Contract Data part one and requiring the *Project Manager* to decide the first assessment date in clause 50.1. I will assume a monthly assessment in the remainder of this description.

The *Project Manager* has to forecast this amount and certify it within 7 days. If the assessment date is, say, the 25th of the month, the *Project Manager* has to forecast what Defined Cost the *Contractor* will have paid by the 25th of the following month. This clearly involves considerable effort in auditing the *Contractor's* accounts and records, but the *Project Manager* is given some assistance by the contract

- Clause 50.2 – the *Contractor* has to submit an application for payment to the *Project Manager* including details of how the amount has been assessed. There is a reference to the Scope for the type of information required.
- Clauses 52.2 and 52.4 – the *Contractor* has to keep accounts and records, and provide access to them for the *Project Manager*. There is a reference to the Scope for requiring additional records.
- Clause 20.4 – the *Contractor* has to prepare and submit forecasts of Defined Cost to the *Project Manager*.
- Clause 26.4 – the *Contractor* has to submit proposed subcontract pricing information to the *Project Manager* when seeking the acceptance of a Subcontractor.

The requirement is to assess what will be **paid**, as distinct from what will be **incurred**. So, in forecasting what will be paid in the next month, many of those amounts will have already been finalised, and the forecast amount will be demonstrable by documents such as invoices. A month later, the actual payment should be capable of verification from banking records.

Remember also that in assessing Defined Cost the *Project Manager* also has to assess Disallowed Cost, as the latter forms part of the definition of the former. The *Project Manager*, as can be seen from the earlier list, can rely upon a series of submissions from the *Contractor* when making the assessment. As with any contractual matter, the onus here is on the *Contractor* to demonstrate its entitlement. If it complies with the various provisions listed, then it should succeed with that demonstration.

I now look at some of these provisions in more detail, starting with clauses 52.2 and 52.4.

Clause 52.2

The *Contractor* keeps these records

- accounts of payments of Defined Cost,
- proof that the payments have been made,
- communications about and assessments of compensation events for Subcontractors and
- other records as stated in the Scope.

Clause 52.4

The *Contractor* allows the *Project Manager* to inspect at any time within working hours the accounts and records which it is required to keep.

The 'keeping' of records is something that any business is required to do. The laws of the country where the *works* take place and the laws of the country where the *Contractor* is domiciled will require this. The requirement to keep the records demanded of clause 52.2 and the Scope should not be unduly burdensome. But the requirement, in clause 52.4, to allow the *Project Manager* to inspect these accounts and records may be seen by some people to be so. Commercial confidentiality and data protection are frequently cited as reasons for denying such access. The time to raise such objections is at the tender stage, not once the *Contractor* has entered into the contract and has already promised to provide access. Legislation, such as the UK's General Data Protection Regulation,[i] is sometimes used by *Contractors* to either deny access or to compel the *Project Manager* to visit head office to ratify any purported Defined Cost for someone. This is not easily achieved in the *period for reply*. This then forces the hand of the *Project Manager* to make an assessment.

There can be problems with a literal interpretation of clause 52.3 and the word 'inspect'. This clause was probably originally drafted in an earlier version of the ECC when there was a document control room and the administration was a paper exercise. As times have moved on, everything is electronic. Therefore, if the *Contractor* chooses to interpret inspect as 'look over my shoulder at the computer screen', then,

[i] General Data Protection Regulation (EU) 2016/679; Data Protection Act 2018 (UK).

albeit not very clause 10.1, it is adhering to its obligations under the contract. Links to online shared sites are much more efficient but can introduce new problems. There is a reliance on the *Contractor* to keep good records, upload them to a shared location and then grant access to that location. This gives the *Contractor* unilateral control over the accounts and records and access. The intent of the contract is not to make the *Contractor* the key holder to all information, but the new way of working with online SharePoint sites grants it this privilege. The *Contractor* must 'sieve' costs data to ensure its relevance rather than just dumping the contents of its accounts system to an online site for the *Project Manager* to assess.

There is an emphasis on payments in all of these provisions. The Parties have agreed to share the risk of the final outturn cost, and hence the *Client* is liable to reimburse actual payments, not accrued amounts or theoretical numbers. Clause 52.1 requires all rebates and discounts to be reflected in the assessment of Defined Cost. That is why the clause requires accounts and records to be kept of payments. The *Contractor's* accounting systems should be capable of demonstrating what has been paid, to whom, when and what for. There should be an audit trail linking the original procurement of the resources, and proof of delivery or completion, assessment, invoicing and remittance. Any accounts system can either store or link these items. Where people costs are being assessed, payroll records should be provided, and some sensitivity should be deployed by the *Project Manager* when inspecting them.

Heaphy and Bone[ii] have identified some of the difficulties of doing these audits in the real world

- people working on the project but whose actual presence in the Working Areas is for lesser periods than their project workload
- using the actual cost of people or the salary costing rate
- benefits in kind in employment contracts
- bonuses
- pay rises for people who are paid for via agreed rates
- buy or hire decisions for Equipment
- value-for-money tests
- Disallowed Cost

The *Contractor's* forecasts, required of clause 20.4, have to be prepared 'in consultation with the *Project Manager*' and must include an explanation of what has changed since the previous forecast. The purpose of these forecasts is twofold. First, to assist the *Client* with its own cash flow planning. Second, as here, to assist the *Project Manager* with assessing payments due to the *Contractor*. While the clause requires the forecast to consider the whole of the *works*, its focus for this task should be on the immediate future. The programme should also guide the *Project Manager*, particularly for those payments that are likely to be made in the next month that aren't currently demonstrated by accounts and records.

The level of audit required will depend on the circumstances of the project and the sums involved. Auditors and the *Contractor* should allocate their time in proportion to the amount involved, but should endeavour to look at all categories of expenditure at least once throughout the project lifecycle.

[ii] Heaphy I and Bone G (2021) Cost assurance and audits on infrastructure projects and contracts. *Civil Engineering Surveyor*, May.

Assessment of compensation events

How do we establish how much money is due for a compensation event?

A reminder follows about the assessment of compensation events, from the core clauses.

> Clause 63.1 (excerpt)
>
> The change to the Prices is assessed as the effect of the compensation event upon
>
> - the actual Defined Cost of the work done by the dividing date,
> - the forecast Defined Cost of the work not done by the dividing date and
> - the resulting Fee.

So, in any main Option we need to establish the effect of the event on Defined Cost and then add the Fee to it, based on the percentage in Contract Data part two.

Don't we just use the rates in the contract to assess compensation events?

Main Option C or D contracts contain significant pricing information in the Activity Schedule or the Bill of Quantities, respectively. But those documents only establish the total of the Prices, or the target. Unlike other forms of commercial contract, the ECC does not default to the existing price data in the contract for assessing the financial impact of changed work or other events that lead to an entitlement. Main Option E contracts tend not to contain much pricing data other than the *fee percentage* and the data needed for the Schedule of Cost Components.

Particularly with a Bill of Quantities, it is tempting to use the rates and lump sums in the bill to assess the financial impact of a compensation event. The use of existing prices is entirely possible in the ECC, but requires the agreement of the *Contractor* and the *Project Manager* to do so.

Clause 63.2, which, as part of the core clauses, applies to each of the main Options, allows this use.

> Clause 63.2
>
> The *Project Manager* and the *Contractor* may agree rates or lump sums to assess the change to the Prices.

So why, in a contract with detailed pricing information (such as main Options C and D), does it not default to that data? The answer is that we expect the Parties to benefit from their original agreement, but, for future changes to the *works* or the manner in which they are provided, neither Party should be required to continue a financial arrangement that is disadvantageous to it. For example, if the *Contractor* has entered into the contract with a series of loss-making rates or sums, then its share will be assessed on that basis. But, without an agreement between the *Contractor* and the *Project Manager*, additional work will not have to be provided at a loss by relying on existing rates. The new works will be paid for on the basis of Defined Cost. The reverse of the analogy works too: the *Client* will not have to continue paying excessively profitable rates either.

Where the Parties do agree to use rates and lump sums, the contract is silent about where they may be found. In main Options C and D the costs data in the Activity Schedule or the Bill of Quantities is likely to be very helpful and may therefore be used. Equally, data from elsewhere could also be used.

Can we reduce the Prices?

A reminder follows about the effect of compensation events on the possible reduction of the Prices. The starting point is Clause 63.3, which is in the core clauses and so applies to each main Option.

> Clause 63.3
>
> If the effect of a compensation event is to reduce the total Defined Cost, the Prices are not reduced unless otherwise stated in these *conditions of contract*.

I explained the contract's approach to reduced Prices in Chapter 8. Main Option C, D and E contracts allow for the reduction in Prices through the core clauses (63.3 and 63.4) and specific compensation events that expressly allow for the reduction in Prices.

> Clause 63.4
>
> If the effect of a compensation event is to reduce the total Defined Cost and the event is
>
> - a change to the Scope other than a change to the Scope provided by the *Client*, which the *Contractor* proposed and the *Project Manager* accepted or
> - a correction to an assumption stated by the *Project Manager* for assessing an earlier compensation event
>
> the Prices are reduced.

In clause 63.4 the first bullet refers to Scope changes, except those resulting from clause 16.1. The second bullet refers to the *Project Manager's* actions under clause 61.6. These are two examples of where the contract expressly allows compensation events to lead to a reduction in the Prices.

The route for amending the Prices in main Option C, D and E contracts is through clause 63.14 (main Option C) or 60.4 (main Option D). There is no equivalent clause in main Option E contracts. I describe the provisions for changing the total of the Prices in more detail later in this chapter.

> Clause 63.14
>
> Assessments for changed Prices for compensation events are in the form of changes to the Activity Schedule.
>
> Clause 63.15
>
> Assessments for changed Prices for compensation events are in the form of changes to the Bill of Quantities.

Clauses 63.14 and 63.15 allow for the reduction in Prices where appropriate, and indeed their increase, because they refer to 'changes' to the respective pricing document.

Contractor's proposals

Clauses 16.1 and 16.2 allow the *Contractor* to propose changes to the Scope provided by the *Client* in order to reduce the Prices.

> Clause 16.1
>
> The *Contractor* may propose to the *Project Manager* that the Scope provided by the *Client* is changed in order to reduce the amount the *Client* pays to the *Contractor* for Providing the Works. The *Project Manager* consults with the *Client* and the *Contractor* about the change.
>
> Clause 16.2
>
> Within four weeks of the *Contractor* making the proposal the *Project Manager*
>
> - accepts the *Contractor's* proposal and issues an instruction changing the Scope,
> - informs the *Contractor* that the *Client* is considering the proposal and instructs the *Contractor* to submit a quotation for a proposed instruction to change the Scope or
> - informs the *Contractor* that the proposal is not accepted.
>
> The *Project Manager* may give any reason for not accepting the proposal.

In main Option C and D contracts, clause 63.13 deals with the outcome of a *Contractor's* proposal that has been accepted and implemented.

> Clause 63.13 – main Options C and D only
>
> If the effect of a compensation event is to reduce the total Defined Cost and the event is a change to the Scope provided by the *Client*, which the *Contractor* proposed and the *Project Manager* accepted, the Prices are not reduced.

Clause 63.13 dovetails with clauses 16.1, 16.2 and 63.3. The product of these clauses is that the *Contractor's* share will improve with such a proposal. Take, by way of example, the following scenario

- The contract is a main Option C contract with a simple 50% share mechanism, so that both 'pain' and 'gain' are shared 50/50 between the Parties.
- The *Contractor* proposes a change to the specified Plant and Materials that achieves a saving in Defined Cost, and thereby the Price for Work Done to Date, of £2.4 million.
- The Prices are not reduced, by virtue of clause 63.13.
- The share will increase (if 'gain') or reduce (if 'pain') by £2.4 million in the calculation under clause 54.1.
- The Contractor's share, calculated under clauses 54.1 and 54.2 at 50% of the total saving, is therefore increased by £1.2 million.

There are no express provisions in main Option E contracts for dealing with *Contractor's* proposals. A successful proposal will merely reduce the total of the Prices. There are no incentives in a purely cost-reimbursable contract for the *Contractor* to make such suggestions.

Main Option C contracts

The specific clauses that apply to main Option C contracts reflect its use of the Activity Schedule for establishing the Prices. The Activity Schedule is typically created by the *Contractor* during the tender or negotiation period. On the Contract Date it is the *activity schedule* and, as it says in clause 11.2(21), that remains the case until later changed in accordance with the contract. It likely changes and develops through the project due to the effect of changes to the programme and compensation events.

> Clause 11.2(21) – main Options A and C
>
> The Activity Schedule is the *activity schedule* unless later changed in accordance with these *conditions of contract*.

So, how can the Activity Schedule change in accordance with the contract? There are five possibilities

- a compensation event (clause 63.1)
- accepting a Defect (clause 45.2)
- agreeing acceleration (clause 36.3)
- to align with the programme (clauses 31.4 and 55.3)
- an agreed change to the contract (clause 12.3).

The Prices in a main Option C contract are defined in clause 11.2(32).

> Clause 11.2(32) – main Options A and C
>
> The Prices are the lump sum prices for each of the activities on the Activity Schedule unless later changed in accordance with the contract.

The reference to 'in accordance with the contract' is to the six possibilities listed above.

Once implemented, the effect of the compensation event is to change the Activity Schedule (clause 63.14). So, the Activity Schedule will be changed by one or more of the following

- a new item – description and price
- a revised description
- a revised price
- the removal of an item and its price entirely
- the amendment of a grouping, moving an activity to change the sequence of payment.

Once the compensation event has been implemented, it merely affects the total of the Prices, in a main Option C contract that is the target. The assessment of the work in question will be made as part of the Price for Work Done to Date in clause 11.2(31).

Main Option D contracts

The specific clauses that apply to main Option D contracts reflect its use of the Bill of Quantities for establishing the Prices. The Bill of Quantities is typically created by the *Client* during the tender or negotiation period and completed by the *Contractor* in its tender. On the Contract Date it is the *bill of quantities* and, as it says in clause 11.2(22), that remains the case until later changed in accordance with the contract. It likely changes and develops through the project due to the effect of changes to the programme and compensation events.

> Clause 11.2(22) – main Options B and D
>
> The Bill of Quantities is the *bill of quantities* unless later changed in accordance with these *conditions of contract*.

So, how can the Bill of Quantities change in accordance with the contract? There are seven possibilities

- a compensation event (clause 63.1)
- accepting a Defect (clause 45.2)
- agreeing acceleration (clause 36.3)
- a significant change to a quantity (clause 60.4)
- a change to correct an error in item descriptions where they do not comply with the *method of measurement* (clause 60.6)
- a change to correct an ambiguity or inconsistency (clause 60.6)
- an agreed change to the contract (clause 12.3).

The Prices in a main Option D contract are defined in clause 11.2(33).

> Clause 11.2(33) – main Options B and D
>
> The Prices are the lump sums and the amounts obtained by multiplying the rates by the quantities for the items in the Bill of Quantities.

This definition makes the assessment of changed work relatively simple once the compensation event has been implemented and the revised entries are in the Bill of Quantities. In a priced ECC contract, the Prices are what the *Client* pays for the work, here the actual quantities of work multiplied by the relevant rates in the Bill of Quantities.

Once implemented, the effect of the compensation event is to change the Bill of Quantities (clause 63.15). So, the Bill of Quantities will be changed by one or more of the following

- a new item – description and rate or lump sum.
- a revised description.

- a revised quantity.
- a revised rate or lump sum.
- the removal of an item and its price entirely.

There are three compensation events added to the contract when main Option D is used. They are in clauses 60.4, 60.5 and 60.6. These were described earlier in Chapter 6.

Clause 60.4 refers to major changes in quantity, and allows for the consequential change in unit rates. The change in quantity must not come from a change to the Scope, in other words the quantity of work for an item of Scope has changed by 0.5% of the original contract value in financial terms. A common example is earthworks, particularly where difficult ground conditions are encountered. If the level of excavation increases significantly, then its unit rate is likely to reduce.

Clause 60.5 refers to any change in quantities; there is no 0.5% limit here. There is a compensation event for the effect of delays to Key Dates or Completion Dates.

Clause 60.6 refers to technical errors in the Bill of Quantities and any ambiguities and inconsistencies. Where the Bill of Quantities has been inconsistent with another contract document, the Bill of Quantities has precedence. The contract assumes that the *Contractor* has taken the Bill of Quantities to be correct.

Once the compensation event has been implemented, it merely affects the total of the Prices, in a main Option D contract that is the target. The assessment of the work in question will be made as part of the Price for Work Done to Date in clause 11.2(31).

Main Option E contracts

The specific clauses that apply to main Option E contracts reflect its wholly cost-reimbursable nature.

The Prices in a main Option E contract are defined in clause 11.2(34).

> Clause 11.2(34) – main Option E
>
> The Prices are the forecast of the total Defined Cost for the whole of the *works* plus the Fee.

Once the compensation event has been implemented, it changes the total of the Prices, according to clause 63.1. The Prices are merely a reporting item for the Parties and the *Project Manager* and do not affect the amount paid to the *Contractor* by the *Client*. The payment to the *Contractor* is based entirely on Defined Cost and the Fee, as explained earlier in this chapter. The assessment of the work in question will be made as part of the Price for Work Done to Date in clause 11.2(31). There is no pricing document in main Option E contracts (compare with the Activity Schedule or Bill of Quantities in main Option A, B, C or D contracts), so there is nothing else to change.

Patrick Waterhouse
ISBN 978-0-7277-6560-4
https://doi.org/10.1680/necdcce.65604.135

Chapter 14
Main Option F contracts: Defined Cost, Disallowed Cost, assessment of Price for Work Done to Date and assessment of compensation events

The role of Defined Cost in main Option F contracts

Defined Cost is used, with the Fee, for the payment of the *Contractor* for all of the work undertaken, whether known about at the Contract Date, or arising subsequently as compensation events.

The Price for Work Done to Date is based on the *Project Manager's* forecast of the future payment of Defined Cost. Defined Cost is also used for the assessment of compensation events.

The Price for Work Done to Date is the amount of the payment that the *Contractor* receives from the *Client* after each assessment. The contract is flexible on how often this is done, but typically it is monthly. The assessment of compensation events adjusts the total of the Prices, which is the forecast of the total.

How do we establish how much money is due for a compensation event?

A reminder follows about the assessment of compensation events, from the Core Clauses.

Clause 63.1 (excerpt)

The change to the Prices is assessed as the effect of the compensation event upon

- the actual Defined Cost of the work done by the dividing date,
- the forecast Defined Cost of the work not done by the dividing date and
- the resulting Fee.

So, in any main Option we need to establish the effect of the event on Defined Cost and then add the Fee to it, based on the percentage in Contract Data part two. I explain the specifics of how compensation events are assessed in main Option F contracts later in this chapter.

Defined Cost in main Option F contracts

Defined Cost is defined in each of the main Options. In main Option F contracts, this is clause 11.2(25).

> Clause 11.2(25)
>
> Defined Cost is
>
> - the amount of payments due to Subcontractors for work is subcontracted without taking account of amounts paid to or retained from the Subcontractor by the *Contractor* which would result in the *Client* paying or retaining the amount twice and
> - the *prices* for work done by the *Contractor*
>
> less Disallowed Cost.

Disallowed Cost acts as a further regulator (together with clause 52.1) on what the *Contractor* is paid.

Disallowed Cost in main Option F contracts

The definition of Disallowed Cost in Option F differs slightly from that used in main Options C, D and E. It reflects the *Contractor's* reduced role in directly delivering works compared with the earlier main Options and the reliance on Subcontractors.

Disallowed Cost is a simple name for a simple concept that, when explored further, becomes more complicated when the detail is understood. The role for Disallowed Cost is to govern the costs paid to the *Contractor* and to ensure that these have been properly incurred and do not result from the *Contractor's* breach of other obligations or its inefficient working. The *Contractor* may have costs disallowed that it can demonstrate through accounts and records, but that were incurred inefficiently or in breach of other obligations and therefore will not fall for the *Client* to pay. Equally, it may incur costs legitimately but not be able to provide accounts and records, and will similarly struggle to obtain payment.

The provisions of clause 11.2(27) need to be considered by *Contractors* when establishing costs management systems. Some flexibility in reporting functionality is possible in accounting systems, but manual human intervention is usually needed to identify which of the *Contractor's* costs fall within Defined Cost and which, by exception, are in the Fee. Where wrongly categorised costs are reported to the *Project Manager* in payment applications, they should be disallowed either for the fact they are not Defined Cost or for the fact that they fall within the definition of Disallowed Cost.

Disallowed Cost is defined, for main Option F contracts in clause 11.2(27).

> Clause 11.2(27)
>
> Disallowed Cost is cost which
>
> - is not justified by the *Contractor's* accounts and records [DC1],
> - should not have been paid to a Subcontractor or supplier in accordance with its contract [DC2],
> - is a payment to a Subcontractor for
>   - work which the Contract Data states that the *Contractor* will do itself [DC11] or
>   - the *Contractor's* management [DC12],

- was incurred only because the *Contractor* did not
  - follow an acceptance or procurement procedure stated in the Scope [DC3],
  - give an early warning which the contract required it to give [DC4] or
  - give notification to the *Project Manager* of the preparation for and conduct of an adjudication or proceedings of a tribunal between the *Contractor* and a Subcontractor or supplier [DC10].

and the cost of preparation for and conduct of an adjudication, payments to a member of the Dispute Avoidance Board or proceedings of the *tribunal* between the Parties [DC6].

[I have added the Disallowed Cost (DC) references to the definition for ease of explanation in this book. They do not feature in the ECC.]

The reference to accounts and records in the first bullet of clause 11.2(27) links to clauses 52.3 and 52.4. Those latter clauses require the *Contractor* to keep certain records, largely about payments of costs, and to allow access to them for the *Project Manager*. There is the ability to state additional requirements in the Scope, and this is also a common topic for Z clauses. Accounting systems should maintain records of amounts paid, for example linking a payment made to a Subcontractor with that Subcontractor's invoice. The item or service in question needs to be capable of being discretely identified.

The first four elements of Disallowed Cost, numbered DC1, DC2, DC11 and DC12 by me, refer to failures in the *Contractor's* administration.

DC1 requires a cost to be 'justified' by accounts and records. Accounts systems are rarely 100% effective, so there may not always be a perfect trail of documents to justify Defined Cost. But something should always be available. Typically, it is the smaller amounts of expenditure that cause difficulties in audit. The *Project Manager* and *Contractor* should remain flexible in how costs are demonstrated. The *Project Manager* should only use this restriction when the records do not justify the payment of a cost.

DC2 guards against payments to Subcontractors or suppliers that may not be contractually required in respect of the *works*. It should be relatively easy to show that a payment was in accordance with a subcontract or supply agreement. If the Subcontractor was properly appointed in accordance with clauses 26.2, 26.3 and 26.4, then the *Project Manager* will already have a copy of the subcontract documents. If the costs relate to a supplier, then the *Contractor* will need to provide a copy of the supply contract to the *Project Manager* if requested. *Contractors* should consider this issue when concluding final account or settlement agreements with Subcontractors where the terms fall outside the ECC.

DC3 relies on the Scope containing an acceptance or procurement procedure. Where large sums of the *Client's* money are expected to be reimbursed through the contract, the *Client* has a justified expectation that the money will be spent effectively. Procedures for procurement and acceptance are part of the contract, if included in the Scope, to ensure that items or services are provided to the right quality and price. Such requirements are much easier to enforce where they are written objectively and with clear wording. The *Contractor* will need to show that it has followed the procedures in question. Acceptance procedures may apply to accepting the type or quality of specification, and subsequently to the quality of finished work, for example dovetailing with clause 42.1. Procurement procedures will specify how proposed suppliers are selected, how many should be approached and the rules for tendering. These should be consistent with clause 52.1 and the Schedule of Cost Components.

DC4 refers to the failure to give an early warning that was required. This is a similar provision to clauses 61.5 and 63.7 in the core clauses, but it is not identical. Those clauses refer to an early warning that **could** have been given. Here, the reference is to early warnings that were **required**. I interpret this restriction as referring to

- the first part of clause 15.1 (i.e. something affecting one or more of the four bullets, but not something that only affects the *Contractor's* total costs)
- clause X10.3 – creation or use of the Information Model
- clause X12.3(3) – achievement of another Partner's objectives

The aim of this provision is to encourage the *Contractor* to give early warnings where they are required, and to avoid the *Client* paying for the additional costs that have been incurred as a result of that failure to warn.

DC10 recognises that the *Project Manager*, *Supervisor* or *Client* may have a role to play in disputes between the *Contractor* and its supply chain members. Sometimes the disputes will involve both the main contract and a subcontract, for example over the quality of work or whether Completion was achieved on a certain date. In such situations the *Project Manager* may be able to help with resolving the dispute. The considerable expense of adjudication, arbitration or litigation often exceeds the costs of a sensible compromise. By requiring a notification, the contract allows the intervention of the *Client* and its appointees. Where such a notification has not been given, the *Client* will not be required to pay costs that could have been avoided if it had known of the proceedings. The worst-case scenario could be if the first that the *Client* knew of the dispute was when it received a notice of adjudication itself under the main contract pursuant to clause W1.3(4) or W2.3(3).

DC6 is an obvious requirement, but not so obvious that it can be omitted. No *Client* will want to find itself paying for the costs of legal action taken against it. Additional rules apply to the payment of the other Party's costs in adjudication in the UK that would make any contrary position unenforceable anyway. Payments to the Dispute Avoidance Board's members are shared equally in the NEC4 Dispute Resolution Service Contract (clause 3.9), so these should not be charged back to the *Client*.

DC11 and DC12 ensure that the *Client* does not pay twice for the same *works* or management activities. The *Contractor* is paid on the basis of its *prices* in main Option F contracts, linked to stated activities in Contract Data part two and to clause 20.2. The *prices* are fixed unless there is a compensation event that requires a change under clause 63.17. If some of the *works* or management activities that were originally allocated to the *Contractor* were then undertaken by a Subcontractor, the *prices* would remain unchanged but the *Client* would pay for the additional cost of the Subcontractor doing the management or activity in question.

The Price for Work Done to Date in main Option F contracts

The Price for Work Done to Date is typically assessed monthly in NEC contracts. It is important because it represents the majority of the *Contractor's* income in an ECC contract by virtue of clause 50.3. After assessment by the *Project Manager*, the amount is then due for payment by the *Client* within the timescales set out in clause 51.2, possibly amended in a Y or Z clause and the Contract Data.

In main Option F contracts the amount is assessed as follows.

> Clause 11.2(31)
>
> The Price for Work Done to Date is the total Defined Cost which the *Project Manager* forecasts will have been paid by the *Contractor* before the next assessment date plus the Fee.

I said earlier that typically these assessments and the associated payments occur monthly. The contract is flexible on this frequency, setting the *assessment interval* in Contract Data part one and requiring the *Project Manager* to decide the first assessment date in clause 50.1. I will assume a monthly assessment in the remainder of this description.

In main Option F contracts, the primary component of Defined Cost is payment to Subcontractors, so this should be supported by assessments and invoices.

The *Project Manager* has to forecast this amount and certify it within 7 days. If the assessment date is, say, the 25th of the month, the *Project Manager* has to forecast what Defined Cost the *Contractor* will have paid by the 25th of the following month. This clearly involves considerable effort in auditing the *Contractor's* accounts and records, but the *Project Manager* is given some assistance by the contract;

- Clause 50.2 – the *Contractor* has to submit an application for payment to the *Project Manager* including details of how the amount has been assessed. There is a reference to the Scope for the type of information required.
- Clauses 52.3 and 52.4 – the *Contractor* has to keep accounts and records, and provide access to them for the *Project Manager*. There is a reference to the Scope for requiring additional records.
- Clause 20.4 – the *Contractor* has to prepare and submit forecasts of Defined Cost to the *Project Manager*.
- Clause 26.4 – the *Contractor* has to submit proposed subcontract pricing information to the *Project Manager* when seeking the acceptance of a Subcontractor.

The requirement is to assess what will be **paid**, as distinct from what will be **incurred**. So, in forecasting what will be paid in the next month, many of those amounts will have already been finalised, and the forecast amount will be demonstrable by documents such as invoices. A month later, the actual payment should be capable of verification from banking records.

Remember also that in assessing Defined Cost the *Project Manager* also has to assess Disallowed Cost, as the latter forms part of the definition of the former. The *Project Manager*, as can be seen from the earlier list, can rely upon a series of submissions from the *Contractor* when making the assessment. As with any contractual matter, the onus here is on the *Contractor* to demonstrate its entitlement. If it complies with the various provisions listed, then it should succeed with that demonstration.

I now look at some of these provisions in more detail, starting with clauses 52.3 and 52.4.

Clause 52.3

The *Contractor* keeps these records

- accounts of payments made to Subcontractors,
- proof that the payments have been made,
- communications about and assessments of compensation events for Subcontractors and
- other records as stated in the Scope.

Clause 52.4

The *Contractor* allows the *Project Manager* to inspect at any time within working hours the accounts and records which it is required to keep.

The 'keeping' of records is something that any business is required to do. The laws of the country where the *works* take place and the laws of the country where the *Contractor* is domiciled will require this. The requirement to keep the records demanded of clause 52.3 and the Scope should not be unduly burdensome. But the requirement, in clause 52.4, to allow the *Project Manager* to inspect these accounts and records may be seen by some people to be so. Commercial confidentiality and data protection are frequently cited as reasons for denying such access. The time to raise such objections is at the tender stage, not once the *Contractor* has entered into the contract and promised to provide access. Legislation, such as the UK's General Data Protection Regulation,[i] is sometimes used by *Contractors* to either deny access or to compel the *Project Manager* to visit head office to ratify any purported Defined Cost for someone. This is not easily achieved in the *period for reply*. This then forces the hand of the *Project Manager* to make an assessment.

There can be problems with a literal interpretation of clause 52.3 and the word 'inspect'. This clause was probably originally drafted in an earlier version of the ECC when there was a document control room and the administration was a paper exercise. As times have moved on, everything is electronic. Therefore, if the *Contractor* chooses to interpret inspect as 'look over my shoulder at the computer screen', then, albeit not very clause 10.1, it is adhering to their obligations under the contract. Links to online shared sites are much more efficient but can introduce new problems. There is a reliance on the *Contractor* to keep good records, upload them to a shared location and then grant access for the *Project Manager* to that location. This gives the *Contractor* unilateral control over the accounts and records and access. The intent of the contract is not to make the *Contractor* the key holder to all information, but the new way of working with online sites grants it this privilege. The *Contractor* must 'sieve' costs data to ensure its relevance rather than just dumping the contents of its accounts system to an online site for the *Project Manager* to assess.

There is an emphasis on payments in all of these provisions. The Parties have agreed to share the risk of the final outturn cost, and hence the *Client* is liable to reimburse actual payments, not accrued amounts or theoretical numbers. Clause 52.1 requires all rebates and discounts to be reflected in the assessment of

[i] General Data Protection Regulation (EU) 2016/679; Data Protection Act 2018 (UK).

Defined Cost. That is why the clause requires accounts and records to be kept of payments. The *Contractor's* accounting systems should be capable of demonstrating what has been paid, to whom, when and what for. There should be an audit trail linking the original procurement of the resources, and proof of delivery or completion, assessment, invoicing and remittance. Any accounts system can either store or link these items. Where people costs are being assessed, payroll records should be provided, and some sensitivity should be deployed by the *Project Manager* when inspecting them.

Heaphy and Bone[ii] have identified some of the difficulties of doing these audits in the real world

- people working on the project but whose actual presence in the Working Areas is for lesser periods than their project workload
- using the actual cost of people or the salary costing rate
- benefits in kind in employment contracts
- bonuses
- pay rises for people who are paid for via agreed rates
- buy or hire decisions for Equipment
- value-for-money tests
- Disallowed Cost

The *Contractor's* forecasts, required of clause 20.4, have to be prepared 'in consultation with the *Project Manager*' and must include an explanation of what has changed since the previous forecast. The purpose of these forecasts is twofold. First, to assist the *Client* with its own cash flow planning. Second, as here, to assist the *Project Manager* with assessing payments due to the *Contractor*. While the clause requires the forecast to consider the whole of the works, its focus for this task should be on the immediate future. The programme should also guide the *Project Manager*, particularly for those payments that are likely to be made in the next month that aren't currently demonstrated by accounts records.

The level of audit required will depend on the circumstances of the project and the sums involved. Auditors and the *Contractor* should allocate their time in proportion to the amount involved, but should endeavour to look at all categories of expenditure at least once throughout the project lifecycle.

Assessment of compensation events in main Option F contracts

How do we establish how much money is due for a compensation event?

A reminder follows about the assessment of compensation events, from the core clauses.

Clause 63.1 (excerpt)

The change to the Prices is assessed as the effect of the compensation event upon

- the actual Defined Cost of the work done by the dividing date,
- the forecast Defined Cost of the work not done by the dividing date and
- the resulting Fee.

[ii] Heaphy I and Bone G (2021) Cost assurance and audits on infrastructure projects and contracts. *Civil Engineering Surveyor*, May.

So, in any main Option we need to establish the effect of the event on Defined Cost and then add the Fee to it, based on the percentage in Contract Data part two.

Don't we just use the rates in the contract to assess compensation events?

Main Option F contracts tend not to contain much pricing data other than the *fee percentage* and the *prices*. The use of existing prices is entirely possible in the ECC, but requires the agreement of the *Contractor* and the *Project Manager* to do so.

Clause 63.2, which, as part of the core clauses, applies to each of the main Options allows this use.

> Clause 63.2
>
> The *Project Manager* and the *Contractor* may agree rates or lump sums to assess the change to the Prices.

So why, in a contract with some pricing information, does it not default to that data? The answer is that we expect the Parties to benefit from their original agreement, but, for future changes to the works or the manner in which they are provided, neither Party should be required to continue a financial arrangement that is disadvantageous to it. For example, if the *Contractor* has entered into the contract with a series of loss-making *prices*, then its own work and management will be assessed on that basis. But, without an agreement between the *Contractor* and the *Project Manager*, additional works or management will not have to be provided at a loss by using existing rates. The new works will be paid for on the basis of Defined Cost. The reverse of the analogy works too: the *Client* will not have to continue paying excessively profitable rates either.

Where the Parties do agree to use rates and lump sums, the contract is silent about where they may be found. In main Option F, data from elsewhere will likely be used.

Can we reduce the Prices?

A reminder follows about the effect of compensation events on the possible reduction of the Prices. The starting point is Clause 63.3, which is in the core clauses and so applies to each main Option.

> Clause 63.3
>
> If the effect of a compensation event is to reduce the total Defined Cost, the Prices are not reduced unless otherwise stated in these *conditions of contract*.

I explained the contract's approach to reduced Prices in Chapter 8.

> Clause 63.4
>
> If the effect of a compensation event is to reduce the total Defined Cost and the event is
>
> - a change to the Scope other than a change to the Scope provided by the *Client*, which the *Contractor* proposed and the *Project Manager* accepted or
> - a correction to an assumption stated by the *Project Manager* for assessing an earlier compensation event
>
> the Prices are reduced.

In clause 63.4 the first bullet refers to Scope changes, except those resulting from clause 16.1. The second bullet refers to the *Project Manager's* actions under clause 61.6. These are two examples of where the contract expressly allows compensation events to lead to a reduction in the Prices.

Contractor's proposals

Clauses 16.1 and 16.2 allow the *Contractor* to propose changes to the Scope provided by the *Client* in order to reduce the Prices. In main Option C, D and E contracts their effect on the assessment of compensation events differs from the other main Options.

> Clause 16.1
>
> The *Contractor* may propose to the *Project Manager* that the Scope provided by the *Client* is changed in order to reduce the amount the *Client* pays to the *Contractor* for Providing the Works. The *Project Manager* consults with the *Client* and the *Contractor* about the change.
>
> Clause 16.2
>
> Within four weeks of the *Contractor* making the proposal the *Project Manager*
>
> - accepts the *Contractor's* proposal and issues an instruction changing the Scope,
> - informs the *Contractor* that the *Client* is considering the proposal and instructs the *Contractor* to submit a quotation for a proposed instruction to change the Scope or
> - informs the *Contractor* that the proposal is not accepted.
>
> The *Project Manager* may give any reason for not accepting the proposal.

There are no express provisions in main Option F contracts for dealing with *Contractor's* proposals. A successful proposal will merely reduce the total of the Prices. There are no incentives in a largely cost-reimbursable contract for the *Contractor* to make such suggestions.

Option F contracts

The specific clauses that apply to main Option F contracts reflect its largely cost-reimbursable nature.

The Prices in a main Option F contract are defined in clause 11.2(34).

> Clause 11.2(34) – main Option F
>
> The Prices are the forecast of the total Defined Cost for the whole of the *works* plus the Fee.

Once the compensation event has been implemented, it changes the total of the Prices, according to clause 63.1. The Prices are merely a reporting item for the Parties and the *Project Manager*, and do not affect the amount paid to the *Contractor* by the *Client*. The payment to the *Contractor* is based entirely on Defined Cost and the Fee, as explained earlier in this chapter. The assessment of the work in question will be made as part of the Price for Work Done to Date in clause 11.2(31). There is no pricing document in main Option F contracts (compare with the Activity Schedule or Bill of Quantities in main Option A, B, C or D contracts), so there is nothing else to change.

Main Option F contracts rely primarily on Subcontractors to Provide the Works, and this is reflected in the definition of Defined Cost, which I explained earlier in this chapter. Defined Cost has two components

- Subcontractors
- *prices*.

Subcontractors' payments should be relatively easy to demonstrate through quotations obtained under the subcontracts, and will be subject to the restrictions of clause 52.1. There is no Schedule of Cost Components in main Option F contracts, so the introductory paragraphs there have no relevance here.

Changes to the *prices* are subject to clause 63.17.

Clause 63.17

> If work which the *Contractor* is to do is affected by a compensation event, the *Project Manager* and the *Contractor* agree the change to the price for the work and any change to the Completion Date and Key Dates. If they do not agree, the *Project Manager* decides the change.

This provision provides for the increased costs faced by the *Contractor* to be recovered in the event of a compensation event. It is not limited to an increase: with the right compensation event, it could reduce. As with other compensation events, if the *Contractor* and *Project Manager* cannot agree, then the *Project Manager* has the last say before (if relevant) the matter is referred to adjudication. This clause is not well written in my view, and perhaps should refer to *prices*. But with sensible cooperation the *Project Manager* and the *Contractor* should be able to agree a change to the *prices*.

ICE Publishing

Patrick Waterhouse
ISBN 978-0-7277-6560-4
https://doi.org/10.1680/necdcce.65604.145

Chapter 15
Final assessments

Finalising costs generally

The process offinalising costs at the end of a project is not new. Often referred to as final accounts, there is a mechanism to draw a line under the payments due for the project. This suits both Parties, each knowing that a claim from the other is unlikely after the date of the accounting. The quantity of payment data involved in contracts formed using main Option C, D, E or F makes a finalisation process desirable prior to Completion.

Final assessments

The introduction offinal assessments into NEC contracts with the publication of NEC4 was welcome. With earlier versions of NEC contracts, the loose wording of clause 50.1 always left open the opportunity for either Party to recommence contractual hostilities sometime after Completion. In the UK, a right to adjudication 'at any time'[i] has encouraged some parties to seek a reassessment of amounts due many months or years after Completion, not always successfully. By providing the Parties with the ability to finalise assessments the ECC enables both to draw a line under part or all the project and gain certainty over those payments.

Final assessments work in two ways

- For the assessment of the final amount due and the consequent certification of the final payment. These provisions are in clauses 53.1 to 53.4, and apply to all main Options.
- For the finalisation of Defined Cost for parts of the *works* when using main Options C, D, E and F. These provisions are in clause 50.9.

I will look at the finalisation of Defined Cost in main Options C, D, E and F later in this chapter but, here, I describe what happens at the end of the project.

The process starts with the *Project Manager* assessing the final amount due and issuing a certificate no later than

- 4 weeks after the *Supervisor* has issued the Defects Certificate or
- 13 weeks after the *Project Manager* has issued a termination certificate.

Note that the time limit is linked to when the relevant certificate is issued, rather than when it should be. So, the *Supervisor* or the *Project Manager*, as appropriate, should ensure that the relevant certificate is issued on time. Any delay in doing so will have an impact on the final assessment process, and

[i] Housing Grants Construction and Regeneration Act (HGRA) 1996 as amended, section 112(3A); Construction Contracts Order (Northern Ireland) 1997 as amended, article 11(3A); clause W2.2(1).

potentially could delay the payment of money due. *Clients* should also bear this process in mind when setting the *defects date*. I occasionally see contracts setting the *defects date* as late as 6 years after Completion. While there may be good reasons for doing this in terms of dealing with Defects, *Clients* should bear in mind what other processes will be affected by such decisions. Responsibility for issuing the Defects Certificate should be remembered: *Supervisors* are often dispensed with at Completion. In that situation, their duties should be allocated elsewhere. Similarly, when dealing with termination, almost always a breeding ground for disputes, the *Project Manager* should issue the termination certificate punctually before dealing with the payment aspects of termination.

If the *Project Manager* does not make the assessment within 'the time allowed', then the *Contractor* can make its own assessment and issue it to the *Client* (note, not to the *Project Manager*). There is no payment certificate in this situation where the assessment is made by the *Contractor*.

Whoever produces the final assessment must provide details of how the final amount has been calculated.

There are a few considerations that will assist the Parties

- ensure that someone remains appointed as *Supervisor* and is in position at the *defects date*
- ensure that the *Supervisor* issues the Defects Certificate on time
- the *Project Manager* should issue a termination certificate on time, where one is needed
- the *Contractor* should issue its own final assessment if the *Project Manager* does not
- the *Client* should remain alert to the timing of these actions, particularly where the *Project Manager* is remiss in undertaking the required duties
- close communication between the *Contractor*, *Project Manager* and *Client* will be needed, particularly with the volume of information that will be exchanged, some of which will require detailed explanation.

The finalisation of anything under contract can and does lead to disputes. Clause 53.3 recognises this possibility and provides a route for resolving such a dispute. Three possible routes are provided, one for each of resolving and avoiding disputes: Options W1, W2 and W3. Only one of these Options can apply to each contract: this is identified in Contract Data part one. The three routes for dealing with a dispute on final assessments reflect the differing nature of the three dispute resolution Options. Clause 53.3 says the following.

> Clause 53.3
>
> An assessment of the final amount due issued within the time stated in the contract is conclusive evidence of the final amount due under or in connection with the contract unless a Party takes the following actions...

This clause is wide ranging. Look at the statements 'under or in connection with' and 'conclusive evidence': these really restrict the ability of a Party to challenge a final assessment after the conclusion of the contractual processes.

The three routes to resolving a dispute about a final assessment are

(*a*) Where Option W1 is used, the referring Party refers the dispute
- first to the *Senior Representatives* within 4 weeks of the assessment
- then, for any matters not resolved by the *Senior Representatives*, to the *Adjudicator* within 3 weeks of the *Senior Representatives* producing a list of the issues not agreed
- finally, to the *tribunal* within 4 weeks of the *Adjudicator's* decision being made.

(*b*) Where Option W2 is used, the referring Party refers the dispute
- first to the *Senior Representatives* or to the *Adjudicator* within 4 weeks of the assessment (this choice ensures that the contract complies with the statutory right to adjudication at any time)
- then, for any matters not resolved by the *Senior Representatives* after they have concluded their discussions, to the *Adjudicator* within 3 weeks of the *Senior Representatives* producing a list of the issues not agreed
- finally, to the *tribunal* within 4 weeks of the *Adjudicator's* decision being made.

(*c*) Where Option W3 is used, the referring Party refers the dispute
- first to the Dispute Avoidance Board
- then to the *tribunal* within 4 weeks of the Dispute Avoidance Board's recommendation being made.

These processes have some common themes, and, once triggered, there are time bars for the referring party to adhere to. The processes must be read in conjunction with the other drafting in Option W1, W2 or W3. For example, the reference to the *Adjudicator* in Option W1 or W2 then sees the relevant process take over at that point. All three processes seek to resolve the dispute through informal negotiation first: that is the role of the *Senior Representatives* and the Dispute Avoidance Board. But clearly where that fails there needs to be a formal resolution process that leads to a binding decision, even if not agreement.

Clause 53.4 allows the amendment of the assessment of a final amount due after

- An agreement of the Parties. This should be recorded in writing as a change to the contract in compliance with clause 12.3.
- Or a decision of the *Adjudicator* or a recommendation of the Dispute Avoidance Board where that decision or recommendation has not been referred to the *tribunal* within 4 weeks. In this situation, it will be worthwhile for one Party, or possibly both, to notify the other that the amount due is now considered to be final following the other Party's failure to issue a notice of dissatisfaction. Clear communication at this stage will prevent costly debate later.

Costs finalisation

I have already explained costs finalisation (clause 53.3) earlier in the context of the end of the project and the desirability for the Parties to conclude their work together. Similar provisions exist in the four cost-reimbursable main Options to finalise costs for a specific part of the *works*, most probably before Completion. The same principles apply and the same benefits to the Parties.

Clause 50.9 exists in main Options C, D, E and F, and refers to a 'Defined Cost for a part of the works' being finalised. The 'part' is for the *Contractor* to decide when it submits the relevant data to the *Project Manager*. The *Project Manager* then has 13 weeks to accept the submission or notify the *Contractor* that further work is needed on the assessment.

Users of the ECC should be careful to understand which version of the contract they are using. The wording of clause 50.9 was altered by the NEC in January 2019, and now differs from that published in 2017. The 2017 version referred to 'a part of Defined Cost' being finalised. The current version (post-January 2019) refers to 'Defined Cost for a part of the works'. The current wording appears more restrictive than its predecessor.

All NEC actions are time limited in some way. But 13 weeks is a considerable period. If the *Project Manager* wants more information, then this should be demanded quickly, and I suggest that this should happen much earlier than 13 weeks from submission. Where differences remain between the *Contractor* and *Project Manager*, they should still identify and record the costs on which they do agree, thus reducing the size of any dispute.

Unlike the provisions of clause 53.3, clause 50.9 only reaches a conclusion that part of the Defined Cost is 'correct'. This is a weaker conclusion than clause 53, which states 'conclusive evidence of the final amount due'. Nonetheless, this process is to be commended in reducing the potential for disputes, and contributes to reducing or avoiding a large-quantum debate after Completion.

ice Publishing

Patrick Waterhouse
ISBN 978-0-7277-6560-4
https://doi.org/10.1680/necdcce.65604.149

Chapter 16
Other NEC contracts

The entire suite of NEC contracts follows similar principles despite the differing objectives of the various contracts. The use of Defined Cost and compensation events exists in all of the contracts except for the Framework Contract and the Dispute Resolution Service Contract.

The other chapters of this book have concentrated on the ECC. In this chapter I look at the other contracts in the NEC4 suite and how they use Defined Cost both for routine work and for the assessment of compensation events. Each contract has its own aims, and I have repeated the NEC's advice as to their intended application.

The principles of Defined Cost and compensation events have been applied by the NEC's authors in a consistent fashion. The short contracts use Defined Cost solely for compensation events, as do the main Option A contracts where they exist.

Other engineering and construction contracts

The ECC leads the suite of engineering and construction contracts. It is one of four engineering and construction contracts – the remaining three are described here. The four contracts provide a range of procurement routes to suit main contracts and subcontracts for complex work and for simple work.

The NEC says that the Engineering and Construction Subcontract (ECS) should be used 'for the appointment of a subcontractor for engineering and construction work including any level of design responsibility where the contractor has been appointed under an NEC4 Main Contract', It's a very close match to the ECC, unsurprisingly as that is the NEC4 main contract that it is most likely to be paired with. There are very few differences between the ECS and ECC. The primary one is that there are only five main Options in the ECS, as opposed to six in the ECC. Main Option F is omitted (the management contract).

The assessment of routine payments and of compensation events differs between 'main' contracts and subcontracts in the NEC4 suite, to allow the main contractor time to undertake its own administration. Timescales are typically shortened for the Subcontractor's obligations and lengthened for the *Contractor.*

The Engineering and Construction Short Contract (ECSC) is said by the NEC to be used for 'the appointment of a contractor for engineering and construction work which does not require sophisticated management techniques, comprises straightforward work and imposes only low risks on both client and contractor'. As with all NEC short contracts there are no main Options – there is only one method of assessing payment, using the Price List. Routine payments are based primarily on the Price List. Defined Cost only has a role to play in the assessment of compensation events. There is a definition of Defined Cost in clause 11.2(6), which has four components of cost. Once a compensation event has been implemented, the assessments are put into the Price List by amendment, addition or deletion. The Completion Date may also be changed as a result of a compensation event.

The Engineering and Construction Short Subcontract (ECSS) is used, says the NEC, for 'the appointment of a subcontractor for engineering and construction work which does not require sophisticated management techniques, comprises straightforward work and imposes only low risks on both contractor and subcontractor'. As with all NEC short contracts there are no main Options – there is only one method of assessing payment, using the Price List. Routine payments are based primarily on the Price List. Defined Cost only has a role to play in the assessment of compensation events. There is a definition of Defined Cost in clause 11.2(6), which has four components of cost. Once a compensation event has been implemented, the assessments are put into the Price List by amendment, addition or deletion. The Completion Date may also be changed as a result of a compensation event.

Alliance Contract

The Alliance Contract (ALC) aims to provide a true partnering relationship between the Parties. The NEC says that this contract 'is designed for use on major projects or programmes of work where longer term collaborative ways of working are to be created'. There are no main Option clauses; only one way of assessing and paying for the *works* is included. The Price for Work Done to Date is, primarily, Defined Cost plus the Fee. This arrangement is very similar to main Option E in the ECC, but can be effectively changed to a target arrangement by the use of the Performance Table. Defined Cost is the cost of components in the Schedule of Cost Components. The role of Defined Cost in compensation events is to change the Budget. The Completion Date and Performance Table are also changed if appropriate. Defined Cost is also an element of payments due on termination.

Design Build and Operate Contract

The Design Build and Operate Contract (DBO) is said by the NEC to be used for 'the appointment of a contractor with responsibility for the design, construction or modification and operation of assets necessary to meet the client's operational requirements'. This a very different task to that in the other NEC construction contracts. The *Contractor* is responsible for deciding how to satisfy the *Client's* operational requirements.

There are no main Options in the DBO. The Price for Service Provided to Date is based on two separate parts of the Price List: part A and part B. Payments for part A are based on a series of lump sums and rates in the Price List, and are assessed when the work in question has been completed. Payments for part A do not use Defined Cost. Payments for part B are based on the forecast Defined Cost that will be paid by the *Contractor* during the next period. The use of part B is only likely where discrete section(s) of work are specified and are easily separable from the remainder of the *works*.

The definition of Defined Cost is the cost of components in the Schedule of Cost Components, less Disallowed Cost.

Assessment of compensation events is based on Defined Cost plus the Fee. Implemented compensation events lead to changed Prices in the Price List and, where appropriate, to the Performance Table.

Defined Cost forms an element of any payment due on termination.

Professional service contracts

The Professional Service Contract (PSC) leads the suite of professional service contracts. It is one of three such contracts, all of which are described here. The three contracts provide a range of procurement routes to suit main contracts and subcontracts for complex work and for simple work.

The PSC, says the NEC, is to be used 'for the appointment of a supplier to provide a professional service'. There are three main Option clauses, A, C and E. These broadly reflect the main Option clauses in the ECC. The definitions of Price for Service Provided to Date and Defined Cost depend upon the main Option selected (each has its own Option). The NEC4 version of this contract differs considerably from its NEC3 predecessor, particularly with respect to payments. It has been brought much closer to the ECC in terms of Defined Cost and Schedules of Cost Components. I have seen numerous amendments to these provisions to reflect the traditional reliance by consultants and their customers of agreed hourly rates.

In main Option A the Price for Service Provided to Date is based on the Prices in the Activity Schedule, and does not use Defined Cost for routine payments. The only role for Defined Cost here is in the assessment of compensation events. Defined Cost is the cost of components in the Short Schedule of Cost Components. The role of Defined Cost in compensation events is to change the Prices in the Activity Schedule.

In main Option C the Price for Service Provided to Date is a forecast of the Defined Cost that will be paid by the Consultant in the next period for all service provided, whether routine or compensation events. Defined Cost is also used in the assessment of compensation events. Defined Cost is the cost of components in the Schedule of Cost Components. The role of Defined Cost in compensation events is to change the Prices in the Activity Schedule. The Prices here create the target cost from which the share is ultimately calculated.

In main Option E the Price for Service Provided to Date is a forecast of the Defined Cost that will be paid by the Consultant in the next period for all service provided, whether routine or compensation events. Defined Cost is also used in the assessment of compensation events. Defined Cost is the cost of components in the Schedule of Cost Components. The role of Defined Cost in compensation events is to change the Prices that are the forecast of the total Defined Cost plus the Fee for the whole of the service.

In all three main Options the Completion Date and Key Dates are also changed, if appropriate. Defined Cost is also an element of payments due on termination.

The Professional Service Short Contract (PSSC) is intended by the NEC for 'the appointment of a supplier to provide a professional service that does not require sophisticated management techniques, comprises straightforward work and imposes only low risks on both client and consultant'. As with all NEC short contracts there are no main Options – there is only one method of assessing payment using the Price List and people rates. Routine payments are based primarily on the Price List. Defined Cost only has a role to play in the assessment of compensation events. There is a unique definition of Defined Cost in clause 11.2(5), which has two components of cost. Once a compensation event has been implemented, the assessments are put into the Price List by amendment, addition or deletion.

The Professional Service Subcontract (PSS) should be used, says NEC, for 'the appointment of a subcontractor to provide a service to a contractor or consultant who has been appointed under an NEC4 main contract'. It operates almost identically to the PSC, and no further explanation is needed here.

Supply contracts

The two supply contracts provide a suitable route to procure goods or services for use on projects or services where an NEC contract is used to appoint the lead contractor or consultant.

The NEC says that the Supply Contract (SC) is intended for 'the procurement of high value goods and related services including design'. There are no main Option clauses; only one way of assessing and paying for the *works* is included. The Price for Goods and Services Provided to Date does not use Defined Cost – it relies upon the Price List. The only role for Defined Cost here is in the assessment of compensation events. Defined Cost is the cost of components in the Schedule of Cost Components. The role of Defined Cost in compensation events is to change the Prices in the Price List. The Delivery Date is also changed, if appropriate. Defined Cost is also an element of payments due on termination.

The Supply Short Contract (SSC) is intended, says the NEC, for 'local and international procurement of goods under a single order or on a batch order basis and is for use with contracts which do not require sophisticated management techniques and impose only low risks on both the purchaser and the supplier'. As with all NEC short contracts there are no main Options – there is only one method of assessing payment, using the Price List. Routine payments are based on the Price List. Defined Cost only has a role to play in the assessment of compensation events. There is a unique definition of Defined Cost in clause 11.2(3), which has five components of cost. Once a compensation event has been implemented, the assessments are put into the Price List by amendment, addition or deletion.

Term service contracts

The Term Service Contract (TSC) leads the suite of term service contracts. It is one of three such contracts, all of which are described here. The three contracts provide a range of procurement routes to suit the main contracts and subcontracts for complex work and for simple work.

The TSC, says the NEC, is to be used 'for the appointment of a supplier for a period of time to manage and provide a service'. There are three main Option clauses, A, C and E. These broadly reflect the main Option clauses in the ECC. The definitions of Price for Service Provided to Date and Defined Cost depend upon the main Option selected (each has its own Option).

In main Option A the Price for Service Provided to Date is based on the Prices in the Activity Schedule, and does not use Defined Cost for routine payments. The only role for Defined Cost here is in the assessment of compensation events. Defined Cost is the cost of components in the Short Schedule of Cost Components. The role of Defined Cost in compensation events is to change the Prices in the Activity Schedule.

In main Option C the Price for Service Provided to Date is a forecast of the Defined Cost that will be paid by the *Contractor* in the next period for all service provided, whether routine or compensation events. Defined Cost is also used in the assessment of compensation events. Defined Cost is the cost of components in the Schedule of Cost Components. The role of Defined Cost in compensation events is to change the Prices in the Activity Schedule. The Prices here create the target cost from which the share is ultimately calculated.

In main Option E the Price for Service Provided to Date is a forecast of the Defined Cost that will be paid by the *Contractor* in the next period for all service provided, whether routine or compensation events. Defined Cost is also used in the assessment of compensation events. Defined Cost is the cost of components in the Schedule of Cost Components. The role of Defined Cost in compensation events is to change the Prices that are the forecast of the total Defined Cost plus the Fee for the whole of the service or, where appropriate, a change to the Price List.

In all three main Options any relevant Task Completion Date is also changed, if appropriate. Defined Cost is also an element of payments due on termination.

The Term Service Short Contract (TSSC) is intended by the NEC for 'the appointment of a supplier for a period of time to manage and provide a service which does not require sophisticated management techniques, comprises straightforward work and imposes only low risks on both client and consultant'. As with all NEC short contracts there are no main Options – there is only one method of assessing payment, using the Price List and people rates. Routine payments are based primarily on the Price List. Defined Cost only has a role to play in the assessment of compensation events. There is a definition of Defined Cost in clause 11.2(3), which has four components of cost. Once a compensation event has been implemented, the assessments are put into the Price List by amendment, addition or deletion.

The Term Service Subcontract (TSS), says the NEC, should be used for 'the appointment of a subcontractor for a period of time to manage and provide a service where the contractor has been appointed under an NEC4 main Contract'. It operates almost identically to the TSC, and no further explanation is needed here.

Each term service contract has improved in the development from NEC3 to NEC4 in the way that Defined Cost is treated.

Facilities management contracts

At the time of writing (June 2021), the facilities management contracts are in their pre-publication form, so the following description may not be entirely representative of the final published forms, due in July 2021. The short form facilities management contracts are due for publication later in 2021.

The Facilities Management Contract (FMC) is intended by the NEC for 'the appointment of a service provider for a period of time to manage and provide a facility management service'. There are three main Option clauses, A, C and E. These broadly reflect the main Option clauses in the ECC. The definitions of Price for Service Provided to Date and Defined Cost depend upon the main Option selected (each has its own Option).

In main Option A the Price for Service Provided to Date is based on the Prices in the Price List, and does not use Defined Cost for routine payments. The only role for Defined Cost here is in the assessment of compensation events. Defined Cost is the cost of components in the Short Schedule of Cost Components. The role of Defined Cost in compensation events is to change the Prices in the Price List.

In main Option C the Price for Service Provided to Date is a forecast of the Defined Cost that will be paid by the Service Provider in the next period for all service provided, whether routine or compensation events plus the Fee. Defined Cost is also used in the assessment of compensation events. Defined Cost is the cost of components in the Schedule of Cost Components. The role of Defined Cost in compensation events is to change the Prices in the Price List. The Prices here create the target cost from which the share is ultimately calculated.

In main Option E the Price for Service Provided to Date is a forecast of the Defined Cost that will be paid by the Service Provider in the next period for all service provided, whether routine or compensation events. Defined Cost is also used in the assessment of compensation events. Defined Cost is the cost of components in the Schedule of Cost Components plus the Fee. The role of Defined Cost in compensation events is to change the Prices that are the forecast of the total Defined Cost plus the Fee for the whole of the service or, where appropriate, a change to the Price List.

The Facilities Management Subcontract (FMS) should be used, says the NEC, for 'for the appointment of a subcontractor for a period of time to manage and provide a facility management service where the service provider has been appointed under an NEC4 contract'. It operates almost identically to the FMC, and no further explanation is needed here.

Summary

We have seen in this chapter how each NEC4 contract follows common principles, but that the detail can vary. Contract drafters and users must pay careful attention to the use of terms such as Defined Cost, Price for Work Done to Date, Prices, etc., when working with different forms.

ICE Publishing

Patrick Waterhouse
ISBN 978-0-7277-6560-4
https://doi.org/10.1680/necdcce.65604.155

Chapter 17
The effect of Z clauses

The good, the bad, and the downright ugly

> Look at the Z clauses in a proposed NEC contract and decide whether they represent a proposal of marriage, or a declaration of war.

When working with standard forms of contracts, amendments to adapt the form to the specific needs of the Parties and the project are common. NEC contracts refer to 'additional conditions of contract' as Z clauses. Z clauses can remove or amend standard form clauses and add new ones. Therefore, their impact on payments must be analysed when drafting them and when using them. All NEC clauses have been written to dovetail with one another, and Z clauses should be similarly written. It's a job for people who know what they're doing. I often see bad examples of drafting Z clauses where the drafter has omitted to allow for linkages between the Z clause and other provisions of the contract. My advice for drafting Z clauses, as with many other parts of the contract documents, is the following

- draft Z clauses carefully and with consideration for how the clauses will interact with other parts of the contract
- the *Contractor* and *Project Manager* must consider the impact of Z clauses when assessing payments due under the contract
- conflicts between the Z clause(s) and the standard provisions should be highlighted and resolved at the earliest opportunity.

There are plentiful examples of ill-conceived and poorly drafted Z clauses that have the potential to cause difficulty, and I have provided some later in this chapter.

Not all Z clauses are bad news; indeed, they are necessary in most contracts to align the contract with specific needs and legislation. Many Z clauses provide a sensible and balanced addition or amendment to the contract to reflect specific needs, for example in respect of the *Client's* funding (e.g. access for funding monitors) or security provisions in military projects.

But Z clauses have also gained a certain notoriety among NEC users, as they are frequently used to skew the contract's risk allocation between the Parties. Tricks of the trade involve reducing the *Contractor's* response times (e.g. to notify a compensation event in clause 61.3) or increasing the *Project Manager's* response times (e.g. in accepting a programme in clause 31.3). Each decision of this nature drives slightly different behaviours from the participants than that initially proposed by the contract's publishers. At the time of writing this book, NEC contracts have been in use for 28 years, and the various time provisions have been well proven.

When *Clients* make decisions on any aspect of the contract's structure, they should consider whether each decision will have a positive influence on the Parties' ultimate relationship, and then act accordingly.

Some seemingly simple clauses can have a dramatic impact on the nature of the contract. Although the English case of *ABC Electrification v Network Rail*[i] did not involve an NEC contract, it sent a worrying message to contractors when the Court of Appeal in England and Wales supported an amended clause on disallowed costs in an Infrastructure Conditions of Contract that prevented the recovery by the contractor of any costs associated with any default. Leading engineering adjudicator Bill Edwards[ii] commented afterwards

> In the real world there are many technical breaches of contract by the contractor, from the simple failure to reply to a communication within the period for reply to the cost of correcting defects before completion and many more. By using this amendment [the one featuring in the case] the risk pendulum has definitely swung away from the client and towards the contractor.

Heaphy and Bone said[iii]

> It is also necessary for users of target costs/cost reimbursable contracts to appreciate that they are sharing in the financial performance of the contractor delivering the works. This sharing of risk, supported by an open book approach to cost, leads to greater alignment of objectives and a reduction in the potential for claims and disputes. If users start to try to limit the sharing of financial performance of the contractor by increasing the list of disallowable cost, this can change the nature of the arrangement and lead to problems and more adversarial behaviour.

As an adjudicator I am often asked to take a view on whether clauses are fair or reasonable, but that usually misses the point. The adjudicator's role is to give effect to the contract. Where a Party has agreed to a term that is now inconvenient, it is irrelevant to determine if that term is fair or not. Subcontractors, particularly, suffer from some ridiculous Z clauses that should act as a warning to steer clear of the organisation proposing them. The time prior to the contract's formation is the time to seriously consider (*a*) whether the Z clauses proposed are sensible and can be relied upon or (*b*) whether the Z clauses are indicative of a likely confrontational and unprofitable relationship.

There now follow a series of Z clauses and a short commentary on each. The majority of these come from contracts formed using the Engineering and Construction Subcontract (ECS). Typically, although not exclusively, ECS contracts tend to contain more Z clauses than ECC contracts because they will also flow down the Z clauses from the main contract. I have amended details in each example to avoid identification of their provenance.

---

[i] *ABC Electrification Limited v Network Rail Infrastructure Limited* [2020] EWCA Civ 1645.

[ii] Edwards W (2021) The death knell tolls for target cost contracts? *Civil Engineering Surveyor*, Feb.

[iii] Heaphy I and Bone G (2021) Cost assurance and audits on infrastructure projects and contracts. *Civil Engineering Surveyor*, May.

Examples of Z clauses

Forms of agreement

Order of precedence

In the event of any ambiguity or inconsistency between any of the documents forming the subcontract, the order of precedence shall be as follows:

- The agreement
- Subcontract Data part one
- Subcontract Data part two
- The Z clauses
- The core clauses
- The main Option clauses
- The secondary Option clauses
- The subcontract works Scope

This is a common type of Z clause, seeking to provide certainty in the event of a conflict between any of the documents in the contract. It doesn't deal with a frequent cause of conflict, that between documents that form the Scope. Where they fall within the Scope prepared by the *Client*, the resolution of such conflicts would be the *Client's* risk if an instruction was given under clause 14.3. Of course, a further Z clause of the type shown later in this chapter may transfer that risk to the *Contractor*.

7.1 This contract incorporates the conditions of contract being the NEC3 Engineering and Construction Contract issued in April 2013 (as amended and supplemented by the additional conditions of contract) incorporating the following Options:

7.1.1 main Option A

7.1.2 dispute resolution clause Option W2

7.1.3 secondary Option clauses X2, X4, X7, X16 and YUK3, and

7.1.4 additional conditions of contract Z

together with the following volumes of documentation annexed to and forming part of this contract:

- Volume 1 Contract Data part one and additional conditions
- Volume 2 Contract Data part two
- Volume 3 Scope
- Volume 4 Specification
- Volume 5 Site Information
- Volume 6 Drawings Design

8 Priority of documents.

8.1 If there is any ambiguity or inconsistency in or between the document comprising this contract the priority of the documents is in accordance with the following sequence:

8.1.1 the contract

8.1.2 the completed Contract Data

8.1.3 the additional conditions of contract (the Z clauses)

8.1.4 the other conditions of contract

8.1.5 the Scope (volume 4)

8.1.6 any other document forming part of the contract.

This is a badly drafted attempt to provide more certainty in the interpretation of the contract. It provides the opposite, unfortunately. First, we see reference to documents entitled 'Specification' and 'Drawings Design' that aren't mentioned anywhere else in the contract, so what role do they play? Remember that the *Contractor's* overriding obligation is to Provide the Works in accordance with the Scope. So, should it follow the Specification or the Drawings Design? If so, how should the conflicts be dealt with? Clause 14.3 only allows the *Project Manager* to instruct a change to the Scope.

The second problem here is the use of the term 'contract' in 8.1.1. The drafter probably intended to say 'conditions of contract', based on the statement in 7.1. But in referring to 'the contract' the clause is now meaningless, as it is illogical. This is an error resulting from a lack of attention to detail, and has only achieved to add uncertainty when its aim was the opposite.

General conditions

> **11.2(8)** Delete and insert the following:
>
> The Early Warning Register is the register annexed at Numbered Document No. A7 (Early Warning Register).

Here the Parties have agreed that the Early Warning Register is already included in the contract. The original drafting of the ECC does not intend the Early Warning Register to be a contract document, but instead to be prepared and used after the Contract Date. By omitting the details from clause 11.2(8), the reference to early warnings has been removed. There is a conflict with clause 15.2, which requires the *Project Manager* to issue the first Early Warning Register within 1 week of the *starting date*. This drafting is well intentioned but hasn't included all of the changes necessary to give effect to its objectives. It is rare that only a single clause can be changed in this scenario – usually there are others connected to it.

> Any notification to be served under this subcontract is sufficiently served if it is sent by first class Royal Mail Recorded Delivery post or by facsimile transmission addressed to the other Party at its office that administers this subcontract (such notice is duly served in the case of postal delivery at the expiry of 48 hours after the time of posting and in the case of facsimile transmission at the time when confirmation of such transmission is received).

This clause from the ECS contract takes the communications provisions back 30 years. Clauses 13.1 and 13.2 recognise the benefits of electronic communications, yet the drafters of this clause want to rely upon post or fax (assuming either firm still has the necessary apparatus to send and receive faxed messages). The danger for the Parties and the *Project Manager* here is that the word 'notification' has a wide meaning in NEC contracts and includes many routine items of contract administration such as early warnings, compensation events, acceptances and so on. Each of these must now be printed prior to transmission to the other side. Whoever drafted this may not realise the effect it will have on the daily workload and response times of those who have to manage the project.

Add the following at the end of core clause 13.3:

Communications (other than a notice of termination, suspension or a notice to refer a dispute) may be given by email or other electronic form where the Contractor has expressly authorised that this is permitted in relation to this subcontract and subject to any restrictions in respect of the same stated in the Subcontract Works Information.

This is another clause from an ECS contract that betrays the ignorance of its drafter as to the existing communications provisions. Clauses 13.1 and 13.2 already allow for email or electronic forms without this clause. The *Contractor* has already 'authorised' such use through the use of the core clauses. The exclusion of email notices for the three reasons given is understandable and is a common feature. But this is an example of a clause that creates more doubt than it relieves.

15.4 Add at the end of this clause:

Without limiting the obligations and liabilities of the Parties under the subcontract, the Early Warning Register shall not itself allocate contractual risks or liabilities to either Party and shall be treated as a management tool only.

I see this Z clause and many similar versions on a regular basis. Clearly, there are many contractual Parties and advisors that are concerned about the potential effect of something being agreed in an early warning meeting. The contract does not place any additional obligations on either Party in clause 15, and therefore this clause appears to be unnecessary.

17.1 Delete core clause 17.1 and substitute:

The Subcontractor examines the Scope and all other documents forming this contract and warrants to the Contractor that they are not aware, as at the Contract Date, of any ambiguity or discrepancy within or between any of the contract documents that might adversely affect the carrying out of the works for the tendered Prices in accordance with the conditions of contract.

17.2 Insert the following at the end of the core clause 17.2:

Such instruction is not a compensation event where the Contractor assesses:

- that the ambiguity or inconsistency in question is one for which the Subcontractor is responsible under this subcontract; or
- that a prudent and experienced subcontractor familiar with works similar to the works would have identified such an ambiguity or inconsistency at the Subcontract Date from the information then available to them.

17.3 The Contractor examines the Scope and all other documents forming this contract and warrants to the Employer that they are not aware, as at the Subcontract Date, of any ambiguity or discrepancy within or between any of the contract documents that might adversely affect the carrying out of the works for the tendered Prices in accordance with the conditions of contract.

Clause 17.1 is designed to reduce or remove the risk of abortive work being done because of errors in the contract documents. The risk in such inadequacies in the published form rests with the Party that drafted the document(s) in question: see clauses 60.2 and 63.10 by way of example. This clause from an ECS contract seeks to push all of the risk onto the Subcontractor. Here, under clause 17.2, the Subcontractor is required to take responsibility for the inadequacies in all documents, including those prepared by the *Contractor*. That hardly seems fair or logical, and gives the *Contractor* little incentive to make sure that its own documents are correct. Does this create the right incentives for collaboration? Would a *Subcontractor* notify an ambiguity or inconsistency if it might lead to expensive, additional work for which it wouldn't receive payment?

> **17.1** Delete clause 17.1 and add a new clause 17.1 as follows:
>
> The Contractor or the Subcontractor notifies the other as soon as either becomes aware of any mistake, inaccuracy, discrepancy or omission in the design of the subcontract works or in the Subcontract Scope or any other document forming part of this contract or if Subcontract Completion Date needs to be extended or the Defined Cost of the subcontract works will increase due to such a mistake, inaccuracy, discrepancy or omission. The Contractor gives an instruction as to how the mistake, inaccuracy, discrepancy or omission is to be dealt with. Compliance with such an instruction shall not constitute a compensation event, and the cost of compliance with such instruction shall be a Disallowed Cost.

This is another example of a reversal of the risks from clause 17.1 instructions. Potentially, here the Subcontractor will be required to undertake additional works, or more expensive works, at the whim of the *Contractor* and then be paid nothing for it. The mistake, inaccuracy, discrepancy or omission may well be in documents prepared by the *Contractor*.

The *Contractor's* main responsibilities

> **Z62** The Client requires the Contractor to design and construct a scheme that is fit for purpose. Nothing contained in the Scope nor within the wording of the Acceptance Procedures (including certificates) shall be taken as diminishing or detracting from the obligation to design and construct a scheme that is fit for purpose.

This clause adds to the *Contractor's* existing obligation to Provide the Works in accordance with the Scope. There is an interesting choice of words saying that the *Client* requires something, as opposed to the *Contractor* providing it. The phrase 'fit for purpose' is used extensively in the industry, but there is not a single meaning – it is very much case specific as to what it means. The *Client's* aim here is to create an asset that does what is required and that, usually, any clause that purports to reduce the design standard to reasonable skill and care will not be effective. For this clause to work, the *Client's* desired purpose will need to be stated clearly in the Scope, together with any agreed methodology for demonstrating that the purpose has, or has not, been achieved.

> **20.5** The Subcontractor shall Provide the Subcontract Works and carry out the obligations of the Subcontractor set out in this subcontract in accordance with its terms and shall comply with all reasonable instructions given to them by the Contractor on any matter connected with the subcontract works subject to reasonable notice and adjustment of the Prices and the Accepted Programme.

The NEC's drafters, since 1991's first consultative publication, have sought to minimise the use of subjective words such as 'reasonable', so its reintroduction in clauses such as this one is unlikely to help a constructive relationship. The agreement to have the *works* changed is already contained in clause 14.3 of the ECS, so a statement here is unnecessary. Adjustment of the Prices and the Accepted Programme will have a significant effect on the Subcontractor's revenue. Imagine, for example, the effect on the assessment of compensation events if the *Contractor* is able to adjust the Accepted Programme unilaterally. Much of what this contract says is already included in the ECS, but the confused wording may obstruct clear interpretation.

> **25.3** Delete the last sentence.

Many Z clauses, on the face of it, look simple and innocuous. Yet, once checked, their true commercial harm to the *Contractor* is discovered. This is one such example. It removes the sole remedy provision from clause 25.3 that limits the *Contractor's* liability in the event that a Condition is not achieved by the relevant Key Date. Clause 25.3 requires the *Contractor* to compensate the *Client* for such failures – usually the costs relate to delay and disruption caused to another contractor working on the same project that has been affected by the default. But the payments due under that clause are sensibly limited in a number of ways, for example there are no consequential costs recoverable away from the project. By removing the sole remedy provision, it opens up the possibility that the *Client* will be able to recover additional costs that were not initially intended by the drafters of the NEC as part of the overall collaborative provisions.

Time

> **36.3** Add the following words to the core clause:
>
> If the Contractor does not accept a quotation for an acceleration, or does not accept the Subcontractor's reasons for not submitting a quotation, then the Contractor may issue an instruction to the Subcontractor to accelerate and the Subcontractor uses reasonable endeavours to accelerate in accordance with that instruction and the Contractor makes their own assessment of the compensation event.

The NEC's acceleration provisions in its construction forms do not require the *Contractor* to accelerate unless it agrees to do so. The provisions are entirely voluntary, and can be invoked either by the *Project Manager* or the *Contractor*. The principle is to allow the *Contractor* the full duration of time agreed in the contract to achieve Completion. This Z clause from an ECS contract allows the *Contractor* to require the *Subcontractor* to accelerate and to make its own assessment of the outcome. The clause refers to the assessment of 'the compensation event', but nowhere in the contract does it say that acceleration is a compensation event. Where the default contract is followed, clause 36 allows a commercial agreement to be reached between the Parties without the restrictions of the compensation event provisions. Here, the reference to a compensation event is unreferenced and does not dovetail with the remaining provisions in the contract. The drafter of this Z clause has not considered the full implications of requiring this acceleration and the unilateral assessment of its impact.

Payments

> **50.2** Delete the second paragraph.

Another short and simple Z clause here. This removes the obligation of the *Contractor* to consider the application submitted by the *Subcontractor*. Anyone pricing a subcontract package from a proposed new customer must surely hear alarm bells sounding here. What type of relationship does this organisation envisage? Presumably when faced with the predictable series of adjudications that is likely to follow the unilateral assessment of amounts due, this company will cite surprise? One of the basics of any business relationship is that there must be discussion of the payments due between the Parties. Where a Party, as here, effectively says that it will decide what is to be paid, then its is clearly planning a master- servant relationship. Anyone agreeing to this provision should be aware of what is likely to occur. The *Contractor* intending to ignore its *Subcontractor's* application, if working in the UK, may find that legislation does not allow it to ignore payment notices.

52.5 The Subcontractor provides the Contractor with detailed daily labour and plant returns showing resources and activities. The Subcontractor submits returns on a weekly basis, for clarity in this context a week means Monday–Sunday. Returns are to be submitted by no later than 1.00 pm on the Wednesday following the end of the previous week.

This clause adds to the accounts and records provisions in clause 52.4. The drafter of this Z clause appears not to be familiar with NEC terminology. 'Labour' is not used in NEC contracts – which use the word 'people'. More confusingly, the reference to 'plant' appears not to recognise that the word is defined in the ECC and refers to permanent works. Presumably the drafter here intended to refer to Equipment. This clause has probably been copied from the company's standard list of requirements for its subcontractors under any form of subcontract and hasn't been adjusted to suit the ECS. Simple mistakes such as this one can lead to disputes later on when each Party will have a financial incentive to prefer one meaning over another.

54 Final payment.

Z26.1 Not later than 2 months after Completion of the whole of the subcontract works the Subcontractor shall send to the Contractor by Royal Mail Signed For post all documents necessary for the purpose of assessing the final amount due under the subcontract and shall confirm to the Contractor the final amount that the Subcontractor consider is due to them and the basis upon which such sum has been calculated ('Final Payment Application').

Another clause requiring the use of an outdated system of communications, despite clauses 13.1 and 13.2 recognising digital communications. This Subcontractor is required to print everything and take it to a Post Office for onward transmission to the *Contractor*. Quite apart from the administrative cost and inconvenience of such a requirement, surely all payment assessments now rely on digital files? Spreadsheets, drawings, text files and so on. Why would anyone, other than a dinosaur, want to take us back to the 1970s? The cynic in me suspects that this clause may have been written to set a trap for the Subcontractor so that it cannot fully comply. Any documents missing from the physical submission may then be ignored by the *Contractor* is its assessment.

53.3a The Project Manager makes a preliminary assessment of the Contractor's share at any assessment date. If the forecast final Price for Work Done to Date is less than the final total of the Prices, this share is included in the amount due following Completion of the whole of the works. If the forecast final Price for Work Done to Date is more than the forecast final total of the Prices, this share is retained from the amount due.

This is taken from a main Option C contract, and is a common provision in target contracts. Imagine a target contract where the target is £10 million. If the *Contractor's* costs and fee reach £11 million, the *Client* will have to pay monthly assessments up to £11 million before the *Contractor* is required, after Completion, to repay the agreed share percentage. Some *Clients*, particularly those in the public sector, worry about the potential loss of the repayment in the event of insolvency, so they insert Z clauses such as this one. Here, the *Project Manager* assesses the likely share at each assessment date, and the *Client* has no obligation to pay amounts beyond the target price.

> **11.2(29)** Delete the clause and replace with:
>
> The Price for Work Done to Date is the total of a proportion of each lump sum price composed in the Prices, which is the proportion of the work covered by each activity that the Subcontractor has completed but excluding any Disallowed Cost. Completed work is an activity that is without Defects that would either delay or be covered immediately following work.

This is a Z clause taken from a main Option A ECS contract. On one hand it is generous to the Subcontractor, allowing payment for part-completed activities when the default position only provides for payment on completed activities. On the other, though, we can see that Disallowed Cost has been brought into a main Option A contract (presumably by another Z clause), which is a tactic used by many *Clients* and (main) *Contractors* as a way of controlling costs.

Schedules of Cost Components

> **Z72** Short Schedule of Cost Components – not used.

This clause was taken from a main Option B contract, and its objective is unclear. The definition of Defined Cost refers to the Short Schedule, so by removing the reference to the Short Schedule, and not replacing it with something else, the assessment of compensation events suddenly becomes difficult. The contract lacks a way of assessing the financial impact of a compensation event, and perhaps the drafter is hoping that clause 63.2, using rates and lump sums, will become the default method. But if that is required, it needs to be stated.

> **Z22** If main Option A or B used:
>
> Under clause 11.2(23) before 'Schedule of Cost Components' delete 'Short'.

This is a common Z clause, using the Schedule of Cost Components (the Full Schedule), not the Short Schedule, for the assessment of Defined Cost, for compensation events, in main Option A and B contracts. It is relatively uncontroversial, but the Parties should bear in mind that the Short Schedule has been written to limit the contract administration in contracts where there is less administrative resource available to do it. Using the Full Schedule is likely to require more work.

Compensation events

> In clause 60.1(1), replace 'an instruction' with 'a written instruction to carry out works in addition to the subcontract works issued in accordance with the Pre-Order Meeting Minutes'.

This is an attempt to tighten up what the drafter perceives as a weakness in clause 60.1(1) of the ECS. The aim is to avoid a compensation event for instructions that involve works known about, or even just discussed, at the meeting in question. The common practice of including meeting minutes in a contract is not a good one, as it generates the possibility of conflict between the minutes and the other contract documents. It is far better to amend the contract documents to reflect anything of importance agreed at the meeting. This Z clause introduces the need to make instructions in writing, which may or may not include electronic communications, and therefore a doubt is brought in as to whether clauses 13.1 and 13.2 apply here.

> If the Contractor issues an instruction omitting all or any part of the works, the Subcontractor is not entitled to claim loss of profit or breach of contract for not providing the works in its entirety regardless of whether or not the Contractor engages another subcontractor to provide the part of the subcontract works omitted.

This clause is linked to the ability of the *Contractor* to instruct a change to the Scope and remove items of work. The contract's provisions explain how such omissions are dealt with in clauses 63.1, 63.4 and 63.6. The ability to remove work in this way is often viewed as a cheaper way of terminating the Subcontractor's involvement than using the termination provisions. Here, the Z clause is preventing a claim for consequential losses from the *Subcontractor*. The removal of work from one supplier, in order to award it to another, conflicts with the law in some jurisdictions. But even where a *Contractor* does this, it merely becomes a breach of contract for which the (sole) remedy is a compensation event under clause 60.1(18). *Subcontractors* agreeing to this provision may need to consider how they are paid for any up-front mobilisation or Equipment purchase costs.

> Add the following before the full stop at the end of the third bullet point of clause 60.1(5): 'the Site Information or the Subcontract Data'.

If this subcontract has been properly written, then the two documents referred to shouldn't include any obligations for the *Client*, the *Contractor* or Others. Clause 60.1(5) compensates the Subcontractor for the failure of the *Client*, *Contractor* or Others to do things, either in accordance with the Scope or with the Accepted Programme. This Z clause increases the documents where an action could be included, and could be to the benefit or detriment of either Party. Its purpose isn't clear, and any effort to nullify the effect of the Site Information and the Subcontract Data would be better spent making sure they were written properly instead.

> **60.5** The Subcontractor shall be entitled to an addition to the Prices but not entitled to a change to the Subcontract Completion Date or any Key Date for any delay to Completion of the whole or any section of the subcontract works arising from a difference between the final total quantity of work done and the quantity for an item stated in the Bill of Quantities.

This is taken from a main Option B ECS contract. Clause 60.5 provides for a compensation event where the actual quantity of work for an item exceeds the estimated quantity stated in the Bill of Quantities. Here, the contract has been amended to deny the Subcontractor additional time in the event it is actually needed. The *Contractor's* generosity does allow for payments for prolongation. The denial of additional time may lead to increased risk of payments under clause 25.3 (Key Dates) and secondary Option X7 (delay damages) by the Subcontractor where it is delayed in this scenario. This clause has partially transferred the risk in the accuracy of the Bill of Quantities from the *Contractor* to the *Subcontractor*.

> Add clause 63.5A:
>
> In judging delay for the purpose of assessing a compensation event, the Contractor may reduce the impact on any change to the Subcontract Completion Date or Key Date to reflect that the delay is also caused or contributed to by any negligence, default or breach of this subcontract by the Subcontractor and/or any of the Subcontractor's employees, agents or subsubcontractors or any failure by the Subcontractor and/or the Subcontractor's employees, agents or subsubcontractors to take all reasonable and proper steps to mitigate such delay.

Taken from an ECS contract, this Z clause deals with concurrent delay and seeks to avoid some or all of the liability for a delay when the *Subcontractor*, or any of its supply chain, can be shown not to have mitigated the delay where possible. The final ten words set a high bar for the *Subcontractor*. To avoid any sanction here, it must have taken **all** reasonable and proper steps. This may allow the *Contractor* considerable leeway in justifying any denial of relief.

> **60.2** Sub-surface Conditions – add to existing clause 60.2.
>
> **Z28.1** The Subcontractor has had an opportunity to inspect the conditions of the Site and is deemed to have become fully acquainted with the same and satisfied itself before commencement of the subcontract works or any part or task thereof that the surfaces, work, etc., to which its work is to be applied are in a satisfactory condition to receive its work and made allowance for any risk, condition, contingency and other circumstances that may influence or affect the carrying out of the subcontract works. Should the Subcontractor consider any surface to be unsatisfactory, it shall notify the Contractor, in writing, as soon as the circumstances giving rise to its dissatisfaction are apparent or ought reasonably to have been apparent and, in any event, before the Subcontractor's work to such surfaces, work, etc., is commenced. In the absence of such notification in accordance with this provision, the Subcontractor shall be responsible for the rectification of any defects in its work and of all damages incurred by the Contractor and resulting therefrom and is not entitled to any additional payment (whether by way of addition to the Prices or as damages for breach of contract or in tort (including negligence)) or any change to the Subcontract Completion Date in respect of breach of this clause or any actions required to be taken by the Subcontractor to deal with the same.

This clause was added to an ECS contract.

A lawyer must have had fun writing this one – perhaps pay per word was the form of engagement! But looking closely at it we can see that some of its provisions are included in the ECS already. Whether the Subcontractor has or has not had the opportunity to inspect the Site is immaterial: clause 60.2 assumes that it has done so, and there is no need to add to this statement. The reference to surfaces could be important in some situations, for example the piling mat for a heavy piling rig or the temporary haul roads for self-propelled modular transporters. But surely such notifications would be better served by being included in the Scope (see the second bullet of clause 60.1(16))? Again, we see that the drafter doesn't understand the contract's communication provisions because the requirement for something to be in writing has crept in, no doubt from force of habit. This clause is a good example of the need to use a drafter who understands the contract when amending its standard provisions.

> **20.11** The Subcontractor has had an opportunity of inspecting the Site and its surroundings and all existing structures thereon (including physical conditions and other conditions (sub-surface or otherwise) of or affecting this site) and shall be deemed to have fully acquainted itself with the same and to have obtained all the same information as to risks, contingencies and all other circumstances which may influence or affect the works and no failure on the part of the Subcontractor to discover or foresee any such condition, risk, contingency or circumstances whether the same ought reasonably to have been discovered or foreseen or not shall entitle the Subcontractor to an addition to the Prices or to a change In the subcontract completion date or to claim indemnities or otherwise any additional sum. The Subcontractor shall not be entitled to rely upon any survey, report or other document prepared by or on behalf of the Contractor (including the Subcontract Works Information and the Site Information) regarding any such matter as is referred to in this clause and the Contractor makes no representation or warranty as to the accuracy or completeness of any such survey, report or document (including the Subcontract Works Information and the Site Information) or any representation or statement whether negligently or otherwise made therein. In the event of any conflict between this sub-clause 20.11 and clause 60.1(12) this sub-clause shall have priority.

Seemingly another pay-per-word candidate here from an ECS contract. The drafter is moving the risk of physical conditions away from the *Contractor* to the *Subcontractor*. Again, we see a reference to the *Subcontractor* being deemed to have acquainted itself with the Site, which already exists in the standard form. The suggestion that the *Subcontractor* is deemed to have inspected things sub-surface shows immense confidence in anyone's ability to forecast what lies below ground. Without effective site investigation, no one can forecast what the actual conditions will be. By including this clause and exempting itself from any liability for Site Information, the *Contractor* is passing the uncertainty of the conditions to the *Subcontractor*, which may not be as capable of managing and mitigating that risk as the *Contractor*, so potentially this clause is counterproductive.

> Delete clause 60.3.

> Delete clause 60.3 and replace with:
>
> If there is an ambiguity or inconsistency within the Site Information (including the information referred to within it), the Subcontractor is assumed to have taken into account the physical conditions less favourable to doing the subcontract works.

> Amendments to clause 60.3:
>
> **Z22.1** The Contractor provides Site Information and other documents relating to the condition of the Site by way of information only. The Contractor does not warrant or represent their accuracy, reliability or completeness.
>
> **Z22.2** The Contractor does not warrant the accuracy or completeness of any data or information provided to the Subcontractor by the Contractor or the Contractor relating to the location, size, nature or condition of services in, on, over or under the Site or in the vicinity of the Site.
>
> **Z22.3** The Subcontractor acknowledges that they neither have nor will have any claim of any kind against the Contractor based upon the accuracy or completeness of any such data or information.

These three clauses, taken from different ECS contracts, try to make the *Subcontractor* liable for any inadequacies within the Site Information. The standard form allocates this risk to the *Contractor*; the second example here merely reverses the clause. The first one may be counterproductive. By removing the clause entirely and not replacing it, the contract is silent on how such problems are dealt with, and this may count against the *Contractor* should such a claim arise. The third example is aiming to shut out any common law claims that the *Subcontractor* may bring against the *Contractor* in the event that the Site Information is wrong.

Geotechnical engineering is not a precise science, and the allocation of risk in a contract cannot remove that risk, only move it from one Party to another. Parties using Z clauses in this way must remember that contractual drafting cannot stop physical events such as difficult physical conditions, and that, when they occur, the Parties will need to collaborate to deal with them. Where one Party feels constrained commercially, its behaviour will be self-preserving and possibly not as collaborative as its counter-party wishes. The default clauses 60.2 and 60.3 provide a delicate balance of these risks that has been shown to work.

> Delete existing clause 61.1 and substitute:
>
> All compensation events, including those arising from the Contractor giving an instruction or changing an earlier decision, are notified by the Subcontractor to the Contractor in accordance with clause 61.3.

This clause achieves little on its own, and was taken from an ECS contract that lacked any further Z clauses on this subject. As often happens in Z clause drafting, the author had not understood the full effect of the remaining clauses. This Z clause requires the *Subcontractor* to notify the *Contractor* of all compensation events. For some reason the *Contractor* needs telling that its instructions create compensation events. It is likely that this clause was intended to apply the 7 weeks time bar to all compensation events, with an increased probability that the *Subcontractor* would fail and that the *Contractor* could escape liability for some of the events. But without an accompanying change to the final paragraph of clause 61.3, that will not happen, because it is that sentence which creates the time bar. The next example, taken from a different contract, does add the time bar to all compensation event notifications.

> **61.3** Delete the following wording:
>
> unless the event arises from the Contractor giving an instruction, issuing a certificate, changing an earlier decision or correcting an assumption.

Here, by removing these words from the end of clause 61.3, the time bar will apply to all compensation event notifications made by the *Subcontractor*. This does seem to work, provided no other Z clauses in that contract contradicted it. Potential subcontractors considering working with a *Contractor* that proposes such provisions really need to question the motivation of such organisations and whether a constructive relationship will be possible.

> Notwithstanding clauses 63.1 and 63.4, the Prices are not increased for any compensation event referred to in clause 60.1(13) or 60.1(19).

> **Z29.1** Delete clause 60.1(12), clause 60.2 and clause 60.3 (physical conditions).
>
> **Z29.2** Delete clause 60.1(13).

These are examples of Z clauses taken from two different ECC contracts that limit the *Client's* obligation to pay additional amounts in the event of bad weather (clause 60.1(13)), force-majeure-type events (clause 60.1(19)) and physical conditions (clause 60.1(12)).

The first clause prevents additional money being paid for such a compensation event but allows for the Completion Date and Key Dates to be moved to a later date. The second and third clauses remove the two compensation events entirely, and therefore leave the *Contractor* exposed to additional costs and damages for delay when these events occur. All three of these clauses are commonly encountered. Those tendering for contracts that include these provisions must include realistic time and cost allowances in their proposals to provide for protection when these events occur.

> **62.6** Delete the third sentence and insert:
>
> If the Contractor does not reply to the notification within 5 weeks, and unless the quotation is for a proposed instruction or a proposed changed decision, the Subcontractor's notification is treated as acceptance of the quotation by the Contractor.

This is a common Z clause from an ECS contract, increasing the time that the *Contractor* has to reply to a quotation received from a *Subcontractor*. The increase, from 3 weeks to 5 weeks, is innocuous but will lengthen the time taken to fully deal with the commercial aspects of a compensation event.

> **63.5** At the end of this clause add:
>
> Where any delay to the planned Completion Date (or to a Key Date) is caused concurrently by a compensation event and by any matter that is an act, omission or breach of contract by the Subcontractor (whether or not the said event and matter commence or conclude simultaneously) the delay to the Completion Date (or to the relevant Key Date) shall be assessed as nil.

This Z clause removes any entitlement from the *Contractor* in the event of concurrent delay. The reference to 'planned Completion Date' doesn't quite follow the contract's logic, but it's clear to see what the drafter intended here. Where any delay caused by, or at the risk of, the *Client* occurs, then the *Contractor* will not be entitled to additional time if that delay coincides with delays at the risk of the *Contractor*.

> At the end of clause 63.7 insert the following:
>
> Any additional cost that is incurred that would not have been incurred if any early warning had been given that an experienced Contractor could have given does not form part of the assessment of the compensation event. The compensation event is assessed as though the additional cost was not incurred. Furthermore, any delay to the Completion Date that would not have occurred if an early warning had been given that an experienced Contractor could have given, and that could have been mitigated by appropriate steps having been taken at the time when an early warning could have been given, does not form part of the assessment of the delay to the Completion Date.

This is another pay-per-word clause. The additional 113 words added to clause 63.7 provide further, but unnecessary, explanation of how clauses 61.5 and 63.7 should work. The existing core clauses provide for the assessment that this drafter seeks, and therefore this Z clause is unnecessary.

> Clause 63.8:
>
> Delete this clause.

By removing clause 63.8 there is no longer an express provision allowing for risk allowances to be included in compensation event assessments. This is nonsensical. No activity can be estimated, either in time or money, without different risks being allowed for. By inserting this clause, the drafter is trying to short change the *Contractor*, but it is hard to see how a proper assessment of Defined Cost under clause 63.1 or time under clause 63.5 could ignore such things, even in the absence of clause 63.8. This Z clause will cause considerable difficulties for both Parties when compensation events occur.

> Amendment to secondary Option clause X2 (changes in the law):
>
> After 'Subcontract Date' insert: 'unless the change and its effects could reasonably be expected to have been anticipated by an experienced and prudent subcontractor prior to the Subcontract Date'.

This amended clause from an ECS contract misses the point of secondary Option X2. The aim of the standard provisions is to transfer the risk of changes in law from the *Subcontractor* to the *Contractor* so that the former does not need to include any allowances in its prices. By making this change, the *Subcontractor* is at risk of changes in law that perhaps were publicised by the government prior to the Subcontract Date but were not commenced until afterwards. The inclusion of risk allowances for changes in law is therefore more likely, not less, with this clause.

> The Subcontractor shall have no greater right to changes to the Accepted Programme, any Key Dates, or any other right or relief (excluding the right to payment) in relation to the subcontract works than the Contractor under the main contract in so far as it applies to the same facts, except where and to the extent the issue relates to a breach by the Contractor of this subcontract or to an instruction or direction given in writing by the Contractor to the Subcontractor but that does not give effect to an equivalent instruction or direction under the main contract.

This clause taken from an ECS contract provides a link to the main contract. *Subcontractors* should always be wary of equivalent relief provisions, particularly where there is no visibility of main contract correspondence. The failure of a claim under the main contract may be caused by something that is independent of the *Contractor–Subcontractor* relationship, but how would the latter know this? *Subcontractors* should be very slow to agree provisions like this one.

ICE Publishing

Patrick Waterhouse
ISBN 978-0-7277-6560-4
https://doi.org/10.1680/necdcce.65604.171

Chapter 18
Disputes concerning Defined Cost and compensation events

Disagreements

Disagreements happen frequently in business, and most are resolved without further assistance or the involvement of third parties. Disagreements in NEC contracts involving Defined Cost and the assessment of compensation events are common. Typically, Parties may disagree on the following

- Has a compensation event occurred at all?
- What delay(s) to sectional Completion, Completion or Key Dates should be allowed?
- What is the effect on Defined Cost?
- What is the effect on Disallowed Cost?
- Is a particular cost Defined Cost, or in the Fee?
- Was something necessary to Provide the Works?
- Assessment of Defined Cost in Price for Work Done to Date certifications and the impact on the share in the target cost options.

Where the Parties to an ECC contract cannot resolve a disagreement, they can use the dispute resolution procedures. While the ECC is well suited to Parties avoiding disputes, its provisions for resolving them are also aimed at the Parties cooperating to do so. That cooperation cannot be taken for granted, as can be seen by the many disputes, and therefore the adjudication provisions can be concluded even with the reluctant involvement, or even no involvement, of one of the Parties.

The role of the *Senior Representatives* is included in some NEC4 contracts, a technique that has worked in other commercial contracts for many years. The mere identification of these people won't, on its own, provide a useful input unless those people genuinely are senior and get involved in the process.

Adjudication remains the primary ECC dispute resolution provision in Options W1 and W2. The Dispute Avoidance Board in Option W3 provides for a group of independent people appointed at the start of a project regardless of the dispute status of the project. The members of the board visit the Site regularly and remain in touch with progress. If and when a dispute arises, the board makes a recommendation for its resolution. The success of a board depends upon the quality of the people appointed to it and the methodology used in its work.

Reference of a dispute to arbitration or to the courts can only be made when the dispute has been decided upon by the *Adjudicator* or where the Dispute Avoidance Board has made a recommendation. The final dispute resolution is at the *tribunal*, identified in the Contract Data.

Senior Representatives

This is more of a dispute avoidance process than one of dispute resolution. Although the aim of using *Senior Representatives* is to resolve any dispute put to them, it is not stated that they act as dispute resolvers. It equally does not prevent them from acting in this role either. They are completely free to attempt to resolve the dispute or get assistance from others, within the time allowed.

In the ECC, whether using Option W1 or W2, the use of *Senior Representatives* takes a similar path. In Option W1, the Parties are first obliged to use this process, and if the disagreement is not resolved by the *Senior Representatives*, then it is referred to and decided by the *Adjudicator* under clause W1.1(1).

There are a few differences in the use of this process between Options W1 and W2. The first is that in Option W2 the Parties need to agree that a dispute arising under or in connection with the contract is referred to the *Senior Representatives* (clause W2.1(1)). This is done to preserve the Parties' right in UK statutes for adjudication at any time for certain contracts caught by the Housing Grants, Construction and Regeneration Act 1996 and its equivalent in Northern Ireland. In Option W2, a Party may refer a dispute to the *Adjudicator* at any time even if the dispute has been referred to the *Senior Representatives* (clause W2.2(1)). In Option W1, a dispute arising under or in connection with the contract is referred to the *Senior Representatives* in accordance with the Dispute Reference Table. No such table exists in Option W2, and any dispute at any time can be referred to the *Adjudicator* as mentioned before. The table in Option W1 has time limitations for referring disputes to the *Senior Representatives*. The *Senior Representatives* will need to be satisfied in the first instance that they can act as provided for in the contract when Option W1 is used.

It may be that the *Senior Representatives* can quite quickly agree that their dispute is of a nature where perhaps only adjudication and the *tribunal* can give it the justice it deserves. Or maybe it is for such an inconsequential amount that they simply negotiate. That is the beauty of this process: between the Parties and the *Senior Representatives*, they remain in control of their dispute and take it in whichever direction they feel is appropriate, unlike most other forms of dispute resolution where the Parties lose control and are in the hands of others making sure the requirements of the process are very carefully followed.

In the ECC, the *Senior Representatives* are stated in the Contract Data part one by the *Client* at the tender stage, and in Contract Data part two by the *Contractor*, again at the tender stage. There is no minimum number of *Senior Representatives* to be provided, but I consider it naturally follows there should be the same number appointed by the *Client* and the *Contractor*.

The *Senior Representatives* are not bound by clause 10.1 or 10.2. They are not mentioned in these clauses, but they will surely have to agree some sensible ground rules for their conduct, or else they may struggle to use the time wisely.

What they do is to follow the provisions in the contract, found in clause W1.1 or W2.1 as appropriate. The 'threat' to the *Senior Representatives* is time and outcome. If they cannot agree an outcome within the time allowed, the dispute may be referred to and decided by the *Adjudicator*. This should be uppermost in the minds of the Parties, so can they get somewhere they can both live with: neither Party likely wishes to proceed to a more formal dispute resolution process, which probably has significant time, cost, cashflow, resource and no end of other implications. A dispute occurs, and generally one Party will decide to formalise this. Whoever that Party is, they notify the *Senior Representatives*, along with the other Party and the *Project Manager*, of the nature of the dispute it wishes to resolve. From that notification, the referring Party has just 1 week to submit its statement of case. The Parties can agree on the length of the statement of case, but if they do not, then the default is ten sides of A4 paper. There can be supporting evidence, and no limit is put on this.

Under clause W1.1(3) the *Senior Representatives* then have quite a free hand on what they do next. They can hold one or many meetings. They can negotiate. They can decide to refer the matter to mediation or conciliation, or to any other procedure, to try to resolve the dispute over a period of no more than 3 weeks. Hopefully, the first meeting is one of honesty, realism and pragmatism. They can reflect on the statement of case, which at this point they only have from the referring Party. They might set a week aside to obtain a similar document from the other Party. They might agree perhaps that the disagreement is so complex and unusual that the best place for this is in litigation, but that is not what the contract wants as an output from the *Senior Representatives*. They must 'try to resolve the dispute' (clause W1.1(3)): that is their job. The *Senior Representatives* must have a go – at least attempt to negotiate.

When the time allowed is up, the *Senior Representatives* are obliged to produce a list of the issues agreed (clause W1.1(3)), and these are put into effect by the *Project Manager* and the *Contractor*. If what is agreed is that the *Project Manager* should give an instruction to change the Scope, then that is what should happen. If it is agreed that the *Contractor* is to submit some design for acceptance that it considered it did not have to do, the *Contractor* puts that into effect. If the Parties need to change a term of the contract (clause 12.3), then one Party will have to initiate this and agree matters with the other – the *Project Manager* does not have any authority to do this. At the end of the process, the *Senior Representatives* should also produce a list of the issues not agreed (clause W1.1(3)), and either Party may initiate adjudication if they so choose to.

For this entire process, clause W1.1(4) says that no evidence of the statement of case or any discussions during the 3 weeks can be used or referred to should there be subsequent proceedings before the *Adjudicator* or the *tribunal*. This is a similar position when using mediation, the process being carried out in confidence such that the Parties cannot later be held to something they said or did, perhaps in an attempt to reach a settlement.

The provisions of the contract are extremely brief in respect of what the *Senior Representatives* do. I think that is a good idea, as to constrain them might potentially mean missing out on allowing the *Senior Representatives* to have a real go at resolving a dispute in a timely and cost-effective fashion, avoiding all sorts of problems and hardship going forward.

The *Senior Representatives* have the job of 'creatively' trying to resolve any dispute within 3 weeks of receiving a statement of case and supporting evidence from the referring Party. I say 'creatively', as there is such a limited time allowed, which I support, that traditional dispute resolution processes simply cannot be accommodated. The *Senior Representatives* have a completely open-ended brief to resolve the dispute. The contract does not even use words like 'negotiate' or 'mediate', but they are some of the processes that are designed to bring time benefits to disputing parties. Obviously, the Parties should try to resolve their disputes even before the *Senior Representatives* act – and this is entirely possible. The *Contractor* can turn to the *Client* and say 'We have a problem here, how would you like to sit down and discuss it with me in a bid to resolve it?' While I have looked in Option W1 at the time allowed to refer a dispute to the *Senior Representatives* and note for some of the disputes there could be a 4 week period before a Party is compelled to refer it, that does give them time to try a reach some sort of settlement within that period. The 'threat' therefore of even *Senior Representatives* getting involved, let alone the more formal dispute resolution processes, might be the thing that helps the Parties to avoid disputes in the first place.

How are disputes dealt with formally?

Where the Parties cannot agree on the assessment of compensation events, then adjudication, and possibly the *tribunal*, will become the next options. Of course, there is the possibility of mediation and the role of the *Senior Representatives* that I described earlier.

Where a Party wants to dispute the assessment of Defined Cost and/or a compensation event, it may do so

- Clause W1.1(4): either Party may dispute a decision of the *Project Manager*, and it may refer the dispute to the *Adjudicator* within 4 weeks of the Party becoming aware of the decision. This seems difficult to establish. When did someone become aware? That's possibly difficult to establish, so the referring Party might need to establish, through a document audit trail, when the responding Party became aware. I think that this clause would be better referring to when the referring Party had been notified of the compensation event notification. However, this clause refers to a wider set of issues than just compensation events, hence the looser wording.
- Clause W1.1(4): the *Client* can dispute the circumstances of a compensation event communication being treated as accepted. This must be done within 4 weeks of the communication being treated as accepted.
- Clauses W1.3(7) and W2.3(7): the *Adjudicator* must assess issues of cost and time affecting the *Contractor* in the same way as a compensation event is assessed. In other words, the *Adjudicator* must act in the same way as the *Contractor* and *Project Manager* should have acted earlier.
- Clauses W1.4(2) and W2.4(2): where the *Adjudicator's* decision still leaves a Party dissatisfied, then that Party must issue a notice of dissatisfaction to the other Party within 4 weeks of being informed of the *Adjudicator's* decision.
- The *tribunal* then deals with the dispute that is referred to it, which may be the entirety of the *Adjudicator's* decision or just a part of it.

In disputing a compensation event assessment, Parties should consider the following

- Have the negotiation options and the *Senior Representatives* route been exhausted?
- Consider the Notice of Adjudication carefully and define the *Adjudicator's* jurisdiction precisely. In essence, set the *Adjudicator* a question that (*a*) can be answered and (*b*) is likely to assist your contract position.
- When referring a dispute to the *tribunal*, review how the adjudication went, and potentially amend the case before asking the *tribunal* to consider it. Clauses W1.4(4) and W2.4(3) allow this amendment of a case to take place. The dispute referred to the *tribunal* cannot change from the one decided by the *Adjudicator*, but the way it is described may be.

ICE Publishing

Patrick Waterhouse
ISBN 978-0-7277-6560-4
https://doi.org/10.1680/necdcce.65604.175

Chapter 19
Defined Cost in termination

Termination in any contractual environment presents challenges to the Parties and, with the ECC, also the *Project Manager*. Termination is occasionally a mutually acceptable arrangement, but is more often associated with insolvency or dispute. It is important that the contract's provisions for dealing with payments are clear, to minimise the potential for disagreement. This chapter addresses only the references to Defined Cost in the termination provisions, not the remainder of the payments due.

The ECC contains provisions to terminate the *Contractor's* obligation to Provide the Works, as distinct from terminating the contract itself. There is a system of

- reasons, labelled R1 to R22 for termination; an additional entitlement for the *Client* to terminate for any reason is in secondary Option X11, if included in the contract
- procedures, labelled P1, P2, P3 and P4, to be followed on termination, the selection of which depends upon the reason for termination
- amounts to be paid after termination, labelled A1, A2, A3 and A4, again dependent upon the reason for termination.

The reasons are listed in clause 91, the procedures in clause 92 and the amounts in clause 93.

Under clause 53.1, the payments due after termination have to be certified by the *Project Manager* within 13 weeks after the termination certificate has been issued and paid by the *Client* within 3 weeks of the date of that certificate.

Amount A1 is paid in all termination scenarios; the inclusion of any of the other three payments in the final amount due depends upon the reason for termination. Amount A1 pays the *Contractor* the remaining amounts due for permanent works, and includes two references to Defined Cost in its list of five entries

- the Defined Cost for Plant and Materials
  - within the Working Areas or
  - to which the *Client* has title and of which the *Contractor* has to accept delivery,
- other Defined Cost reasonably incurred in expectation of completing the whole of the *works*.

The amount due for Plant and Materials, qualified in two respects, can be assessed by reference back to the definition of Defined Cost in whichever main Option is relevant. The definition will point you either to the Schedule of Cost Components (the Full Schedule) or to the Short Schedule, and to the components for Plant and Materials in section 3 of either schedule. The reference to title is only to those items outside the Working Areas, and covered by clauses 70.1 and 71.1.

The reference to other Defined Cost with two qualifications creates the scope for disagreements. What is the measure of 'reasonably incurred?' How does that sit with clause 52.1 and the introductory paragraph of the relevant schedule? When could the *Contractor* have stopped expecting to complete the whole of the *works*? On receipt of the termination notice, or were the signs there previously? Remember that the *Contractor's* obligation to Provide the Works under clause 20.1 continues until it receives the termination certificate under clause 90.4, so it would be in breach if it did not keep making arrangements for the procurement of resources prior to termination.

Amount A2 is paid in situations where the termination has not resulted from the *Contractor's* default. The forecast Defined Cost of removing Equipment refers to component 26 of the Full Schedule and component 24 of the Short Schedule.

Amount A4 contains a reference to Defined Cost in main Option E or F contracts. This applies the Fee to the difference between the first forecast of the Defined Cost over the Price for Work Done to Date less the Fee. This payment provides the *Contractor* with the payment of its off-site overheads and profit that would otherwise have been paid but for the termination. The first forecast would effectively be the estimate on day 1 of the likely total cost of the *works*.

Finally, with contracts using either main Option C or D the *Project Manager* must assess the share after certifying termination. Clauses 93.4 and 93.5 both say 'The assessment uses, as the Price for Work Done to Date, the total of the Defined Cost which the Contractor has paid and which it is committed to pay for work done before termination.'

Patrick Waterhouse
ISBN 978-0-7277-6560-4
https://doi.org/10.1680/necdcce.65604.177

Index